The General Strike

by the same author

THE WOBBLIES: THE STORY OF SYNDICALISM
IN THE UNITED STATES

THE GENERAL STRIKE

Patrick Renshaw

 Eyre Methuen · London

First published 1975
© 1975 Patrick Renshaw
Printed in Great Britain for
Eyre Methuen Ltd
11 New Fetter Lane, London EC4P 4EE
by The Bowering Press Ltd
Plymouth

ISBN 0 413 27610 4

*To Mary, who lived through
these nine days with me*

Contents

Illustrations

A*

Acknowledgements and thanks for permission to reproduce the plates is due to the Radio Times Hulton Picture Library for plates 1, 2b, 3a, 3b, 4a, 4c, 5b, 7c, 8b, 8c, 9 and 10; to Paul Popper Ltd for plates 2a, 4b, 6a, 6b, 7a and 8a; to Associated Newspapers Ltd for plates 5a and 7b; and to the Greater London Council for plates 11 and 12.

Foreword

Many books have been written about the General Strike in Britain. Why write another? The main justification for this one is its new sources. When Parliament opened for the first time Government documents which were thirty rather than fifty years old, it released a vast store of Cabinet papers, departmental records, correspondence and memoranda to the historian. They provide the basis for this study. Rather than recount the story of the Nine Days once more in minute detail it tries to put it in context. Much of the text deals with the coal crisis of the 1920s which culminated in the General Strike. But this is placed in a wider perspective by starting with the origins of that crisis and ending with the legacy which has lasted until today. The General Strike was a crucial event in modern history. It raised questions about the nature of obligation and dissent which go to the heart of democratic theory in an industrial community. It influenced labour relations for a generation and more, and left its mark not only on the Labour Government of 1945–1951 but on politics since then.

Indeed, while this book was being written there was a general strike in Ulster and Britain's mineworkers twice went on strike – their first national stoppages since 1926. The tactical similarities between the two situations in the 1920s and the 1970s were intriguing. In both periods the miners were made to bear the brunt of an incomes policy which had a direct impact on their wages. Even the figure in dispute – around 13 per cent – was the same. The difference was that in 1926 the miners were being asked to accept *wage cuts* of 13 per cent. They managed to win their first confrontation with the Government in 1925, as they did in 1972. On both occasions Conservative Cabinets chose to see this as a humiliating defeat and were determined not to be humiliated again. The rhetoric about 'who rules – the miners or the Government?' which Ministers resorted to in the 1920s was used again in the 1970s. There were the same Government promises to reorganise the industry, improve conditions and treat the miners as a special case. Little or nothing came of all this talk, and all the miners wanted was cash on the table.

The result in 1926 was a disastrous dispute which dragged on for months, inflicting enormous damage and leaving bitterness which still survives. Yet Government policy was in a sense vindicated. Wages and prices fell, so that the purchasing power of the pound increased. Life for the majority of people was better. But the price of this improvement was very high. Though history does not repeat itself, the mining disputes of the 1970s show that the legacy of the 1920s is still very real among the miners. Indeed, their reaction to the Coal Board's productivity plan in 1974 showed that some of the old, regional rivalries of the 1920s were still alive. Of course, there was one important difference between the situation in the 1920s and in the 1970s. Today the mines have been nationalised. In the 1920s they were privately owned. And the great gap in previous accounts of the General Strike has been the mineowners' case. The traditional picture of these men is well known : selfish, grasping, small-minded people prepared to risk everything to force the miners' wages down below starvation level.

Is this a fair picture? It may be, but it has been based on scanty evidence. Lord Birkenhead dismissed the mineowners as 'the stupidest men in England'. When asked what he thought of the mineowners' case, one of my colleagues snorted, 'They didn't have one.' This book tries to modify that oversimplified picture by identifying the owners more clearly and discussing the divisions in their ranks. These divisions were based on regional differences which influenced profitability, markets, the selling price of coal and so on. They were just as deep, and just as important, as similar divisions among the miners. The intransigent policies adopted by both masters and men were based on a desire to bridge their internal divisions. Ultimately, they led to a collision which provided the most dramatic event in British history between the wars.

Acknowledgements

This book was written at intervals over several years in time taken from teaching and research in other fields. The Department of Medieval and Modern History at Sheffield University gave me leave from normal duties to spend a year's exchange at Syracuse University, New York, where much of the text was written. An award from the Fulbright Commission paid my transatlantic travel and the Maxwell School of Citizenship and Public Affairs made me a Senior Research Fellow so that I could continue working when my teaching semester ended. Sheffield University Research Fund also provided several grants to help travel and research.

The staffs of many libraries helped the work. In particular, I would like to thank the Public Record Office, the TUC Library, the British Museum, the Newspaper Library at Colindale, London University and the London School of Economics, the Bodleian and Nuffield College Library, Oxford, Cambridge University Library, Sheffield University Library, Leeds University Library and the Brotherton Collection, Leeds Public Library and Sheffield Public Library, Cusworth Hall Museum Library, Doncaster, Yorkshire Area NUM Library at Barnsley and Nottingham Area NUM Library at Mansfield, the BBC Written Archives, Caversham Park, the BBC Sound Archives, London, the International Institute of Social History in Amsterdam, Syracuse University Library, the New York Public Library and the Industrial and Labour Relations School Library at Cornell University, New York. Some of the material used in Chapter 8 first appeared, in somewhat different form, in an article of mine in *History Today* in June 1971.

Many people gave freely of their time to read the manuscript at various stages and offer criticism and advice. Michael Bentley, Dr Clyde Binfield,

Professor Melvyn Dubofsky, Anthony Fletcher and Professor Peter Marsh all removed mistakes of fact, interpretation and expression, but are not responsible for any which still remain, nor for any opinions expressed here. Dai Smith, of Swansea University, kindly lent the text of a paper on company unions. My brother, Geoffrey Renshaw, of Warwick University, improved the economic sections with his comments, and Clive Barker, of the Department of Drama and Theatre Arts, Birmingham University, allowed me to listen to his extensive tape-recorded interviews with strikers.

Mrs. J. H. Smith was a fast, efficient and very accurate typist.

Finally, I would like to thank Dean Alan K. Campbell and my colleagues and friends both at the Maxwell School and in Syracuse for all their kindness.

Sheffield   P.R.G.R.
November 1974

Dark Testament

The drivers are dead now
But the drivers have sons
The slaves are dead too
But the slaves have sons
And when the sons of the drivers meet the sons of the slaves
The hate, the old hate keeps grinding on.

Pauli Murray

Introduction

At the end of the first week in May 1926, prosperous London business-men and stockbrokers driving to work one sunny morning in the City from comfortable suburban homes were surprised and shocked. As they approached town their cars suddenly became entangled in military convoys carrying heavily armed troops. 'Long files of armoured cars,' a *New York World* reporter observed, 'choked the country roads in Surrey. Troops continue to pour into town. The ordinary barracks and different quarters of the city are gorged with soldiers in service uniforms. Thousands of marines are packed into the Duke of York Barracks. Sentries guarding Royal residences have exchanged their usual ceremonial dress for khaki and carry 150 rounds of ammunition in their packs.'

Why all these alarming military preparations? Was Britain in danger of foreign invasion? The businessmen and stockbrokers might have feared the threat was already in their midst. For an official Conservative Govern-ment newspaper had been thundering for a week about the necessity of waging 'total war' and demanding 'unconditional surrender'. But 'the enemy' the Government was mobilising all its resources to defeat was not a foreign power. It was the British organised labour movement. The Trades Union Congress had called a General Strike and $3\frac{1}{2}$ million trade unionists had stopped work. Public transport was halted. Factories, mines and mills were closed. Most newspapers had ceased production. Though the strikers had promised to maintain essential services, such as food and power supplies for hospitals, the Government had felt obliged to transport perishable goods by armoured convoys.

That very morning, in the East End of London, a convoy of 105 Army lorries, each carrying Grenadier Guards, escorted by 20 armoured cars, was being loaded with food in London docks under the protection of machine guns before being driven to Hyde Park, which had become a vast food storage centre. That afternoon 170 lorries made the same journey, and the following day a much larger armoured convoy of 267 lorries broke the strikers' dockland blockade. 'The sullen mass of strikers,' the *New York World* reported, 'were awed by the military . . . backed . . . by enough artillery to kill every living thing in every street in the neighbourhood.' Battleships anchored off large ports like Liverpool with their guns trained on the harbourside. These ominous military preparations were backed up by belligerent policies. The Chancellor of the Exchequer, Winston Churchill, had promised, in the columns of the official *British Gazette*, which he edited, that any action taken by the armed forces 'will receive, both now and afterwards, the full support of His Majesty's Government'.

Nor was this all. Churchill pressed urgently for the immediate mobilisation of the Territorial Army. The Home Secretary had broadcast an appeal for 30,000 more special constables to be enrolled at once to swell the total to 200,000 – some 40,000 of them in London alone. Police measures were being greatly tightened throughout the country at the weekend and the Government had announced the formation of a special steel-helmeted Civil Constabulary Reserve. The Home Office had issued a *communiqué* about a new phase in the legal and Constitutional aspects of the emergency which might make it necessary to take special powers, and extra troop movements had been ordered. There were no deaths during the strike, and the 4,000 arrests represented a negligible fraction of the total number of strikers. But 604 of these arrests were made without warrant and there was much more violence than was commonly realised then or subsequently.

The weekend of 8–9 May, with the strike six days old, saw police baton charges at a dozen places in London alone. Outside the capital there were ugly riots at Plymouth, Southsea, Swansea and Nottingham. Shots were fired at a passing train at the important railway centre of Crewe, while the Flying Scotsman, the nation's most famous express, was derailed. At Preston, a mob of 5,000 people who tried to storm the police station and release an arrested striker were only beaten back by repeated baton charges. There were similar scenes in such important industrial centres as Middlesbrough, Newcastle and Hull, where there were 25 arrests and 41 hospital admissions. At York another mob tried to release a prisoner, while Edinburgh and Glasgow both saw violent scenes stretching over four or five nights with missiles being thrown and hundreds of arrests.

As one observer wrote :

> At the end of the first week of the strike a ripple of violence had spread
> through South London. Vast crowds had gathered at New Cross tram
> depot to prevent the emergence of blackleg trams; a police charge had
> dispersed them, but the volunteer drivers had been so intimidated that
> they remained shut up in the depot under the protection of the police.
> At Deptford Broadway . . . a recent meeting had ended in a riot between
> strikers and police; bottles had been thrown and mounted police
> unseated and mauled. Men had been injured on both sides and tempers
> made permanently ugly.

Most of the 600 arrests without warrant had been of Communists and
revolutionaries and by order-in-council 13A the Government had taken
the extraordinary measure of prohibiting banks from transferring funds
from overseas, especially from Russia but also from European socialist
and labour organisations which might be used to aid the strikers. There
was a strong rumour in Labour's ranks that the Government meant to
break the strike by violence and arrest national strike leaders like Arthur
Pugh, Ernest Bevin and J. H. Thomas. 'General opinion that the fight
would be short but violent,' was the diary entry of the novelist Arnold
Bennett, a well-informed London clubman and friend of Cabinet
Ministers. 'Bloodshed anticipated next week.'

The General Strike of 1926 was the most dramatic single event in
British domestic politics between the two world wars. As such, it has
passed into folk-lore, like Peterloo and Tolpuddle. Like all such national
myths, it is surrounded by colourful memories and misconceptions.
Although it lasted only nine days, from 3 May until 12 May, it seemed
to have brought Britain to the brink of revolution. At the same time, it is
full of a kind of quaint period charm, redolent of the Gay Twenties.
People who know nothing else about the strike recall that undergraduates
from Oxford and Cambridge drove buses and railway locomotives, while
in Plymouth the strikers actually played football with the police.

Yet in reality there was nothing cosy about the Nine Days. They were
born of the bitterness and desperation felt by millions of industrial wage-
earners during the great inter-war trade depression, when pay was low
and unemployment high. The idea of a General Strike had been much
discussed in labour and revolutionary circles for a generation and more.
But it had not been used in Western Europe on a nation-wide scale. Now,
for the first time in British history, industrial life came to a virtual
halt.

What had brought the nation to a standstill, and to what looked like the brink of revolution? The immediate origins of the General Strike are familiar enough. It had been called by the general council of the Trades Union Congress in support of the Miners' Federation of Great Britain. The MFGB represented a million mineworkers, who had been locked out by the mineowners for refusing to accept new terms of employment which meant longer hours and lower pay. But apart from its immediate origins it also had roots deep in the squalor and misery of the Industrial Revolution. Although it seemed to run counter to British traditions of moderation, the idea of a general strike had first been advocated a century earlier by an extraordinary British Quaker radical, labour agitator and pamphleteer named William Benbow. Benbow's passionate talk of 'armed revolution' during the repressive years which followed the defeat of Napoleon in 1815 won him a wide audience. And in the year of the First Reform Act in 1832 he had published a best-selling pamphlet which set out his revolutionary ideas clearly.

Benbow pointed out that while 'All men enjoy life' they did not 'enjoy it equally'. He continued, 'The only class of persons in society, as it is now constituted, who enjoy any considerable portion of ease, pleasure or happiness, are those who do the least towards producing anything good or necessary for the community at large.' Benbow added that one person out of every 500 controlled the remaining 499, who toiled ceaselessly for others. They toiled, Benbow concluded, because they did not understand the power labour might wield if only it were organised. His solution was a 'Grand National Holiday', or stoppage of labour, which would last until the employers had granted the workers equal rights in the fruits of that labour. From Benbow's idea grew the whole theory of the General Strike as the revolutionary weapon with which the working class would seize political power.

Benbow's beliefs were by-passed in Britain, where trade unions had rejected his messianism in favour of bread-and-butter bargaining and Parliamentary reformism which led to the birth of the Labour Party early in the twentieth century. His ideas had also been rejected by labour leaders in other countries such as Germany where the theory of the General Strike was dismissed as 'general nonsense'. But Benbow's philosophy fell on more fruitful soil in France. Here, after the death of the Second Empire in 1871, democracy gradually reappeared during the Third Republic. As part of this increasing freedom trade unions emerged once more, and a group of revolutionary philosophers, like Emile Pouget and Fernand Pelloutier, discussed how these working-class organisations could be used as the spearhead of revolution. French trade unions were known as *syndicats*, and the philosophy of using them as the spearhead of revolution was called syndicalism.

The syndicalists developed Benbow's somewhat simplistic beliefs about the social revolution into a more elaborate theory that industrial workers would seize political as well as economic power by a sustained and pitiless campaign of direct action and strikes, leading eventually to general strike and revolution. The workers would 'take and hold' the industries where they worked, lock the employers out and finally force the Government to capitulate. After this seizure of power, the workers themselves would take over the administration of the workers' state. By the early 1900s the syndicalists had won temporary control of the relatively weak French labour movement, and drawn up the Charter of Amiens, reaffirming their belief in direct action and the general strike as a means of overthrowing the Parliamentary system, which they described as a 'sink of jobbery, corruption and compromise'.

A whole generation of journalists and popular writers broadcast such ideas. The French philosopher Georges Sorel, author of a widely read book, *Reflections on Violence*, spread them as a kind of 'social myth' which took on an almost religious significance in some revolutionary quarters. Syndicalism certainly alarmed the middle class. But despite its appeal to some young intellectuals, syndicalism gained little support from the workers themselves. The syndicalists soon lost their hold on the French labour movement, and never established a major foothold outside Latin countries, where the labour movement was weak and lacking political power. Yet the Charter of Amiens of 1906 was undoubtedly a watershed in labour history. It marked the first serious syndicalist challenge to the existing political and social order. This syndicalist challenge lasted in Europe until the ultimate failure of the General Strike in Britain, and gives the period 1906–26 a historical unity of its own.

During these years syndicalism had undoubtedly helped create propaganda in Britain for sympathetic strike action on the widest possible scale. Yet it was not seen as the road to revolution, except by a tiny minority, but simply as a means of winning particular strikes. This tendency towards wider strike action was encouraged by events on the political side of the British labour movement. Labour's success in the general election of 1906 had not produced any dramatic results. Divisions within the party, the leadership's apparently slavish dependence on the goodwill of the Liberal Government, and its failure to do anything practical about inflation drove the labour movement sharply to the left. The years of 'labour unrest' – in the docks, the transport industry and, above all, coal mining – were the result. And the symbol of this new and aggressive labour solidarity was the celebrated triple industrial alliance. The triple alliance, formed in 1914, was a loose, informal agreement between railwaymen, transport workers (including dockers) and miners, by which each union promised to support the others during trade disputes and strikes. Here was something which seemed to justify middle-class fears about the general strike.

For the triple alliance appeared to be a powerful weapon in the armoury of organised labour, and seemed certain to sharpen class conflict. Then the First World War suddenly cut short the triple alliance's plans for united action and imposed an uneasy industrial truce. For the moment all was calm. Nevertheless, the miners in particular hoped to use the triple alliance to win more concessions from the mineowners. They had been most active in forming the new alliance. The coal industry was booming in the years before the war, and the miners were determined to use their industrial strength to win a greater share of this prosperity based on their labour. The celebrated syndicalist pamphlet, *The Miners' Next Step*, written by two South Wales militants, appeared to presage a generation of conflict. Above all, the miners wanted national, as opposed to regional, pay agreements and nationalisation of the mining industry. Yet the industrial truce lasted in the mines more or less throughout the war. So did the pre-war boom. When hostilities ended, owners and miners alike expected this boom to continue. Instead, they found the bottom had fallen out of the coal trade. Far from fighting over ever-rising profits, both sides found themselves fighting to save what they could from a sinking industry.

So the stage was set for the titanic mining disputes of the 1920s. The mood was apparent as early as 1919, when the Government promised it would relinquish war-time control of the mines and return them to private ownership. The mere threat of united action by the triple alliance was enough to persuade the Government to change its mind and appoint a royal commission on mining. This recommended nationalisation; but the Government refused to accept this plan. Instead, Lloyd George's Coalition renewed its pledge to return the coal industry to private hands in April 1921. The owners, faced on their return with plunging profits, proposed huge wage cuts. The miners refused to accept them and were locked out. The triple alliance lumbered up again to help; but this time unity collapsed on 15 April 1921 and the miners were left to fight on alone for months before hunger drove them back to worse terms than they could have had at the beginning. This humiliating defeat was known as Black Friday.

After Black Friday employers everywhere had the upper hand. The miners were regarded as the pacemakers of British industry. Coal was still the core of the nation's economy; the miners were comparatively well paid and incomparably well organised. If their wages could be forced down, everyone's could. But by 1924 things were beginning to pick up a little. Events abroad made British coal more competitive in export markets. Then came the new Conservative Government's gamble of returning to the gold standard in April 1925. At one stroke this over-valued sterling and destroyed coal's competitive edge overseas. Profits tumbled again and the owners proposed more sweeping pay cuts. Despite the collapse of Black Friday, the threat of united action by the unions behind the miners on 31 July 1925 forced the Government to pay a subsidy in support of current pay and profits and establish another royal commission into mining. Such was Red Friday.

The Government subsidy was to last nine months. When it ended, the next mining crisis seemed certain to come in May 1926. During that nine months Baldwin's Government had made careful plans for coping with the impending conflict. The unions did nothing effective. However, the railwaymen and transport workers had also made it clear that they were becoming a little tired of always having to come to the support of the miners. The Trades Union Congress agreed. They promised that the next time the miners needed support it should come from the TUC. So, almost as a casual administrative decision, the TUC ensured that future united action in support of the miners would be a general strike. In March the royal commission recommended reorganisation of the coal industry in the long term. But its only immediate proposal was a pay cut, which the miners could not accept. When the nine months expired, Baldwin refused to extend the subsidy; the owners imposed their pay cuts; the miners refused them and on May Day 1926 they were locked out. Three days later the TUC's sympathetic strike call had brought industry to a halt across the country. The General Strike had begun.

The next nine days saw a political event of the first importance. But the sufferings of the miners, their wives and children, were the reality behind the drama of high politics. The strike also brought into direct confrontation some of the most colourful and powerful political personalities of the time. On the union side there was J. H. Thomas, whose image of a hard-drinking, untrustworthy fixer hid the skills of an accomplished bargainer; A. J. Cook, the miners' secretary, who was so dangerously emotional and eloquent in public, so disarmingly rational and frank in private; and Herbert Smith, the union's president, who seemed taciturn to the point of parody in his attempts to protect the dignity of his men. At the TUC, Ernest Bevin and Walter Citrine, cool and calm administrators, spoke for the new generation of labour leaders, pragmatic technicians taking the vital strategic decisions in a war they had never believed in or supported.

On the Government side stood Winston Churchill, breathing fire and smoke, demanding total defeat of the Labour 'enemy' in the *British Gazette* during the strike, but then behaving more magnanimously than any of his Cabinet colleagues after it. Lord Birkenhead, brilliant and arrogant, acted like a dove before the strike began and a hawk once it had started. Above them all, his surface appearance of indolent calm hiding an intensely nervous yet calculating temperament, was Stanley Baldwin. The Prime Minister, a man of endless fascination, faced this supreme crisis with a studied air of unconcern which shocked his Civil Servants, yet never missed a trick in dealing with obstreperous Cabinet colleagues, intransigent opponents or a general public whose feelings he sensed with uncanny skill.

Beside Baldwin sat Tom Jones, deputy Cabinet Secretary, an inveterate gossip and go-between, whose diary is packed with mordant comments on men and events. For the mineowners, Evan Williams, president of the Mining Association, 'an insignificant little man' in Jones's phrase, had to try to bridge divisions in his ranks with a policy which conceded nothing to the Government or the miners. Sir Adam Nimmo, another owner, 'the greatest stumbling block to peace' (the phrase is again Jones's), huffed and puffed as he blew the crisis up to bursting point. In the middle were men like John Reith, at thirty-six, head of the infant British broadcasting system, anxious to achieve Government support for a new charter, but trying to maintain his independence by resisting – with little success – Churchill's efforts to turn his organisation into a Government propaganda agency. Sir Herbert Samuel, former Governor of Palestine, future leader of the Liberal Party, chairman of the controversial 1925 royal commission into the mining industry, also failed in his attempt to act as honest broker during the strike. Randall Davidson, appropriately conventional and conservative as befitted an Archbishop of Canterbury, staunchly opposing the strike yet vainly seeking a settlement, was refused permission by Baldwin to broadcast an appeal for peace, as he grappled hopelessly with forces he did not understand.

After the collapse of the General Strike on 12 May 1926, and the defeat of the miners in November, the Government lost no time in securing the spoils of victory. In 1927 it passed the Trade Disputes Act, punishing both the TUC and the Labour Party for the General Strike by hitting at the Labour Party's financial links with the unions and declaring the General Strike retrospectively illegal. Not surprisingly, the labour movement lost faith in united industrial action. Instead, Walter Citrine and Ernest Bevin helped prepare the path for the Mond-Turner talks[1] on cooperation between management and labour. Denounced by the Left as an example of class collaboration, the Mond-Turner talks had few concrete results in 1928. But they influenced TUC thinking for years to come, as the pendulum swung back to political action. Yet the second Labour Government of 1929 was, like its predecessor of 1924, still only a minority administration, and just as ill-starred. Its ignominious collapse in 1931 emasculated the party, and led to the desolation of the 1930s.

That dismal decade ended with war; and when Labour at last won real power in Parliament in 1945 it looked out upon a changed world. Significantly, two of its first actions were to repeal the Trade Disputes Act and nationalise the mines. A peaceful, but momentous, revolution followed – a revolution which it is perhaps hard for those who did not live through the inter-war depression to appreciate. Full employment, social security, a free health service, proper care for the old, the sick, the young, widening educational opportunities, less crude class distinctions, a chance for ordinary working men to face their employers with dignity and effectiveness – all these were things the beaten strikers had dreamed of in 1926. And they were being achieved twenty years later, by a Government in which many of the 1926 strike leaders were prominent – men like Ernest Bevin, the Foreign Secretary from 1945–50, and Aneurin Bevan, a strike organiser in South Wales in 1926, who was architect of the National Health Service.

For the labour movement this was sweet revenge for all the hurt and humiliation which the failure of the General Strike had symbolised. The vengeance was not bloody or brutal, as it had been in other countries, but it was no less satisfying. More important, this political turning-of-the-tables took place within a vastly different economic context. After 1945 the unions were able to reverse, at long last and in years of severe labour shortage, that same legal bargaining strength which the employers had used against them during the inter-war period of trade depression and mass unemployment.

Such is the wider historical perspective of the General Strike. But as always with historical narrative there is the problem of when to begin.

At the end of the war in 1918? During the turbulent years before 1914? With the birth of the Labour Party in 1900 or the Miners' Federation of Great Britain in 1888? With Benbow and the idea of a general strike in the 1820s? Yet if there is a problem about *when* to begin there is really no problem about *where*. In his powerful novel *Germinal*, which tells of the failure of a desperate mining strike in his homeland, Emile Zola predicted that a black, avenging army, toiling endlessly in the bowels of the earth, would slowly germinate so that one day it would rise in blind, unappeasable rage to overturn the world. Any account of the tragedy of 1926 must begin, as it must end, with that avenging army of coal miners.

Part One:
The Nine Decades
1825-1915

Chapter One

The Making of the Mines

Coal mining is as old as Britain itself. The Roman army of occupation burned coal.[1] Its use almost died out during the Anglo-Saxon settlement. The Saxons and Danes were wood users; and Domesday Book says little or nothing about coal mines. Yet after the Norman Conquest the ancient tradition revived again, and the Middle Ages have left records of a flourishing mining industry, despite the efforts of Edward III's grandfather to forbid the use of coal in London.[2] But such royal proclamations proved so ineffective that in the middle of the sixteenth century the annual output of coal in the British Isles was already about 200,000 tons. Coal was clearly playing a more significant part in the economic life of Britain than of other countries.

Coal's primary use was as a household fuel. Thus in the hundred years after the 1688 Revolution, coal output rose three-fold – or about the same rate as the rise in population. Yet the use of coal in furnaces of all kinds, in pottery kilns and in iron-smelting, together with such inventions as James Watt's steam engine, was an important spur to more coal production. However, the amount of coal burned in the hearths of British homes was still very much greater than that consumed by industry. So the pre-industrial base of the coal industry was sounder than that of the iron industry. Even before the industrial revolution, the coal industry's output could be measured in millions of tons.

The really spectacular increase in the demand for coal came in the 120 years after 1790, when coal production multiplied twenty-five-fold. As late as 1842, the smoky fireplaces of British homes still burned more than two-thirds of Britain's domestic coal supply. But as the first phase of British industrialisation, based on wool and textiles, reached its peak around 1850, it was overtaken by an even more profitable phase, based on capital goods industries, like coal, iron and steel. Coal output in 1840 was about 30 million tons a year; by 1850 it had risen by nearly two-thirds to 49 million tons; and by 1880 it had tripled to 147 million tons.[3] An increasing proportion of this coal was exported, to supply the rapidly expanding European industries, and to help pay for the imports of cheap food available since the repeal of the Corn Laws for Britain's own mounting population. Thus the value of coal exports rose from under £$\frac{3}{4}$ million in 1840–2 to more than £3 million in 1857–9 and to something like £60 million a year by the turn of the century.[4]

On the eve of the First World War, coal had established a pre-eminent position in the British economy. It was the only industry to employ more than a million workers.[5] Its output was 287 million tons of coal in 1913 – a figure never surpassed before or since – of which 98 million was exported. This product was worth more than £250 million a year. Coal provided one-tenth of British exports in value, and no less than four-fifths in volume. By furnishing outward cargo for a large amount of shipping, it cheapened freight-rates for the import of such vital commodities as food. It was the foundation of the iron and steel industry, of shipbuilding and engineering, of the railways, of Britain's whole industrial life. One-tenth of the population was directly dependent for its livelihood upon the prosperity of the coal industry.[6]

The economic importance of coal was matched by the political importance of the coalowners. By the end of the eighteenth century it had become clear that the magnates who owned land where coal had been found would become increasingly important as a social class. This politically decisive landlord class had a direct interest in the coal which happened to lie under their lands. Unlike their continental counterparts, the landlords rather than the king exercised undisputed ownership of the coal. This concept of the private ownership of minerals, which played a crucial part in the mining crisis of the 1920s, was by no means universal. In most countries mineral rights were the property of the state. Among major industrial nations Britain and the United States were virtually alone in allowing mineral rights to be privately owned.

Coal in Britain was thus the property of the owners of the land where it happened to be found. But it was rarely mined by them. Instead, the companies which mined the coal paid the landowners royalties in return for mining rights, and what were known as wayleaves for the right of most direct access to the coal.[7] This royalty system increasingly became the cause of great bitterness in an industry where the work was unusuall hard and dangerous. As the industrial revolution progressed, most industrialists could argue that their rewards, even if they sometimes seemed excessive, were the result of their skill and enterprise. In the coal industry such rewards looked like the result of a happy accident, for they went to landlords, often absentee landlords at that, who had simply had the good fortune to find themselves sitting on top of an underground mountain of coal. Not surprisingly, by 1914 there was growing pressure to nationalise the industry.

Coal deposits were found all over the British Isles. Regional differences in the type and quality of coal often gave rise to differences of interest between different groups of owners and miners which were becoming clearly defined by 1914. First among the principal coalfields in age, and in many ways in importance, was the north-eastern region of Northumberland and Durham : Northumberland produced some 'soft' coal, Durham mostly 'hard' steam coal. As late as 1889 the region had produced more than any other coalfield in Britain. Yet by 1914 South Wales had surpassed the north-east as Britain's greatest coal producer, while Yorkshire had surpassed Durham. During those twenty-five years, 80 per cent of the coal mined in the north-east was either exported or sent south.[8] The region's heavy dependence on the highly competitive and fluctuating export trade had an important influence on hardening the attitudes of both owners and miners towards wage bargaining.

By contrast, the Cumberland coalfield in the north-west was much smaller and far less dependent on risky export markets. But the greater cost of Cumberland coal production meant it was steadily undercut by coal from its west-coast neighbours, Scotland to the north and Lancashire to the south. Nevertheless, the amount of coal mined in Cumberland to supply local iron, steel and coke industries virtually doubled between 1889 and 1913. Its pits were the biggest in the country, with seams ranging up to fourteen feet thick, which meant that miners could work two coal-cutting shifts a day, instead of one as was more usual elsewhere. Yet irregular seams, geological faults and the distance of the coal faces from the pit heads made mining difficult and expensive. Dirt brought up with the coal meant much costly washing which was a constant source of disputes between masters and miners.[9]

The Lancashire coalfield developed near one of the cradles of the industrial revolution with production based on cotton textiles. This created a demand for machinery, and thus for coal for the iron and steel industry. Later, the cotton mills themselves were converted from water power to steam, which further increased the demand for coal. Thus, the Lancashire coalfield sold its product almost exclusively in its own backyard. When the bottom fell out of the cotton textile trade in the 1920s exhaustion of the upper coal seams was already forcing Lancashire mineowners to sink deeper shafts, so driving up the cost of mining. Similarly, the North Staffordshire coalfield, with which Lancashire was geologically connected, was past its best by 1918, with output increasing only slowly. The North Wales coalfield, in Flint and Denbighshire, which produced both steam and soft coal for local consumption, was another area facing incipient decline.[10]

Yorkshire, on the other hand, was booming. Coal mining there, as in Lancashire, really began with the industrial revolution. The metal industries of the West Riding of Yorkshire began later than in Lancashire, while steam power came to cotton mills before it came to wool and worsted. So Yorkshire's coal mines developed later than Lancashire's. Yet between 1889 and 1920 Yorkshire's coal production doubled, nearly all of it being consumed locally or in the Midlands. However, the fact that the southern region, with its deeper, thicker seams, its modern coal-cutting equipment, its much greater division of labour and its large-scale undertakings, paid much higher wages than the western region had become a potent source of friction among miners by 1914.[11]

The Yorkshire coalfield formed a geological whole with the great North Midland coalfield covering Nottinghamshire and Derbyshire: the celebrated 'Barnsley Bed' seam was worked almost continuously nearly fifty miles south-east. But these two counties, unlike Yorkshire, did not enjoy close proximity to a large, profitable local manufacturing market. Thus in the 1880s Derbyshire produced mainly house and gas coal, the famous 'Derbyshire Brights', while Nottinghamshire's soft coal and steam coal were both dependent on a small local market which grew very slowly. The discovery of excellent hard steam coal near Mansfield changed this picture in the 1890s, and by 1913 a quarter of Derbyshire's coal production and half Nottinghamshire's was hard coal.[12]

The South Midland coalfield, in contrast, was predominantly a soft coal area. Its principal districts, Cannock Chase, South Staffordshire, Warwickshire and Leicestershire, were generally grouped together; but there were great differences between them, especially as regards wages. Yet they were alike in general quality of coal, and this market was mainly domestic for gas and manufacturing purposes, either locally or in Midland towns. Cannock Chase, mainly a house-coal region in the 1880s, had by 1914 greatly increased its steam coal, which was sold locally, while much of the soft coal was sent south. Leicestershire was handicapped by lack

1. J. H. Thomas, founder of the National Union of Railwaymen, addressing a meeting at King's Cross during the great railway strike of 1911.

2a. David Lloyd George, Prime Minister from 1916 to 1922, takes a stroll round his official country house at Chequers with Lord Reading in 1921.

2b. Andrew Bonar Law, Lloyd George's strong-man and his successor as Prime Minister in 1922, helps Glasgow students welcome the Prince of Wales to the city in 1921.

of local markets, and practically all its coal had to be sent by rail, much of it to London. Yet despite this, production in Warwickshire and Leicestershire grew far more rapidly between 1889 and 1913 than in any other district in Great Britain.[13]

Three more of less separate mining districts were found in Somerset, centred at Bristol, Newbury and Radstock, producing coal of varying qualities suitable for domestic, gas, and manufacturing purposes. Before 1914, the district changed from purely house coal to gas and manufacturing production as well, which meant less seasonal fluctuation. But as an old coalfield, it had to fight increasing competition as other districts developed. Local markets were supplied from other regions by cheaper transport, although demand grew with increasing population and the development of some large ironworks. Closeness to Bristol was not much use : little of the local coal was suitable for bunkering, and it was too costly to export. Moreover, manufacturing in Bristol did not develop much between 1870 and 1914. Thus, and because the Somerset coalfield was in the heart of an agricultural area, wages were about the lowest in any mining district in Britain.[14]

Even today the Forest of Dean is a world to itself. Sixty years ago it was even more socially isolated. Geologically connected with South Wales, as is Somerset, its coal had been worked for centuries. Yet the industry was altogether independent – indeed, its economic connection was with the Midlands rather than South Wales. In the 1880s the small Forest coalfield produced mainly house coal, most of it consumed locally, the rest shipped to Ireland and south-west England. Thus competition was with the Midlands rather than South Wales and wages tended to follow suit. By 1914 half the pits produced steam coal, but the Forest always lacked capital. Pits were mainly family concerns and the owners, like Lord Bledisloe, local men. This delayed modernisation and meant more costly working. Transit of coal from the face to the surface was often antiquated, double winding was rare and there was a lack of large pumping machinery. The peculiar system of mineral rights, a feudal survival, allowed 'free-miners' to mine coal themselves, a custom which was often a source of friction.[15]

The South Wales coalfield, which includes Monmouthshire, produced mainly steam coal for export, perhaps the finest in the world. But even in 1914 much coal was sold for home industries, and this had been even more true in the past. The old districts, such as Ebbw Vale, Tredegar and Merthyr, had been built up to supply the demands of home industry by great local ironmasters like D. A. Thomas, who considered their coal

B

mines of secondary importance to their main business of making iron and steel. The 1860s slump in iron prices turned their attention to coal. They at once found this profitable because their mines were more fully developed than those only recently started elsewhere, and because they paid less.[16] Wages in the Rhondda and Aberdare valleys were 15 to 25 per cent above those paid in the older Merthyr district.[17] By the 1880s the South Wales coalfield was more dependent on the export trade, and expansion was enormous. Production more than doubled between 1889 and 1913; yet during the whole period there was a more or less acute shortage of labour, despite large movements of migrant workers from England and Ireland, and a chronic shortage of housing. Pits were not sunk near large towns but in country districts, and labour had to be attracted there. The cost of living in mining villages tended to be high, because transport was more expensive. Employment was less regular in the highly fluctuating export trade than it had been when most of the coal was sold at home. So while wages were usually higher than in the home trade districts of South Wales, poor housing, high living costs and seasonal unemployment made South Wales miners more militant than most.[18]

In South Scotland, coal was mined almost everywhere, but there were three principal districts – Lanarkshire, Fifeshire and Ayrshire. Of these, Lanarkshire was easily the largest. Its rapid rise to pre-eminence had been based on three factors. Its shallow seams were easy and cheap to work; the famous local 'Blackband' ironstone had needed coal to smelt it; and the rise of the Clyde valley as a shipping and manufacturing centre created a huge local demand for coal and provided a convenient export outlet. Fifeshire had enjoyed none of these advantages, and its seams were both deep and costly to work. Yet by the start of the First World War the Fifeshire coalfield was slowly overhauling Lanarkshire. In 1889 Fife had produced only $2\frac{3}{4}$ million tons as against 13 million tons from Lanarkshire, but by 1913 Fife produced about 9 million tons while Lanarkshire's production had risen to $17\frac{1}{2}$ million tons. The royal commission on coal supplies in 1905 estimated that this trend would continue, judging that Fifeshire had more coal resources than any part of Scotland, and that its output was certain to surpass all others eventually.[19]

In the Ayrshire field seams were generally fewer, thinner and of poorer quality than in the other two major Scottish coalfields. Mining there was also more costly because of rock faults. Yet between 1889 and 1913 production rose from three to four million tons, a rate of increase equal to that in Lanarkshire. But Lanarkshire's importance was based not only on the amount of coal it produced but on its variety, which enabled the

Lanarkshire field to sell its coal in manufacturing, railway and domestic markets. In 1914 most of this production was consumed locally, and the export trade was still subsidiary, though of growing importance. However, the general level of wages was much the same in all three coalfields, although the leaders of the Scottish Miners' Federation tended to come from Lanarkshire.[20]

So by the eve of the First World War the British coal industry had established a pre-eminent position in the British economy. It employed more men than any other, while in both value and volume its product outstripped that of any other enterprise. Mining had laid the foundation of British industrial supremacy, while coal exports paid for the country's imports of cheap food. But already it was clear that important regional divisions were opening up in the coal trade, particularly between those mining regions which exported their coal, such as South Wales and Durham, and those like Nottinghamshire and Yorkshire which sold at home. In times of boom the exporting regions tended to be more prosperous. But it was impossible for them to control the terms of trade, and if they were hit by fierce foreign competition from Germany, Poland or other European coal-exporting countries, the resulting depression could bite very hard. In 1914 both owners and miners expected the industry's prosperity to continue indefinitely. No one could foresee the rapid change in fortunes which lay just a few years ahead.

Chapter Two

The Making of
the Miners

The sacrifices of the men who dug the coal from these pits are an indelible part of British social history. Working long, back-breaking hours in cramped, ill-lit conditions, facing the constant danger of fire, falls, floods and explosions, living in isolated mining villages often made up of squalid miners' hovels, colliers were regarded by both owners and workers in other trades as little better than beasts of burden. Children, often as young as five or six, had commonly worked eleven or twelve hours a day underground until near the middle of the nineteenth century. Frequently these children were in charge of some non-productive, but literally vital, operation such as winding the cages which took the men to and from the coal seams. Women worked with their men underground for fourteen and sixteen hours a day. The death rate was high and even if they survived fatal or crippling accidents, miners were usually worn out and finished at forty, and dead at fifty as late as the 1920s.[1]

The public conscience was slow to stir about such brutalising and inhuman conditions, as indeed it was about conditions in other industries or about the abuses of child labour. There were Acts of Parliament dealing with miners, but not with their conditions of work. The rapid expansion of mining between 1800 and 1842 greatly increased the number of mining disasters, and forced public opinion to face up to the problem of safety in the mines. Sir Humphry Davy's safety lamp might have been expected to reduce the number of fatal explosions. In fact, the Davy Lamp aroused widespread expectations which it could not fulfil. Mine shafts were driven deeper and mining operations undertaken with greater recklessness than ever before during the years of rapid expansion, so that a select committee of the House of Commons heard in 1829 that loss of life had actually increased.[2]

In the 1830s, concern about conditions in the mines of Britain began to spread. In 1835 another Commons select committee suggested better systems of pit ventilation; improved safety lamps; more accurate plans of the entire workings of pits; and greater education for the miners. It also urged the owners not to neglect their responsibilities, and suggested regular visits to the mines by scientists and philanthropists. The findings of the epoch-making royal commission on the mines of 1840–2 revealed 'a state of things not only disgraceful but perilous to the country'.

Shaftesbury's Mines Act of 1842, a watershed in the history of mining legislation, was passed in the face of bitter opposition from the mine-owners. It tackled the most glaring abuses of the times. Yet 'even this fragment of legislation met with the disapprobation of the colliery owners', wrote one historian of the coal industry.[3] And it was received with indifference by the miners themselves, who were more conscious of wage cuts and unemployment during the 'hungry forties'. Yet the Mines Act of 1842 marked the first step on the long, hard road of reform.

The 1840s also saw the miners take their first, hesitant steps towards founding stable labour unions. Miners were – and have largely remained – villagers. Their way of life and their struggle often seemed strange to the workers in other industries, with whom they had little contact. In the period of rapid growth after 1850, colliers tended to seek out the highest wages, usually paid where new pits were being sunk, so that mining became for a time a migratory trade.[4] Despite the growth of trade unionism, and of more stable mining communities, during the second half of the nineteenth century, this social isolation of the miners was not fully broken down even by the 1920s, as the General Strike was to show.

After the repeal of the Combination Acts in 1825, miners, like other workers, had the legal right to organise. But the Miners' National Union, formed in 1842, never amounted to much. Despite this disappointing start, the agitation for further Parliamentary legislation to improve mining conditions, the Mines Inspection Acts of 1850 and 1855, and the whole long struggle for a 'better Mines Act', which dominated the history of the mineworkers from 1850 until 1910, inevitably had powerful reper-cussions on the campaign to establish mineworkers' unions. And this campaign took place against a background of mounting strength and authority for trade unionism in general. After 1850 the trade union move-ment began to put down strong and permanent roots, and by the 1870s had joined forces to launch the Trades Union Congress and achieve a legal status which remained largely unchanged nearly a century later. In 1858 the Yorkshire Miners had formed the first successful local federation of mineworkers, and soon other county and regional miners' federations were appearing.

The main focus of union activity among miners was the campaign for safety and the appointment of checkweighmen. The Mines Act of 1860, which reinforced the 1842 Act and added new rules governing ventilation, safety, haulage, winding, education and inspection, also enforced the use of true weighing where miners were being paid by the weight of the coal they cut. Most important, the miners were pressing to secure the right to appoint their own checkweighmen. The provision of elected checkweighmen to supervise the honesty of payment by weight was of great importance in the growth of trade unions among the mineworkers. Miners' leaders were determined to have their best union organisers elected as checkweighmen. The owners, well aware of these tactics, and determined to frustrate them as much as possible, put all kinds of obstacles in the way of such elections.

The struggle over checkweighmen became crucially important, not only in determining the level of wage rates, but as the symbol of trade union activity within the mining industry. The colliers eventually triumphed, and the system of electing checkweighmen became law. The Coal Mines Regulation Act of 1872 established the principle that in future all face workers must be paid by the weight of coal they cut. Moreover, the Act extended and improved checkweighing procedure so that miners could control the honesty of their payment by results through their elected checkweighmen. 'Never before . . . did any section of the working class so thoroughly leave their impression on any Act of Parliament,' commented the Scottish miners' leader Alexander Macdonald. 'No class of working men are better united than the miners,' he added, 'and they have the power of their unions to bring to bear . . . a power no government could afford to despise or ignore.'[5]

In fact, the power of the united mineworkers was much less than Macdonald imagined. Severe trade depression at the end of the 1870s hit their unions hard. Only the Northumberland and Durham district associations survived; but the spirit of trade unionism remained. Wages were still automatically regulated by prices according to a sliding scale. With no floor to wages, and prices tumbling, there was a general belief among miners that the sliding scale would have to go. And just as the campaign to secure proper safety regulations and elect checkweighmen had helped create unions in the 1860s, so opposition to the sliding scale provided the focus for a new burst of unionisation in the 1880s. The Derbyshire Miners were created from a combination of smaller local unions in 1880, while other county and regional associations were appearing. In 1881 the Yorkshire miners united and ended their pay scale; Lancashire miners, not to be outdone by their great rivals across the Pennines, did likewise; and in 1885 the Midland Federation, covering miners from Staffordshire to the Forest of Dean, was established to abolish sliding scales and introduce the eight-hour day.[6]

All this represented improvement over the bleak picture of the 1870s. Nevertheless, it is easy to exaggerate the strength and importance of trade unionism among the miners at the end of the decade. Only in Northumberland and Durham were the unions capable of carrying on organised negotiations with mineowners which had any real impact on the course of labour relations. Yet mineworkers in other districts often regarded these north-eastern unions as reactionary, because they still obstinately upheld the principle of the sliding scale and were strongly opposed to the eight-hour day for underground workers.[7] The new unions in Yorkshire, Lancashire and the Midlands had few members and influenced little beyond the general wage structure. Miners in West Scotland were virtually unorganised, while those in South Wales belonged to many small local unions pursuing independent and ineffective policies. In the smaller coalfields, the story was the same: nothing was being done to establish standard minimum rates for a district, let alone for the country as a whole, while there were very few agreed wage rates. And it remained true, of course, that miners' unions were effectively confined to coal hewers and other underground men. Little was being done to organise surface workers.[8]

The first step towards achieving an industrial union for mineworkers came in 1888 when the miners' unions took the momentous step of banding together to form the Miners' Federation of Great Britain. The MFGB marked a decisive split in the mineworkers' ranks. The old miners' union was still in existence, controlled by (and almost entirely composed of) men from Northumberland and Durham, and still unalterably opposed to the eight-hour day and the end of the sliding scale. Yet despite these divisions and weaknesses, the birth of the MFGB was a real watershed in the history of the miners and of the British labour movement as a whole. It marked the beginning of a period of rapid growth which, within a generation, was to make the MFGB the mightiest union in the land. Initially, at least, this growth can be attributed to a rapid rise in the selling price of coal. After 1888, trade improved, and wages followed the rapid rise in prices. Coal went from 4s 10d a ton in 1887, for example, to 8s 3d a ton in 1890 – a rise of more than 80 per cent in three years. At a time when profits were rising rapidly, the newly-created MFGB was able to provide a nation-wide bargaining unit which could deal with mineowners from a position of comparative strength.

The growth of the mineworkers' unions stimulated the growth of employers' organisations. From 1865 onwards district associations of colliery owners had been forming and improving their organisation and communications systems. The employers traditionally had been rugged individualists, intent on driving each other out of business and scooping the pool. But increasingly, as their workmen began to organise effectively, they were forced to recognise that their individual problems of wages, profits, investments and so on, and the control of both labour and market prices, were all common ones. So in 1870 and 1871 conferences were held between different regional groups of owners, who could then present a more united front in dealing with their workers.[9] In 1888 the owners in areas where the sliding scale was not in force combined to form joint conciliation boards to regulate collective bargaining. These boards – in the Yorkshire–Derbyshire–Nottinghamshire area and in the Lancashire, North Wales, West Midlands, Cumberland and Somersetshire coalfields – consisted of equally balanced representatives of miners and owners.[10] Finally, in order to match the national bargaining strength of the MFGB, the employers formed the Coal Owners' Association and later the Mining Association. The scene was now set for future conflicts.

Chapter Three

Prelude to Conflict

At its foundation in 1888 the MFGB had represented 36,000 workers : by 1893 this figure had grown to over 200,000. In that year the union fought its first struggle on a national scale. Coal prices had fallen sharply in the early 1890s and the employers in all coalfields demanded sweeping reductions in wages. Three hundred thousand men in Yorkshire, Lancashire and the Midlands came out on strike in July, and there were also strikes in South Wales and Scotland : altogether nearly four-fifths of the total numbers employed underground at that date were involved. The MFGB declared that wages were not to be reduced because prices had fallen, and that the old principle of the sliding scale must be put aside once and for all. Wages had risen with prices 40 per cent since 1888. By December the men were back at work, and the owners' original demand for a 25 per cent reduction had been modified to one of 10 per cent. But the owners had reasserted the principle that wages must in the main follow prices.

This failure taught the miners many lessons, but it mainly served to convince them of the value of organisation. As a direct result of the strike, the Scottish Miners' Federation was formed in 1894. But there was no county union in Lancashire, at this time the biggest district of all, till 1896. South Wales also felt the need, and by 1898 had formed and consolidated the South Wales Miners' Federation, and linked it with the MFGB, which in 1900 had more than 360,000 members, nearly half the total number of all colliery workers. Only Northumberland and Durham still remained outside, though the latter had tried to join.

The stumbling block to complete unity was the question of the eight-hour day. For the MFGB steadily and persistently pursued this. At every annual conference a resolution in favour of legislation was carried : every

B*

year since 1894, almost without exception, MPs supported by the MFGB brought a Bill before Parliament. Gradually the belief spread in Northumberland and Durham that after all it was possible to rearrange the existing working conditions, under which there were two short shifts of hewers to one long shift of transit workers, and to find the extra boy labour necessary. When the miners' Eight-Hour Day Committee was appointed, two trade union leaders from Northumberland gave evidence, one in favour and the other against, and each was supported by about half the membership. Eventually in 1908 the Eight-Hour Act was passed. Not the least important of its effects was to make complete unification possible. The old National Union was dissolved, and Northumberland and Durham joined the MFGB.

The Eight-Hour Act, which secured an important objective of the MFGB, was clearly a major step forward for the miners. Within a few years it was followed by others. Another long-standing aim of the MFGB was a minimum wage. No national or uniform system of wage regulation existed in the coalfields. The forms and methods of payment were fantastically complicated. Rates varied greatly from district to district and pit to pit, and it took a lifetime to master the intricacies of assessment.[1] Miners were paid Xd a ton for cutting coal, Yd a ton for loading into tubs, Zd a ton for setting pit props and so on. However, many men in the mining industry, especially surface workers, were paid by time. The full complexity of this system would require a book in itself to unravel;[2] but the main point was that in every coalfield payment was based on a so-called 'standard', or basic rate. These standards represented the actual level of wages in a particular year in the past. Three years – 1877, 1879 (the low-water mark for colliery wages at the end of the coal trade depression) and 1888 – were used in different areas as the basis for calculating wages. Actual rates were determined by percentage advances 'on standard'. Thus, in the Federated Area (comprising roughly the Yorkshire–Derbyshire–Nottinghamshire, Lancashire, North Wales and West Midlands coalfields) wages in 1912 stood at 55 per cent above the standard of 1888.[3]

The conciliation boards set up in 1888 to regulate wages and collective bargaining reached regular agreements which were renewed from time to time. These agreements usually set parameters for wage variation. But the original standards were *local*, and stood for one amount in South Wales, another in the various districts of Scotland, and still another in the Federated Area. So to understand wages one really had to have detailed historical knowledge of the coal industry region by region.

As these wage standards became increasingly obsolete in the early years of the twentieth century, unsuccessful attempts were made to replace them by new standards based on present conditions or, better still, replace them by national wage agreements. But the vexed question of standards was only the beginning of the complexity of the wage system in the coal-fields. The majority of miners worked on piece rate, and were paid according to an elaborate price list, which stated the rate for each particular job. Normally each colliery had its own price list; sometimes there were several lists for different seams, especially where conditions varied a good deal.[4] In South Wales, for example, with difficult geological conditions, elaborate price lists varied greatly from place to place, and once fixed were seldom changed. In Durham, on the other hand, where conditions were much easier, piece-work prices were adjusted regularly under the so-called 'county average' system. By this method, if average actual earnings in a particular pit or seam varied by more than 5 per cent above or below the county average, which, like the standard, was a figure agreed some time before, either miners or owners could apply for the price list to be changed. Again, in Scotland, percentage variations were usually added to or subtracted from piece-work rates.[5]

The complexity and increasing unreality of this system came under mounting fire from the miners until the Minimum Wage Act of 1912 partially undermined this system and secured a second major MFGB objective. The MFGB was originally drawn into this dispute by the South Wales federation, which became markedly more militant in the years before 1914. The rich steam coal of South Wales was located in unusually narrow seams; and the dispute had grown out of a demand over payment for work in 'abnormal places' – coal faces where, through no fault of his own, a hewer was unable to make his usual earnings because of natural conditions which made coal cutting more difficult. The difficulty of defining an abnormal place led, naturally enough, to a simpler yet more fundamental idea : a general minimum wage for all underground workers. The struggle lasted from 1910 until 1912 and resulted in some long and bitter miners' strikes, especially in South Wales.

With the passing of the Minimum Wage Act, the power of the MFGB had been amply demonstrated, and the loyalty of the men successfully put to the test. The MFGB immediately arranged for a general campaign by ordering that no agreements were to be made for any period extending beyond 1915. Until the longest existing agreement had run out, no national action could be taken, and the years 1913 and 1914 were spent in working out the details of the Minimum Wage Act. The outbreak of the

First World War postponed the proposed campaign for an advance in wages and conditions and under the general industrial truce no national move was made until the spring of 1919. But the years before 1914 saw a great increase in union strength. In 1907 the membership of the MFGB was 458,000; the next year, with the adhesion of Northumberland and Durham, the total was 590,000; by 1913 it was 670,000. Many districts had secured closed shop agreements, by which employers promised to hire only union labour.

Much still remained for the miners to do. Even after the Minimum Wage Act there was no national system of wage regulation. The Act put a floor on wages; but this floor consisted of district minimum rates, which still varied greatly from district to district. The wage system in the mines remained entirely on a local or area basis; and it was a prime MFGB objective to replace this district system by a system of national wage agreements. Indeed, national agreements and nationalisation of the mining industry were the outstanding MFGB demands in the years before the war. But the years since the birth of the MFGB in 1888 had revealed a cleavage between miners whose coal sold at home, and those who produced for the more competitive export market. The coalfields of Yorkshire, Lancashire, Nottinghamshire and the Midlands were by the end of the nineteenth century selling almost exclusively in Britain. They were thus not affected by the erratic conditions of foreign markets and could openly declare that wages must control prices and not *vice versa*, as had been the case with the sliding-scale system. Miners in Scotland, the North-East and South Wales, on the other hand, who were more dependent on overseas sales, could not blind themselves to the fact that it was impossible for them to control prices in the same way.

Yet despite this fundamental dichotomy, great changes had been taking place in the general conduct of industrial relations. The real energy of the miners' leaders since the 1860s had been concentrated in building from the bottom upwards. No district association could do much unless the pit branches, or 'lodges', of which it was composed, were vigorous and healthy centres. The 'paper strength' of 1888–93 had not only increased greatly, but become increasingly real strength. Trade unionism began to exercise a day-to-day influence in the life of the individual miner. Price lists were no longer posted by the management, but were fixed by joint negotiation. When there was an injury by accident, the miners' agent dealt with the case, and saved the miner from losing money because of the law's delays. The unions gradually began to enforce some sort of standard rates for different grades throughout the districts. At some pits they were able to secure 'make-up' rates for the hewers in specially difficult stalls. The degree of general control exercised varied greatly in different coalfields; but everywhere there was at least an influential body of men strongly organised, and waiting for the opportunity to use their power to the best advantage.

On the national scene, too, the miners were much better organised. They had shown this gradually throughout the nineteenth century by the increasing effectiveness with which they pressed their case for reform of the mining industry. The miners' voice was heard in union lodges and county association meetings, in demonstrations and petitions to Parliament, in deputations to Ministers, in evidence presented to Parliamentary select committees and royal commissions and, as the century neared its end, increasingly in the speeches and votes of miners' MPs, Liberals and later the so-called 'Lib-Labs'.[6] Miners' MPs were sent to Parliament by the votes and financial contributions of miners themselves. This mounting pressure had made its mark on public opinion, on the mineowners, and on the law, so that reform and improvement gradually came. The leadership of the Miners' Federation showed the direction events were taking. Ben Pickard, the first president of the MFGB, a typical tough, gritty, uncompromising Yorkshireman, was known as the 'iron man' by the miners because of his great stubbornness in negotiating with the mineowners. His successors, the Scottish socialist Robert Smillie, and the laconic Herbert Smith, another tough Yorkshireman, were moulded in the same way as Pickard. Under their leadership the MFGB grew and prospered.

In 1900 the MFGB, in company with the trade union movement as a whole, moved more directly into the political arena with the formation of the Labour Representation Committee, which later became the Labour Party. In the 1890s several court decisions had reversed the traditional picture of the legal rights of trade unions as they had been apparently defined in the 1870s. Unions suddenly found that their rights of picketing were severely restricted, while their funds were no longer safe from suits for damages brought by employers during strikes. The railway unions were especially hit by these decisions, and were anxious moreover to secure better representation in Parliament, where so much railway legislation was discussed and enacted. In addition, unskilled and semi-skilled workers had been pressing for a greater say in industrial matters since the eruption of labour unions among their ranks in the 1880s following strikes among dockers and gas workers. Other trades, like engineering, printing and shoemaking, were fearful that new techniques would lead to greater redundancy in their ranks. Finally, the growing strength of employers' organisations and the mounting use of 'blackleg' labour to break strikes in the 1890s led to a stronger sense of solidarity.

In fact, the miners had not pressed strongly for the creation of a Labour Party, since they were already well placed to elect their own Lib-Lab MPs. Support for the idea of a Labour party came from the unions already mentioned and from such earlier socialist societies as the Independent Labour Party, whose members included Keir Hardie, the first Labour MP, and Ramsay MacDonald, the first Labour Prime Minister. Other political groups involved were the Marxist Social Democratic Federation and the Fabians. And though the MFGB had been unenthusiastic about the new venture it was one of the first organisations to benefit from it. In the general election of 1900 Keir Hardie, the Scottish miners' leader, was elected in company with a Liberal for the two-member Welsh seat of Merthyr.[7]

Labour's real success came in the next general election, when twenty-nine of its candidates were returned in the Liberal landslide of 1906. Passage of the Trade Disputes Act later that year, which legalised picketing and guaranteed union funds against actions for damages, seemed to show that Labour could bring pressure to bear on the Liberal Government. But internal divisions, its secret electoral pact with the Liberals and apparently slavish dependence on Government goodwill, quickly led to disillusion in some quarters of the labour movement. The victory of 1906 had looked like a triumphant vindication of the British tradition of Parliamentary reformism and gradualism; but the failure of both the Liberal and Labour parties to do anything effective about the rapidly rising cost of living and consequent steep decline in real wages drove some elements of organised labour sharply to the Left in the years before the First World War. The price rise was probably one of the steepest in living memory. Between 1896 and 1910 food prices, for example, rose by 25 per cent, while between 1900 and 1913 the purchasing power of the pound fell to 17s 1d.[8] Parliamentary methods seemed to have failed, and the idea of direct action became suddenly more popular.

The miners were still fairly happy about the path of Parliamentary reform. They had secured passage of the Eight-Hour Act and persuaded the Government to set up the royal commission of 1906 with more comprehensive terms of reference than any previous investigation into the coal mining industry. Management and men were represented equally on the commission; and its hearings bore fruit with the Mines Act of 1911, an important step which was arguably the most advanced piece of legislation of its kind in the world. With four parts and nearly one hundred sections, it vindicated the miners' efforts since the first Mines Act of 1842, and was to provide the legal framework for the British mining industry for the next fifty years.

At the same time, however, the struggle to secure the Minimum Wage Act was drawing the MFGB into the labour unrest which marked the years before the First World War. Two apparently incompatible forces seemed to be at work here. Since the strikes among dockers and gas workers in the late 1880s, and the birth of the Labour Party in the early 1900s, semi-skilled and unskilled workers had been struggling to form effective labour unions and narrow the gap between their wages and those of more skilled and better organised workers. On the other hand, comparatively well-paid groups, like the miners and railwaymen, were struggling to maintain the differential between their pay and that of other workers. The miners, in particular, wished to benefit from the great prosperity in the industry at a time when their own organised strength seemed greater than ever. Yet this apparent incompatibility of aim did not prevent the dockers and transport workers eventually getting together with the railwaymen and the miners.

In 1910 the dockers and transport workers unions combined to form the National Transport Workers Federation, while in 1913 many of the railwaymen's unions, with the notable exception of the footplate men and the booking clerks, established their own nation-wide industrial union, the National Union of Railwaymen. The railway strike of 1911 had important repercussions on organised labour. Its impact was felt not just on the railways but in the wider sphere of cooperation between major groups of industrial workers. The railwaymen's fight for recognition of their union helped reveal the great interdependence of railwaymen, miners and transport workers employed in the docks. Having experienced the benefits of sympathetic action from miners and transport workers during their own strike, many railwaymen wanted to show their appreciation in a practical way.[9] Their chance came during the great dock strike in 1911, and the transport and mining strikes of 1912. The resulting coal shortage had forced factories to close and railways to curtail services drastically. Once again, as during the rail strike of 1911, the increasing interdependence of the big unions had been demonstrated. Why not institutionalise this interdependence? The miners took the initiative; the TUC, recognising the force of the movement for unity, somewhat belatedly joined the discussion and gave the *imprimatur* of official TUC approval to the alliance.

The triple alliance, formed in April 1914, was a loose, informal organisation of $1\frac{1}{2}$ million miners, railwaymen and transport workers for sympathetic action during disputes, when each group agreed to help the other. The outbreak of war in Europe four months later cut short miners' plans for using the alliance to replace district by national wage settlements. But the years before 1914 had seen significant developments elsewhere. In 1909, for example, at Ruskin College, Oxford, an adult trade union centre founded in 1899, radical students had struck for closer contact with the university and a more socialist syllabus. When the strike failed, the students, supported by South Wales miners and the railwaymen, set up the Central Labour College in London.[10]

The CLC influenced the leftward trend of the Labour movement. Its roll-call of students reads like a *Who's Who* of radical labour leaders: Frank Hodges, handsome, intelligent secretary of the MFGB in the early 1920s and Judas-figure of 'Black Friday' in 1921; A. J. Cook, Hodges' successor as miners' secretary, an emotional, silver-tongued and tragic leader in 1926; John McLean, the Clydeside Anarchist and Marxist who died young in 1923; Aneurin Bevan, perhaps the greatest Parliamentarian produced by the British labour movement; James Griffiths, Morgan Phillips, Arthur Jenkins and many more.[11] There were other developments too. Noah Ablett, a South Wales miner and one of the 1909 Ruskin strikers, combined with Cook to write an influential revolutionary pamphlet after the 1912 strike called *The Miners' Next Step*. The preamble called apocalyptically for 'A united industrial organisation, which, recognising the war of interest between workers and employers, is constructed on fighting lines, allowing for a rapid and simultaneous stoppage of wheels throughout the mining industry.' The pamphlet was published by the Plebs League, another product of the Ruskin strike, a nation-wide discussion group for syndicalist and socialist ideas, whose magazine, *Plebs*, helped create an intellectual climate in which talk of direct action, syndicalism and the theory of the general strike was possible.

These developments, the wave of strikes in Britain before the war, and such episodes as the Singer dispute in Glasgow in 1911, created a hard core of militant industrial radicalism which led to more strikes on Clydeside during the war and helped create the militantly left-wing Shop Stewards' Movement, the British Communist Party and the National Minority Movement in the 1920s. In South Wales, for example, leadership of the miners seemed to be passing from solid, respectable pillars of the Nonconformist Chapels, like the celebrated Lib-Lab MP William Abraham, known everywhere by his Bardic name of 'Mabon', to left-wing militants like Ablett and Cook.[12]

Yet it is easy to make too much of all this. The Ruskin strike, the Singer strike, *The Miners' Next Step* and the activities of the Plebs League were all dramatic. But in many ways they took on a significance in retrospect during the bitter conflicts of the 1920s which they had not possessed at the time. The triumph of the great dock strike in 1911 had to be set against the failure of the great transport strike in 1912. In the years before the war all the moral pressure was on the syndicalists to make their ideas seem more viable. Some union leaders hoped the triple alliance would control militancy rather than stimulate it.[13] Meanwhile, Labour MPs seemed to be steadily improving their position. Their support was vital to the Liberal Government: the two elections of 1910 had eroded their Parliamentary majority and made them dependent on Labour and Irish votes. The Labour Party put pressure on the Government to pass the Trade Union Amendment Act in 1913, which reversed the Osborne Judgement of 1909[14] and made it legal once more for unions to help finance the Parliamentary party.

Yet the Liberal Government seemed to possess, in David Marquand's words, 'a miraculous gift for gaining more steam the longer it stayed in office. . . . What the years 1911 to 1914 really saw was not the strange death of Liberal England but its ressurection in modern dress.'[15] The most potent symbol of class conflict was the triple alliance; but the industrial truce brought on by the war cut short plans for united industrial activity. In any case, the strongest element in the triple alliance, the MFGB, had already achieved much of what it wanted. The eight-hour day and the minimum wage had been secured before the war. The MFGB had also been taking steps to secure simultaneous termination of all existing district agreements throughout Britain's coalfields so that they could replace them with a demand for uniform national agreements. Finally, the miners had long been pressing for nationalisation of the mining industry. In 1914, purely as a war measure, the Government took control of the railways. So it made sense later for the Government to take control of coal mining too. The miners, widely recognised as perhaps the most vital element in the war effort, objected to the mineowners making huge profits during wartime. The MFGB had thus secured most of its long-term objectives by 1916 and was anxious not to surrender any of these gains when the war ended. Indeed, it was determined to secure full nationalisation and retain proper national wage agreements. In this post-war struggle, pre-war syndicalism seemed to take on a new and more significant historical perspective.

Part Two:
The Nine Years
1916-1925

Chapter Four

A Land Fit for Heroes

The year 1916–17, which saw serious industrial unrest on Clydeside, Lloyd George overthrow Asquith to put Britain on a total-war footing, and the Government take control of the mines, was really a more decisive time in British history than 1918. Yet the jubilation which greeted the Armistice on 11 November 1918 revealed much more than relief at the ending of the costliest war in history. It expressed the profound hope that four years of sacrifice would not have been made in vain : that 'the war to end war' would indeed usher in a new period of peace and prosperity. British sacrifices in the war had been real enough : nearly 1 million dead, another $1\frac{1}{2}$ million permanently injured by wounds or gas.[1] But the hopes proved illusory. There was no peace in Ireland or in India. War loomed in Russia and the Near East. At home the post-war prosperity proved short-lived; and when the boom burst, mass unemployment rather than good times characterised Britain's industrial scene. The world was in turmoil. Industrial unrest had continued in Britain, on Clydeside and elsewhere, throughout the war. General strikes occurred in Russia as long ago as 1905; in Sweden before the war; and in North America at Winnipeg, Seattle and Vancouver, as well as in Ireland at Limerick, in 1919. The Bolshevik Revolution was a portent of both hope and fear.

At home, material losses during the war had been comparatively slight. The abrupt halt to peacetime activities in August 1914 had been more damaging. More serious in the long-term, the war had promoted further expansion in overdeveloped industries, and done little to help expanding ones. Thus cotton mills had been encouraged, while the automobile industry had been comparatively neglected. The steel industry had too much capital tied up in the wrong places. Much the same story of out-moded investment patterns could be traced in textiles, shipbuilding and engineering – the traditional pacemakers of British industrial prosperity.[2] When the post-war boom collapsed in 1920–1, the blow fell hardest here and the old, staple industries bore the brunt of mass unemployment in the inter-war depression.[3]

These factors were important. Yet in a wider view, hindsight shows that the real cost of the war to Britain had not been material but financial. It had reversed the old-style roles of creditor and debtor nations, trans-forming Britain's position as London ran up large short-term debts to pay for the war. Foreign investments had been sold to help sustain the exchange rate of the pound sterling against the dollar. The real losses were not large, though Britain's principal debtor had been Russia, and the Bolsheviks repudiated all Tsarist international debts.

This repudiation – later emulated by South American countries – was symptomatic of the way the war and its aftermath had destroyed the international financial structure. Free exchange and comparatively free trade – the conditions on which British financial hegemony had been based – had crumbled. Inter-Allied debts haunted international relations for years after the Paris Peace Conference. Britain might have proposed that all debts be liquidated. But this would have broken every rule. And London financiers could not grasp the fact that most European countries were no longer safe debtors, that the central pillars of international finance had fallen, that the rules no longer applied.

The war had been largely financed by inflation : the pound had been pegged artificially at a value of $4.76, against the pre-war parity of $4.86; the dollar, on the other hand, remained pegged to gold. It followed that if Britain was to return to pre-war gold parity a ruthless policy of credit restriction would be necessary to force down prices. Yet no Govern-ment could start the post-war years with a major trade depression. So industry was given its head to encourage a post-war boom and let the pound take the consequences. When the Government suspended the gold standard in 1919, the pound fell to $3.40. But the Bank of England and the Treasury refused to accept the decision to 'go off gold' as final. Both had lost power during the war, when social and military priorities took precedence over 'sound finance'; both were determined to regain their former position and return to gold at the pre-war parity of $4.86 as soon as possible.[4]

These economic and financial changes hit the coal industry especially hard. Coal was still a symbol of Britain's industrial greatness. In 1913 it had produced a record tonnage, of which more than a third had gone for export. The miners had shared in this bonanza and were better paid than many industrial wage-earners in the years before the war. The insatiable demands of the military machine had pushed up the price of everything, including coal, to record heights. Owners and miners alike assumed coal prices would continue rising once the rich export markets, closed by the war, were reopened.

The combative spirit of the pre-war years had been most clearly marked in the coal industry. It was carried over with a vengeance into the post-war period. Coal had always been a hating trade. Mining was hard and dangerous; and though miners were paid better than many industrial workers, their living and working conditions were much worse than most. The colliers were tough, the mineowners obstinate : disputes between them were fought without quarter. Moreover, coal entered every branch of industrial life, so that a coal strike always had a big impact. Finally, coal was easily recognised, and sympathetic railwaymen and dockers, the miners' comrades in the triple alliance, had no difficulty in refusing to handle it during a mining dispute.

Industrial unrest was hastened by the fact that wartime inflation had driven prices spiralling upwards. The purchasing power of the pound, which had fallen to 17s 1d between 1900 and 1913, slumped to 6s 9d by 1920.[5] The Government set up a committee, headed by Lord Sumner, to investigate price increases. The Sumner report concluded that, 'when food is combined with other expenses . . . with no luxuries and including only necessities . . . the final increase in the cost of living as a whole is found to be for skilled workmen 67 per cent; for semi-skilled 75 per cent; and for unskilled 81 per cent'.[6] Price increases which hit the poorest sections hardest continued after the war. Taking 1914 as 100, wholesale prices were over 200 in 1919 and over 300 early in 1920. Yet wages were rising fast too, and unskilled wages faster than skilled, closing the gap between skilled and unskilled wage rates. So the whole problem of pay differentials became more prominent in the post-war period.

The miners had been one of the best-paid groups before the war. Now they felt they had fallen behind in the race to keep up with the rising cost of living. The new 'standard' for pay and profits in the post-war mining industry was 1914 – an extremely good year. Yet as Herbert Smith, president of the Yorkshire miners, put it, 'In comparison with other industries we are far from being fairly treated. The rates now paid to workers in other industries now exceed their 1914 rates by proportions much higher than ours.'[7] Even Evan Williams, president of the Mining Association, agreed that by 1921 the cost of living had risen 122 per cent since 1914, while miners' wages had risen by barely half this figure.

In South Wales, for example, where Williams himself owned important coal companies, wages had risen 78 per cent during the war, the cost of living 120 per cent.[8] The trade unions, militant before 1914, would continue to press for higher wages in the inflationary post-war period. And the Miners' Federation would be in the van of this struggle. The MFGB, which had been growing fairly rapidly before 1914, grew even faster during the war, rising from 670,000 members in 1913 to nearly 900,000 in 1920. With virtually every miner in the country now in its ranks, the MFGB was in a much stronger position than it had been before. It felt especially aggrieved because mining had slipped from being a comparatively well-paid job to being a comparatively badly-paid one. And it could expect backing from the triple alliance now that hostilities had ended.

Yet in the euphoria of victory, and the short-lived economic boom which followed the Armistice, these harsh facts did not make much impact, at least on the parliamentary scene. David Lloyd George, who had seized power from Asquith in the Cabinet *coup* of December 1916, was Prime Minister of the wartime Coalition Government. Born of humble Welsh farming stock in 1863, educated at Church school and trained as a solicitor, Lloyd George was Liberal MP for Caernarvon Boroughs from 1890 until 1945. Brilliant, unpredictable, unprincipled, he was fifty-five in 1918, and at the height of his powers. 'A master of improvised speech and improvised policies',[9] a compulsive womaniser, one of the outstanding parliamentarians of his time, he had become the champion of the new working-class radicalism with his notorious 'soak the rich' Budget of 1909. His present position was unassailable as 'the man who won the war'.

The prestige of this political magician may have been immense. But there was a good case for a general election. Parliament had outlived its legal term by three years; the extension of the vote to all men and many women had more than doubled the electorate; and Britain's representatives at the Paris Peace Conference would need a mandate from the people. Moreover, there was something to be said for getting the election over before the soldiers had time to come home and show what they thought of the politicians. The date was fixed for 14 December 1918. Lloyd George's action in unseating Asquith two years earlier had split the Liberal Party. Though many Liberals supported Lloyd George's Coalition with the Unionists,[10] an important section of the party opposed the 'traitor' of 1916.

This Liberal schism gave Labour its chance to become the second party in the state, and Labour withdrew its wartime support for the Coalition to fight on a clear socialist programme. Yet the main election issue was Lloyd George himself, and the result was a smashing personal vindication. The Coalition won 6 million votes and an overwhelming 533 seats against 4 million votes and 101 seats for its opponents. The Asquithian Liberals were annihilated : every one of their former Ministers, including Asquith himself, was defeated and only 26 independent Liberals were returned. Labour did much better, winning nearly 2.4 million votes – an almost five-fold increase since 1910 – increasing its MPs from 39 to 59. But the Prime Minister's popularity, and Labour's growing strength, could not disguise the fact that this was really a Tory triumph, a sign that for thirty-six of the next fifty years the country was to be controlled by Tory Governments or Tory-dominated Coalitions.

Chapter Five

The Uncertainty of Sankey

The new Parliament reflected clear class divisions. There were more businessmen than usual – 260 against a normal parliamentary average of 200 in the years between 1918 and 1945. 'The old-fashioned country gentlemen,' J. C. C. Davidson wrote with regret, 'and even the higher ranks of the learned professions, are scarcely represented at all.'[1] In the Labour Party, on the other hand, which made up more than half the opposition, all but one of its 59 MPs had been sponsored by a trade union. As Lloyd George said, it was 'the Associated Chamber of Trade on one side and the Trades Union Congress on the other'.[2] All seemed set for a resumption of the class-war combativeness and labour unrest which had characterised the years before 1914. Trade union membership was rising : from just over 4 million in 1913 to just over 8 million in 1919 to just under 8·5 million in 1920.[3] Lloyd George faced crises at home and abroad – in India, in Ireland and on the industrial front.

The first to break was on the industrial scene early in 1919. The miners, railwaymen and transport workers took the triple alliance out of its wartime mothballs and put in demands for higher wages and shorter hours. The Government, which still exercised its wartime control over railways and mines, was at once inevitably involved. Both industries had provided the backbone of British industrial expansion in Victorian times; both had been taken under Government control during hostilities as a war measure. But if by 1919 the railways had been worked out, and much of their equipment worn out, Government control of the coal mines had made little difference either. There had been some tidying up here and there. The abolition of all existing regional pay differentials had certainly satisfied a long-standing demand of the mineworkers. But there had been no real reorganisation or regrouping, while the richest coal seams had been exploited with impatient prodigality. Yet coal mining still remained Britain's largest industry. It was also labour-intensive : 75 per cent of the cost of coal was labour cost. Any trouble in the coal industry was going to mean trouble elsewhere, for the miners had the sympathy – and through the triple alliance the active support – of other wage workers.

So the first and most significant industrial confrontation in the post-war period was in the mining industry. Now the war was over, the owners were anxious to regain control from the Government, get their royalties back and exploit what they imagined would be a favourable post-war market. The miners were equally determined not to surrender their hard-won gains; in particular, the long-standing demand for national wage agreements. They knew that a return to private ownership would mean longer hours and less pay. The other members of the triple alliance threatened united strike action.

The Government, preoccupied with the Paris Peace talks and hard-pressed on Clydeside and the railways, as well as in Ireland and India, was not ready to resist this kind of pressure. It considered legislation[4] to deal with united action by the triple alliance, which would have amounted to a general strike, and discussed a memo prepared by the Home Secretary, Edward Shortt, on the use of troops in the event of trouble. But in the end, after a good deal of talk, no action was taken. Instead, Lloyd George appointed Sir John Sankey, a high court judge, to head a royal commission of inquiry into the coal mining industry.

Since the Government did not expect the Sankey commission to make any radical recommendations, Andrew Bonar Law committed his colleagues 'to carry out in the spirit and the letter' the Sankey proposals.[5] Bonar Law, who had succeeded Balfour as Tory leader in 1911 and made a name for stubbornness in the debates over Irish Home Rule before 1914, relished a good fight. This tough, curiously obscure, Canadian-born Glasgow ironmaster had been Lloyd George's closest friend and supporter in the Coalition since 1916. His prevailing mood of melancholy scepticism deepened with the loss of two sons in the war. Now Leader of the House, he was the real power behind the Coalition. While making conciliatory noises to the mineworkers in public on 21 March 1919, he was assuring the Cabinet in private that the commission would not report in favour of nationalising the mines, and that even if it did he would not be prepared to pass the necessary legislation.[6]

Austen Chamberlain, at the Exchequer, said 'it would be suicidal for the

Government to commit itself to the principle of nationalisation before it was known what was involved'.[7] The Prime Minister agreed, as did Walter Long, spokesman for the Tory squirearchy. Sir Eric Geddes, the minister responsible for railways, felt such a concession would immediately lead to a similar demand for nationalisation of the railways by the railwaymen. Both Government and unions regarded mining as a pacemaker for the rest of British industry.[8]

The Government had underestimated the strength of support inside the commission for really radical reorganisation of the mining industry. Despite this, the Sankey commission was an outstanding example of Lloyd George's inimitable style of political improvisation. It seemed authoritative and fair; it was created by Act of Parliament; and it represented masters and men equally. But this very equality of representation was the Sankey commission's fatal flaw. It was unable to issue a unanimous report, and so left Lloyd George free to play his favourite game of divide and rule. Sir John Sankey himself, later a Labour MP and Lord Chancellor, presided at commission hearings in the splendours of the Royal robing room at the House of Lords, 'a shrewd, good-humoured and open-minded man'.[9] On his right, appropriately enough, sat three coalowners and three industrialists, Sir Arthur Balfour, Sir Thomas Royden and Sir Arthur Duckham. On his left, again fittingly, sat three miners and three economists favourable to the miners.

The dominant personality was undoubtedly Robert Smillie, president of the Miners' Federation of Great Britain, one of the great figures of British labour history, 'his whole personality full of suffering . . . "sadder than any tears and complainings".'[10] Smillie, a mild-mannered, humorous and quietly-spoken Scot, had been a life-long socialist, miners' leader and friend of Keir Hardie. He was an MP and a formidable political opponent. 'When Smillie half-closed his right eye while listening to someone in conference,' one observer remarked, 'there was trouble looming for that speaker.'[11]

The miners' second representative was Herbert Smith, 'the man in the cap', president of the powerful Yorkshire mineworkers' federation. Smith had been born in a workhouse a few months after the 1862 Hartley Pit disaster, in which 214 men and boys died, effectively snuffing out a whole Northumberland village. That catastrophe was the background against which the whole of his lifelong struggle for the miners must be seen. Among his possessions when he died was a bundle of old newspapers, faded and yellowing, which told the story of the Hartley Pit disaster day by day.[12]

Both Smillie and Smith had risen from desperate poverty to become leaders of labour. They had seen dead bodies brought up from pits after mining accidents, seen women and children dragged from their homes by the owners' bully-boys during strikes. Struggle was as natural to them as the air they breathed. Both were deeply influenced by leaders in their own areas in their own respective styles – Smillie warm and charming, Smith shut-mouthed. Smith's laconic public personality – epitomised in his characteristic Yorkshire dialect response to requests for concessions, 'Nowt doin' ' – hid a warmly emotional private life. His son Ernest had been invalided home from the front in July 1918. On Armistice Day he took to his bed and never left it. His eyesight was failing and eventually he went blind. Except for a short period he was in constant pain. But for more than a year before he died in September 1919, his father never missed a chance, in the midst of busy conferences and tough negotiations, of dashing home, often on night trains from London, to sit at his son's bedside in Barnsley and read to him.[13]

Both Smith and Smillie had been pupils of Alexander Macdonald and Keir Hardie and were in the tradition of miners' leaders who did not accept the social order of the times. Now, at the Sankey commission hearings, they met their former masters as political equals with many painful scores to settle. Equally outstanding, though very different from Smith and Smillie, was Frank Hodges, the young secretary of the MFGB, a thirty-two-year-old graduate of the Central Labour College and a most gifted representative of the new generation of labour leaders. He was lean, forceful, quick-witted, an excellent speaker 'with the culture, the manners, the background of a university man of the upper class, but carrying the consciousness of the delegated power of one million working men'.[14]

The experts on the Sankey commission were Sidney Webb, the encyclopaedic Fabian who, with his formidable wife Beatrice, was one of the most influential figures on the British Left in the twentieth century; R. H. Tawney, historian, Marxist, moralist and a key figure in adult education; and the aptly named financial wizard, Sir Leo Chiozza Money, later hero of the Savidge scandal.[15]

The weight of ability on the miners' side was telling. No wonder the coalowners' witnesses often lost their composure at the hearings and felt they were being grilled. Smillie, for example, coolly asking Lord Londonderry, whose income came largely from mining, if he could produce the deeds for his estates, provided one of the highlights of the hearings. 'As time went on,' G. D. H. Cole remarked, 'the character of the commission seemed to change imperceptibly into a tribunal before which the private ownership of the mines was on trial. The miners successfully compelled the owners to remain throughout on the defensive.'[16] Or, as the *Daily News* correspondent observed, 'More than once . . . I have been reminded of reports of revolutionary tribunals in France and Russia.'[17] Yet the Sankey commission was far from being a revolutionary tribunal. In the long-run it can be seen as a significant step on the road to the kind of consensus politics which were to become the hallmark of the inter-war years. It effectively defused a potentially revolutionary situation and dealt a decisive blow to the Labour Party's socialist ideals and the labour movement's industrial militancy.

As Cole explained, 'the entry of labour into the coal commission – acclaimed at the time as a great labour triumph – was the determining factor in tiding over the critical industrial situation in the first half of 1919. . . . [It] gave the Government time to pass the point of danger without the development of a general militant policy on the part of labour.'[18] Inflation and decontrol, while arresting the post-war tendency towards collectivism, would not alone have prevented the advancement of the Labour Party's schemes for nationalisation. Had they been pressed immediately after the war – when their inevitability still seemed credible – they would almost certainly have succeeded, in part at least. That was the measure of Lloyd George's achievement, and the true legacy of the Sankey commission. For seven years after 1919 – until the General Strike cleared the log-jam – Labour and the miners became bogged down in endless discussions of wages and hours. For twenty years and more, the Labour Party lost all real interest and confidence in socialism. It had missed its opportunity. The road was open for Baldwin and MacDonald and the politics of consensus.

The real tragedy of the Sankey commission was that it paid too little attention to general principles of *how* the mining industry should be controlled and organised. As the Labour newspaper editor Hamilton Fyfe explained, 'The dispute between the miners and the mineowners has been mishandled all through. It ought to have been a dispute about the state of the coal industry. It has been allowed to become a dispute about wages.'[19] The truth of this became ever more apparent in the years before 1926. Sir Richard Redmayne, for many years chief inspector of mines, wrote, 'I am firmly convinced that the coal mining industry of Great Britain can be placed on a profitable basis . . . but to accomplish this, drastic reorganisation will be required, the first move being . . . the combination of the collieries into groups of like natural conditions and conditions of trade'.[20] Hamilton Fyfe felt

Far too much has been heard about wages and hours, far too little about the methods which must be employed to prevent any lowering of the miners' standard of life. . . . The chief villain is Lloyd George. He promised to do whatever the Sankey commission recommended. But, he was told by Big Business that he could not nationalise, so he did not keep his promise. All the trouble since 1919 has been trouble arising out of that broken pledge.[21]

Lloyd George, of course, denied that he had broken any pledge, and characteristically used the divided counsels of the Sankey commission to justify his policy. On 20 March the commission rendered three interim reports. The six miners' representatives recommended that the colliers' claims be met in full. The three coalowners recommended a wage increase of 1s 6d a day for a working day reduced from eight to seven hours. Sir John Sankey and the three industrialists steered between these two positions : a seven-hour day, reducing to six in July 1921 if the economic condition of the industry allowed : a pay rise of 2s a day, which would cost £30 million; and a levy of 1d a ton on coal, which would raise £1 million a year, to improve housing and conditions in mining regions. Housing and conditions, the report concluded, were 'a reproach to our civilisation. . . . No judicial language is sufficiently strong or sufficiently severe to apply to their condemnation.'[22]

The commission issued four final reports on 20 June. All recommended the nationalisation of royalties, improved distribution of coal, and the creation of a ministry of mines. Sankey himself went further and recommended state ownership, on the grounds that the present system, with 3,000 pits owned by 1,500 firms, was inefficient and had created 'the present atmosphere of distrust and recrimination' between owners and men.[23] 'The coal industry has been backward,' the report suggested, 'largely owing to its excessive individualism.'[24] The six miners' representatives endorsed Sankey's views in their report, but went further in urging workers' control, a doctrine central to syndicalist beliefs. The coalowners and industrialists, of course, rejected nationalisation as 'detrimental to the development of the industry and the economic life of the country' and recommended no change in the system of private ownership. Its only conciliatory gesture was a nod in the direction of the miners' claim for pit committees, district councils and a national council representing owners and men. The owners agreed these should be established to discuss questions relating to the industry, but not conditions of employment in mining – a restriction which would have rendered the councils pointless.

The fourth report, by the industrial engineer Sir Arthur Duckham, attempted to reach a compromise between outright nationalisation and unreconstructed private ownership. Duckham's proposals were based on the evidence of Sir Richard Redmayne, the chief inspector of mines. They suggested that in each area all collieries should be acquired by a single company, known as a District Coal Board, and operated by the board with a limit on profits. Though this idea was not unlike the eventual structure of the industry after nationalisation in 1947, it was derisively dubbed 'Duckham and water' by the miners in 1919 and soon vanished into limbo.

Thus there was no clear majority finding, though the reports of Sir John Sankey himself and the miners' side put together commanded seven out of thirteen votes for nationalisation. But Lloyd George used this lack of unanimity as an excuse for rejecting nationalisation. Instead, the Prime Minister offered some reorganisation; but the miners in turn rejected this as a bribe to keep them quiet and reorganisation was dropped too.[25] Wages remained the same, the seven-hour day was imposed by Act of Parliament and Government control prolonged. No one was happy with this kind of compromise. As one observer has put it, 'The bitterness and the troubles of the coal mines for the next seven, or for that matter twenty-seven years, derived in great part from the feeling of both miners and owners that they had been betrayed.'[26] The owners, furious that the Government had come so close to conceding nationalisation, were determined in future to stand firm and hang on to what they held. The miners, who had hoped for so much from the commission and had made such an impressive showing at the hearings, felt cheated. Vernon Hartshorn, a South Wales miners' leader who was now a Derbyshire miners' MP, asked indignantly in the House

> Why was the commission set up? Was it a huge game of bluff? Was it ever intended that if the reports favoured nationalisation we were to get it? . . . That is the kind of question the miners of the country will ask, and they will say we have been deceived, betrayed, duped.[27]

Yet, despite Hartshorn's indignation, it was already clear that the militant mood at the start of the year had cooled. A strike for the hypothetical cause of nationalisation at some undefined future date was clearly impractical now.

As if to emphasise this defeatist atmosphere, the miners' campaign, 'The Mines for the Nation', though taken up by the TUC as a whole, created little stir even among the miners themselves. But there were still some

3a. Frank Hodges (left), MFGB secretary from 1918 to 1924, talking to two other members of the first Labour Government in January 1924, Robert Williams (centre) and J. R. Clynes (right).

3b. Robert Smillie, who resigned as president of the MFGB over Black Friday, leaves 10 Downing Street followed by his successor, Herbert Smith (centre), and J. P. Robson, another miners' leader.

4a. Sir Alfred Mond, creator of the huge Imperial Chemical Industries and an important mineowner, going to a meeting at 10 Downing Street in 1922.

4b. Sir Philip Cunliffe-Lister, an enlightened Yorkshire mineowner.

4c. Lord Londonderry, one of the richest and most influential mineowners in Britain.

traces of militancy. The Yorkshire miners, for example, struck for more than a month in 1919. By 21 July all the Yorkshire miners were out, and some 200,000 miners in South Wales and Monmouthshire were planning to strike in sympathy.[28] Sir Robert Horne, the Minister of Labour, told the Cabinet that one disturbing feature of the strike in Yorkshire was that the local union had given orders that the pump men were to quit – though it was standard practice for the safety men to stay at work during disputes. Horne added that at eighty-five mines pumping had stopped altogether, and that at another fifty-eight union officials themselves were doing the pumping. In at least thirty-one pits the fact that pumping had stopped was not likely to ruin the mines, but three were already flooded and it would take months to get these mines in working order again.[29]

Edward Shortt, the Home Secretary, said that 3,500 men from the Navy could keep the Yorkshire pumps going, and the First Lord of the Admiralty, Walter Long, agreed that leave could be cancelled for this purpose. Not to be outdone by the Navy, the Secretary of State for War (combined with Air), Winston Churchill, said he could bring home four divisions of the Rhine Army, two of them immediately, if necessary.[30] All this talk of mobilisation and special measures, combined with the draft of a Bill which would have empowered the Government to arrest top trade union and labour leaders, seems excessive in the situation which actually faced the Government on the industrial front in 1919. After all, they were not dealing with a general strike, or even a national mining strike, but simply a strike of Yorkshire miners with some support from South Wales. But winding up the Cabinet discussion the Prime Minister revealed the trend of Government thinking. The strike was 'practical, and not theoretical, Bolshevism and must be dealt with with a firm hand'. He was rather inclined to agree with the mineowners that a fight had got to come; but if the Government chose the present moment for a showdown with the miners they had to be certain they were on firm ground and had public opinion squarely behind them. 'The whole future of the country might be at stake,' Lloyd George concluded, 'and if the Government were beaten and the miners won it would result in Soviet Government. . . . Parliament might remain [but] the real Parliament would be at the head-quarters of the Miners' Federation in Russell Square.'[31]

Here, seven years before the General Strike, was the scenario of the Government strategy which led to that dramatic nine-day confrontation in 1926. The owners were right and must be given full Government backing; the miners were wrong and little better than Bolsheviks who wanted to take over the country; a showdown would probably have to come, but the Government must wait until public opinion was firmly on its side and then hit hard. In 1919 all this was in the future. Lloyd George doubtless did not believe in the Bolshevik threat, but used it to convince his largely Tory supporters that he was the only man who could solve the crisis. Yet for the moment one thing was clear. Whatever the outcome of this later confrontation, the Government had won the first round. A general strike in 1919 might have destroyed Lloyd George's improvised Coalition and perhaps damaged parliamentary democracy. Instead, by a typical piece of political sleight-of-hand, 'the Welsh wizard' had avoided the necessity of giving battle to the miners at a critical time. He lived to fight another day on better ground.

Chapter Six

Rumours of Revolution

The revolutionary atmosphere of 1919–20 is hardly surprising. Britain had just emerged from a terrible war. The seizure of power by the Bolsheviks in Russia was a frightening portent. All over Europe established Governments and elaborate economic and financial systems were falling.[1] Why should Britain be immune to this infection? So the possibility of a general strike, leading perhaps to a direct challenge to the Constitution, haunted every British Government between the Armistice and 1926. The period 1919–20 seemed to be dominated by strikes and rumours of revolution; by civil disobedience and riots in India; and by street fighting and open warfare in Ireland. Compared with this violence in India and Ireland, or with the Government's anxiety about the Armistice negotiations in Paris, the situation on the home front may not have seemed quite so dangerous. Yet many sober observers saw the disputes of 1919–20 as merely the prelude to a period of general industrial unrest which, if it occurred at the same time as the fighting in Ireland, might bring the country to the verge of civil war and revolution. Documents certainly suggest that Lloyd George took the danger of revolution seriously, and made earnest preparations to deal with it.[2] From the point of view of organised labour, a general strike would have stood a much greater chance of success in 1919 than it did in 1926.

Preoccupation with industrial unrest was clear in Cabinet discussions. For example, Churchill, a man who feared revolution and played a key role in the years ahead, said that if the Government refused to nationalise the mines the miners would call a general strike to force nationalisation.[3] Lord Curzon commented that 'if the miners strike on this question there will be an enormous body of opinion behind the Government'.[4] Perhaps so; but in 1919 no one could be sure. The Minister of Labour, Sir Robert Horne, pointed out that the real question was how long the Government could still continue to control the mines. The agreement with the owners under the Defence of the Realm Act of 1917 was for six months after peace – but the Government could end that agreement at any time.[5] Finally, the Cabinet instructed the Home Secretary, Edward Shortt, to draw up contingency plans for meeting a possible national strike by the triple alliance.[6]

The form these contingency plans took is shown in the Strikes (Exceptional Measures) Bill which the Cabinet had before it in draft during the discussions. In the event of a sympathetic strike by the triple alliance, this Bill would have closed all public houses, placed a moratorium on all uncollected rents during the dispute, closed banks to prevent payment of strike pay, confiscated trade union funds and, finally, made it illegal to incite anyone to take part in such a strike. This would almost certainly have led to the arrest of top trade union leaders and some Labour MPs too.[7] As Churchill remarked – in a phrase which anticipated his attitude in 1926 – 'This would be a very serious thing. We should use a form of words which would allow us to pick and choose the people we arrested.'[8]

In fact the general atmosphere at the very start of the post-war period was much more favourable for concerted action by the labour movement than at any later time. There was much greater unity on the trade union side immediately after the war than at any time subsequently. Men returning to civilian life after the hell of the Western front reacted in a militant mood to the inevitable problems of readjustment and rising prices. Moreover, they had not yet been cowed by years of mass unemployment.

For in 1919–20 the post-war boom was still in full spate. Prices were rising rapidly and demobilised soldiers were determined that wages should keep pace and that the Government must make good its pledge to create 'a land fit for heroes'. The unions were stronger and more united in 1919–20 than they were to be later, while the Government was much weaker. Cabinet papers, personal diaries, the files of Sir Basil Thomson, Director of Intelligence at Scotland Yard, all indicate real alarm about the situation in the first eighteen months after the war. The army was fully stretched, not only in Europe in the aftermath of war, but in Russia against the Bolsheviks, and in the Middle and Far East, where trouble was brewing in the Dardanelles and in India. At home, Ireland was about to explode. G. H. Roberts, the Food Controller,[9] said 'There are large groups preparing for Soviet Government'. Lloyd George was so anxious that he called a special conference to discover whether the country was really as defenceless as Churchill and the Army claimed.[10] Having established that there were eighteen battalions, of which seven were Irish and of uncertain temper, and that this was only enough to hold London, the Prime Minister learned that there were three battalions in Malta, four in Silesia and seven in Egypt.[11]

The Cabinet finally agreed to bring two battalions back from Malta, but this still left a large gap. Lloyd George asked 'How long will it take to get the well-disposed to range themselves on the side of Law?' and General Sir Nevil Macready, commander of the forces in Ireland, replied 'We are taking private steps to secure the aid of a certain class of citizen' – the nucleus of the special constables and others who broke the General Strike in 1926. Walter Long observed that he personally had no pistols less than two hundred years old, and that 'A bill is needed licensing persons to bear arms'. Shortt replied that the Home Office had such a bill ready and Bonar Law emphasised that all weapons ought to be available for distribution to the Government's friends, referring so often to the stockbrokers as a loyal and fighting class that 'one felt that potential battalions of stockbrokers were to be found in every town'.[12] The Cabinet then created a Munitions and Weapons Committee to assist the Industrial Unrest Committee.[13] Clearly, the Government was not ready to meet any serious challenge from the unions on the industrial front, and all the immediate evidence pointed to a rapidly rising tide of militant industrial and trade union solidarity. In this situation the police strike sent a shudder of fear through the propertied classes and the advocates of law and order.

In 1918 the London police had struck for recognition of their union, started before the war. Lloyd George had raised their pay and appointed a new commissioner, General Macready, the adjutant-general of the army. Macready's policy was the direct cause of the second police strike in August 1919. Backed by a bill in Parliament, he forbade policemen to join a union. In London only about 1,000 out of 19,000 men came out; and the strike fizzled in a few days with all the strikers being dismissed. Elsewhere – especially in Liverpool and Bootle in Lancashire – the strike was more serious. On Merseyside nearly half, in Bootle two-thirds, of the force struck, and reinforcements, mostly from Leeds, were drafted into the area after widespread looting and rioting. Some 2,500 soldiers, four tanks, a battleship and two destroyers were sent to Merseyside. Local labour organisations gave full support to the police, despite their frequent clashes with the police in earlier disputes, notably the bobbin-weavers strike in 1912. Threats of direct action and even a general strike in support of the police were made. Yet this formidable display of solidarity did not prevent the ultimate failure of the strike and subsequent mass dismissals.[14]

This police strike was scarcely over before a new threat appeared – this time on the railways. Since the railways were still under Government control, the railwaymen had been negotiating with them. 'If it comes to a fight,' the Minister of Transport, Sir Eric Geddes, warned, 'the railwaymen will say that the Railway Executives' estimates are open to much question and criticism.'[15] When the fight came, the railwaymen's leader, J. H. Thomas, a shrewd negotiator, did just as Sir Eric had feared. Beneath his breezy exterior of cheerful, beery bonhomie, verging on buffoonery, Jimmy Thomas was one of the cleverest political operators in the Labour movement. Born illegitimate in dire poverty in South Wales in 1874, Thomas became an engine driver and the most resourceful organiser the railway unions ever produced. He created the National Union of Railwaymen out of a handful of weak and divided railway unions, and was general secretary of the NUR from 1917 until 1931. As ambitious as he was able, Thomas made no secret of his taste for advancement and good living. 'Jimmy was always heading for the Royal Box,' one observer noted, while David Low, the brilliant cartoonist of the inter-war years, depicted him as 'the Rt. Hon. Dress Shirt' in a series of memorable drawings. Later discredited within the labour movement, he was forty-five and near the peak of his career in 1919.

In the 1919 rail strike Thomas did as Sir Eric had predicted, making the facts public, challenging his fellow-Welshman Lloyd George to trial by propaganda and winning. In October, the Government settled the strike on the basis of no cuts, stabilisation of existing rates, with an increase on the basic rate for the lowest grades, full reinstatement and no victimisation.[16] Early the following year a new offer gave immediate increases to the worst-paid men.[17] It had been a famous victory, a formidable and hitherto unprecedented display of solidarity between the footplatemen and the other grades. 'Before the strike had ended,' the Liberal C. F. G. Masterman commented, 'railwaymen had rallied nine-tenths of the industrial workers to their side.'[18] The Government was seriously worried. The Cabinet Secretary, Sir Maurice Hankey, perhaps the most influential figure in Whitehall between the wars, told his deputy Tom Jones that 'Ministers . . . have the "wind up" to the most extraordinary extent about the industrial situation. CIGS[19] also is positively in a state of dreadful nerves on the subject. Churchill is the only one who is sane on this subject, and on the subject of Denekin *he* is a nuisance.[20] From a meeting yesterday I came away with my head fairly reeling. I felt I had been in Bedlam.

Red Revolution and blood and war at home and abroad!'[21] Hankey added that he felt this panic was unfounded; that Sir Robert Horne was largely responsible for spreading it, and that the situation was less threatening now than it had been a few months earlier.

Jones agreed, but struck a warning note when he said that South Wales – which he knew at first hand – would not be peaceful until the mines and the railways had been nationalised. 'What Churchill and Co forget,' he told his boss, 'is that there are other ways of averting discontent than with civil guards and the military.'[22] Hankey replied that he was 'dead against trying to create a citizen guard or increasing the army in a hurry on any pretext. This will only precipitate the very trouble we want to avoid. And the men won't come without an appeal of such a character as would make trouble inevitable.'[23] Instead, the Government should make absolutely sure of its arms and munitions, and establish the machinery for mobilising a full-scale permanent force if and when trouble arose.

During the next few years the Government quietly reviewed the operational structure of the Supply and Transport Services. All Government departments undertook similar surveys of the situation within their own field of operations, and these official activities were augmented when the semi-official Organisation for the Maintenance of Supplies, the so-called OMS, emerged in 1925. The police force itself had been enlarged and strengthened from 58,000 in 1911 to 69,000 in 1921. Police discipline had been partly militarised, and, as recommended by the Desborough committee of inquiry set up after the troubles, local forces had been brought under central control.

A start had also been made in enrolling the so-called 'citizens guard' of special constables and other vigilante groups. A scheme for providing emergency road transport during a national strike had been drawn up in anticipation of plans later prepared for the General Strike. Drivers had been registered, 25,000 lorries requisitioned and food distribution arranged by a food controller in the wartime Ministry of Food. Wartime regulations were, of course, very useful to the Government and civil servants in the attempts to make secret plans for dealing with a possible future emergency. The Supply and Transport Services, for example, had been set up originally to deal with wartime emergencies. Finally, the whole country had been divided into sixteen areas or regions, each under the control of a special commissioner. The machinery for this kind of nation-wide operation was kept in being, revised and strengthened, as Sir Maurice Hankey had advised.[24]

In contrast with this mounting Government preparation, the unions did little to improve their position. The solidarity of the railwaymen proved short-lived. Though the footplatemen had struck in sympathy with the lower-paid grades in 1919, they did not receive similar support when they struck in 1924. Moreover, railwaymen's wages were now probably the highest in any industry; certainly they had won greater improvements on pre-war rates than any other industrial group.[25] As one locomen's leader put it,

> Throughout the 1920s the employers kept telling us railwaymen that we were in a more-or-less sheltered trade. We had a guaranteed week, a guaranteed minimum, paid holidays, little risk of unemployment and so on, while in addition the railways were a virtual monopoly. But the employers said the wages they were having to pay us made their position impossible.[26]

This comparative affluence, and the fact that they had won these increases *without* calling on the triple alliance for help, did nothing to strengthen solidarity.[27] The railway strike in 1911 had opened an era of working-class unity; that of 1919 was in many ways an expression of incipient division. After the solidarity of 1919, the forces of organised labour grew steadily weaker and more divided, while those of the Government and employers, though far from unified, certainly grew stronger and more prepared. When the great confrontation came in 1921, and the triple alliance was finally called on to conduct a national strike, the labour movement was in for a rude awakening.

Chapter Seven

The End of Post-war Prosperity

Government preparations for dealing with future emergencies continued quietly against a background of apparently growing solidarity and militancy in the ranks of labour and the Left. The Labour Party vote was rising and union membership increasing. The general council of the TUC was emerging as a kind of general staff to coordinate nation-wide industrial action. On the far Left the Communist Party and the National Minority Movement made their appearance and became influential in certain areas, especially among South Wales miners. In the spring of 1920, with Bolshevik forces advancing on Warsaw, Churchill persuaded the Government to send arms to the Poles. This threat of renewed fighting united the Labour movement, Right and Left, in a campaign of industrial action to stop the shipments. Councils of Action, which were to be revived during the General Strike, were set up, and on 10 May London dockers refused to load weapons into the *Jolly George*. 'We were impotent,' Churchill admitted. 'All forms of military intervention were impossible.' It looked like a triumphant vindication of the doctrine of direct action. All this strengthened Lloyd George's resolve to resurrect wartime emergency powers for dealing with national strikes.

Trouble hit the coal industry again in September 1920. The mines were still under Government control, and Lloyd George had earlier forced the owners to relate higher pay to greater output. Negotiations broke down on the tonnages (the so-called 'datum line') at which these pay increases were to operate. The miners struck; and by mid-September the situation had become serious. The triple alliance agreed to support the miners, although more grudgingly than in 1919. But faced with the actual threat of a sympathetic railway strike and a probable road-

c*

transport strike, Lloyd George acted in characteristically devious fashion : he rushed the Emergency Powers Act through Parliament, which seemed to screw the crisis towards snapping point; and then paradoxically settled the strike on the miner's terms.

Lloyd George was simply playing for time, until he was ready for the decisive struggle foreseen in 1919. The significant thing about the 'datum line' strike of 1920 was not that the miners won their 2s a shift pay rise, but that the Emergency Powers Act made permanent the dictatorial powers the Government already possessed under wartime Defence of the Realm Acts. Whenever action was threatened in future by the triple alliance, the Government could use orders-in-council to establish summary courts and take other measures it deemed necessary to supply essential services.

This increasing Government power was not widely known at the time. But the following year the trade union movement, buoyed up by the successes of 1919–20, received a sharp public jolt. The 'datum line' coal strike had been settled temporarily on the miners' terms, pending a permanent settlement, which was to have been reached by 31 March 1921. When no settlement had been agreed, the next coal crisis occurred, but this time it caught the triple alliance in serious disarray. The result was disaster.

Since 1918, Government, mineowners and miners had been living in a fool's paradise encouraged by the short-lived post-war prosperity. The boom burst abruptly in the winter of 1920–1. There is some evidence that the Treasury and the Bank of England forced Britain into this depression in order to hasten return to the gold standard at pre-war parity of $4.86, as recommended by the influential Cunliffe report on currency and foreign exchange in 1918.[1] Europe was in political turmoil, its exchange and money markets in chaos. More important, the British coal industry suddenly met a catastrophic change in the terms of trade.

Encouraged by the demands of war economy, the mining industry had hoped to reap a bonanza in the export markets closed by four years of fighting. Now they found they had grossly overestimated the demand for coal in European countries. Over-production of primary products brought something like ruin to the old British staple industries such as coal mining in the post-war period. Exports of coal plummeted, prices collapsed and unemployment rose rapidly. The same story could be told of other staple industries – shipbuilding, engineering, cotton textile manufacture – the very industries which had once made Britain the workshop of the world. There was a glut of world shipping, while cotton sales abroad fell sharply. The number out of work doubled in the winter of 1920–1 and passed the two million mark the following summer. By the end of March 1921, when the coal industry agreement expired, it was quite plain that this was one of the worst years of depression since the industrial revolution.

The collapse of the post-war boom was selective in its effects. It hit export industries far harder than those who sold on the home market. Industries producing for the home market quickly recovered from the collapse of 1920–1. But mining's richest markets had traditionally been abroad. Moreover, the Government still exercised its wartime control; and as coal profits tumbled in the post-war depression, Lloyd George hurried to divest himself of responsibility. He announced that he would hand back the industry to the owners when the present agreement expired on 31 March 1921.

The private ownership of mineral rights resulted in a multitude of separate colliery concerns – roughly 1,500 companies owned the 3,000 pits. Each individual colliery concern had to negotiate with the individual land-owner, who granted the right to work his coal in return for an annual royalty. In 1921 this royalty was about 6d a ton. The result was that 'There has been no directing authority to control the planning of the coalfields. . . . Growth has been haphazard . . . being largely dependent upon the boundaries of the properties of the surface owners.'[2] Or, as two Communist critics of the coal industry put it, private ownership had resulted in 'inefficient chaos'.[3]

The system also meant that while some collieries made handsome profits, even after paying massive royalties, many others had to struggle to keep going. It was an intrinsic property of any competitive system that wage rates had to be low enough to keep the least efficient pits in existence. However, the mining industry's profitability was more sensitive to small changes in wage rates than almost any other. Miners had at last received during the war the long-standing demand for national wage agreements. Yet wages were far from standardised: indeed, the method of assessing pay was so complicated that rates varied greatly from pit to pit. But the principle of national agreements was so sacred to the miners that they would rather risk lower pay or higher unemployment than abandon it.

Who were the mineowners who had just had the mining industry returned to their full and unfettered control? Though they naturally played a decisive role in the coal crisis, very little has been written about them. Even their names are not easy to discover. A good deal is known about the miners' side of the dispute; virtually nothing about the owners' case.[4] For years one of their principal spokesmen had been the masterful D. A. Thomas, chairman of Cambrian Collieries Ltd, a key figure in the Cambrian Combine Strike of 1910–11, Liberal MP for Cardiff, who afterwards became Lord Rhondda. By 1921 the president of the Mining Association of Great Britain was Evan Williams, another Welsh colliery owner, and the secretary W. A. Lee. Perhaps the best-known coalowner was Lord Londonderry, the 7th Marquess, with an impeccable upper-class pedigree and background: educated at Eton and Sandhurst, he had served in the Guards and been Conservative MP for Maidstone from 1906–15. From 1921–6 he was leader of the Senate and Minister for Education in Northern Ireland, and after returning to England in 1926 to look after his extensive property, he became Secretary of State for Air in the Coalition Government of 1931–5.

Men like Londonderry, Lee, Williams and D. A. Thomas presented the hard side of the mineowners' case, which was to become dominant during the next few years. Londonderry, for example, apparently believed that the MFGB's sole objective was to destroy the private enterprise system, not just in mining but in industry as a whole.[5] Williams, whose period as president of the Mining Association saw it move significantly towards hardline intransigence, expressed similar fears in even more extreme language, shocking the Government with tough talk about wanting to repeal the 1919 Mines Act and setting the clock back to 1908. He further argued that any Government attempt to regulate wages would be 'revolutionary in character' and that the miners already had 'an excessive share' of the industry's prosperity.[6] Other owners, like Sir Adam Nimmo, from Nottinghamshire, and Finlay Gibson, secretary of the South Wales Coalowners' Association, shared these views.

But they were by no means universal. More moderate owners included David Davies, who was also from South Wales, Charles P. Markham, who had extensive interests both in South Wales and the East Midlands, Lord Bledisloe, an enlightened owner from the Forest of Dean, C. B. Crawshaw and W. Burton Jones, of the West Yorkshire Coalowners, and Sir Philip Cunliffe-Lister, another Yorkshireman.[7] The divisions among the owners represented by these men tended to follow economic lines: those from profitable regions, such as Yorkshire and the East Midlands, could afford more liberal views on wages and conditions than owners from less profitable areas, especially those hit by the slump in coal exports, like Durham and South Wales.

Cunliffe-Lister, a strong supporter of the principle of the national minimum wage agreement, put the point clearly.

> Yorkshire knows that Durham and Lancs will *not* pay *less* than a given rate, so Yorkshire will agree firmly to a good rate. But there is a risk that if Durham and Lancs pay less than they ought they will cut prices and force Yorkshire down below what it can pay. . . . The risk is greater if the Durham rate is fixed at a figure which will enable the bad pits to go on. . . . A national minimum . . . will cut out pits that can't work except at starvation wages. But it ought to do so.[8]

Such views were to become increasingly unacceptable to the Mining Association during the 1920s as it came to express the interests of those owners who were struggling to survive. The whole function of the Mining Association came to be the fixing of wage rates which *would* enable the bad pits to go on. Cunliffe-Lister came from a profitable region which sold in the easy domestic market. Evan Williams, the president of the Mining Association, came from the area hardest hit by the collapse of the export trade.

As it pursued this hardline policy, the Mining Association grew more unrepresentative, silencing moderate and liberal opinion among the owners. Of course, the plight of many of the owners, and with them the miners they employed, became increasingly grim as time passed. Yet the Eastern Division, which was the most profitable in the country, also produced more than one-third of the country's coal. However, South Wales and Durham, both regions badly hit by the decline of exports, between them produced slightly more coal than the Eastern Division.[9] The obvious answer would have been to pool the profits of the entire industry in some way, so that the more profitable areas could help the weaker ones, and the good years could be used to tide the industry as a whole over bad spells. Such proposals were shortly to be made. But the owners, facing the post-war crisis, never achieved the unity or foresight which enabled them to accept such ideas. Instead, they fell back increasingly into positions of rivalry and suspicion, with moderates from more prosperous pits unable to persuade hardliners from more difficult areas. By the same token, the increasing militancy among the miners tended to be related to the relative prosperity of their coalfields. Owners in the Eastern Federation were willing to offer more, since they had more to offer, while miners from this region seemed more willing to accept it. In South Wales and Durham, on the other hand, both masters and men tended to retreat into intransigent positions as they fought to divide the shrinking proceeds of coal sales. This conflict, among both owners and miners, would most likely be settled by attitudes in the other areas, which between them produced the remaining third of Britain's coal. But since many of these other areas, such as the smaller mining regions of the North, Midlands and West, were finding it harder to survive, while some Scottish pits were also hit by foreign competition, hardliners on both sides made the running.

In addition to these crucial divisions based on profitability, there was another source of friction. The unusual British system of private ownership of mineral rights meant that the mineowners, who operated the colliery companies, had to pay royalties and wayleaves to those who owned the land where they mined. The coal companies often objected to paying such royalties, which were levied on each ton of coal and amounted to very substantial sums. Principal royalty owners included Lord Bute, who was paid £115,000 a year, the Duke of Hamilton, who made a similar amount, Lord Tredegar, who made £84,000, the Duke of Northumberland, who made £83,000, Lord Dunraven, who made £64,000, and Lord Durham, who made £38,000. One of the biggest royalty owners was the Church of England which, through the Ecclesiastical Commissioners, drew some £400,000 a year from coal.[10] Though the royalty levy in 1921 was only 6d a ton, the total paid in royalties was over £4 million. The royalty system irritated the owners. But it made the miners especially bitter. They felt they were working themselves to the limit in conditions no other group of industrial workers would tolerate, simply to make the royalty owners richer. Yet despite the huge royalties the colliery owners were forced to pay, and their claim that many pits were losing money, it was clear from their own figures that in most years huge profits were being made. Though 1922 was a year of abnormal depression, the profit on coal sold at the pit head was still 1s 6½d a ton, and in 1923 the profit rose to 2s 6d a ton, which made a total profit for the industry as a whole of £27 million.[11]

However, at the immediate impact of the 1921 depression, with coal prices tumbling crazily in the export markets, losses were very large: 5s a ton for the first three months, or £5 million a month between January and March, when Government control ended.[12] Even more worrying perhaps was the sharp decline in productivity. Output per miner had fallen from 256 tons a year in 1913 to 178 in the year ending 31 March 1921, while cost per ton had risen from 9s 5½d to 40s 3d per ton in the same period.[13] Faced with these figures the owners felt they had to act. But their actions seemed to bear out the received, if simplified, picture of the owners as selfish, mean-spirited and grasping. Lord Birkenhead called them 'the stupidest men in England'. They might have reorganised the industry, as every commission of inquiry urged, on resuming control. But they seemed incapable of overcoming their own internal divisions and agreeing on a reorganisation plan. The only economy they all seemed to understand was lower wages : coal mining was, of course, highly labour-intensive. When the owners resumed control on 1 April 1921 – All Fools Day – they posted notices at every pithead in the country announcing drastic wage cuts. These cuts – as much as 49 per cent in some regions, such as South Wales, where profits had been hardest hit by the collapse of export markets – were not the only blow. Worse, perhaps, the new proposals destroyed the existing system of national agreements and returned to the hated old system of district rates.

The vexed question of national wage agreements was thus at the centre of the coal crisis of the post-war years. The miners refused to abandon the sanctity of national agreements; the owners argued that pits in the less profitable regions, such as the Forest of Dean, could not afford existing wage rates, while more profitable regions, like Yorkshire or the East Midlands, could afford them. The average wage of the mineworkers in Great Britain in the first quarter of 1921 was 89s 8d per week,[14] and the owners said that when they resumed control this would have to be cut sharply. The miners tried to resolve this problem by proposing the idea of a national pool. The main object of the national pool was to fix a levy on every ton of coal raised and so assist the poorest collieries by providing a national fund on which they could draw to cover any losses and meet wage bills. If it really was impossible for a very large number of companies to pay a living wage, as the owners suggested, then the only alternative either to closing down or to cutting wages savagely was to accept the national pool.

Frank Hodges, secretary of the MFGB, first proposed the idea of a national pool on behalf of the MFGB early in 1921 at a joint conference between the Government, the MFGB and the Mining Association at 10 Downing Street. Herbert Smith disliked the idea of the national pool. It was too abstract. But he loyally accepted the Federation's decision if it was the only way to stop crippling pay cuts or thousands of miners being thrown out of work when unprofitable pits were forced to close.[15] In the opinion of an independent observer, 'It [the national pool] was a most sensible proposition . . . a sane and reasonable project in harmony with . . . the abnormal need of the period. . . . But even its name terrorised the nation. The alternative put forward by the owners . . . meant . . . ruthless competition.'[16]

In short, the owners opposed the pool because they believed in the merits of competition and higher profits for the more competitive pits, even if this meant the less profitable pits would have to close and thousands of colliers be thrown out of work. So they rejected the miners' demand for a national pool to equalise wages; the miners refused to accept the new terms; and on 1 April 1921 they were locked out. Clearly, the triple alliance would be asked to call a rail and transport strike in support of the miners. The trial of strength foreseen by Lloyd George in 1919–20 was close at hand. It came on Black Friday, when in the legends of the labour movement weak and self-seeking labour leaders betrayed the miners, crippled working-class solidarity and destroyed the triple alliance.

Chapter Eight

Black Friday

If the triple alliance strike call became effective, more than two million workpeople would stop work in support of the miners. The Cabinet viewed this threat with the utmost concern, and resolutions confirming the regulations to be issued under the 1920 Emergency Powers Act were introduced into the Commons on 5 April 1921. The Secretary of State for War, Sir Laming Worthington-Evans, told the Cabinet that eighteen infantry battalions and ten battalions of Guards were ready in Britain, but it might be desirable to withdraw some of the fifty-one battalions then serving in Ireland.[1] Two battalions were ordered back from Malta, four from Upper Silesia, and the army reserve was mobilised.[2] In addition, a sub-committee on supply and transport was established to explore the possibility of creating a 'special defence force of loyal ex-servicemen and loyal citizens' to combat the strike. All leave was cancelled, and preliminary troop movements were made 'in view of the possibility of a sudden railway strike'.[3]

These preparations were far more forceful than they had been in 1919. The Government had declared a State of Emergency, mobilised 80,000 special constables and made some ominously effective military preparations, including calling reservists to the colours, placing machine-gun posts at some pitheads, and sending troops in battle order to many working-class areas. On the union side the prospect looked less pleasing. The economic situation made 1921 a time for caution. The post-war boom had collapsed. Prices were tumbling, unemployment was rising: by the summer, two million were jobless. Clearly, this was no time for a national strike. Moreover, the solidarity of the triple alliance was more apparent than real. True, the transport workers and dockers were led

by one of the most promising and effective members of the rising generation of labour leaders, Ernest Bevin. Now aged just forty, Bevin had been
born in Bristol, poor and illegitimate, like Jimmy Thomas of the railwaymen. Again like Thomas, he had unified weak and divided unions within
his industry. His masterly advocacy of the London dockers' case before
an arbitration tribunal in 1920 had won the dockers big wage increases
and a recommendation for decasualisation,[4] and Bevin a formidable
reputation as 'the dockers' K.C.'. Like Thomas he was destined to hold
Cabinet office in future Labour Governments. And like Thomas he was
doubtful about the success of a national strike in 1921.

Herbert Smith might urge his comrades in the triple alliance in his
Yorkshire accent, to 'Get on t'field. That's t'place'; but for all his notorious
opportunism (indeed, because of it) Jimmy Thomas was a much shrewder
judge of the tactical situation in 1921 and the need for the utmost caution
on the union side. His own railwaymen were far from united: the 1919
railway strike had been an exception, as the 1924 strike was to make
abundantly clear. Moreover, the railwaymen and the transport workers
were becoming tired of always having to support the miners. It was comparatively easy to keep a miners' strike solid and make it last for months:
a handful of determined men could defend a pithead against strikebreakers almost indefinitely. Goodsyards and dockyards, transport depots
and miles of railway track were much more vulnerable and practically
impossible to picket effectively for long. As Thomas put it succinctly,
'The mines are blackleg proof. The railways are not.' Frank Hodges
recalled that Thomas declared that he had once led a rail strike that
had lasted eleven days and 'said it as though it were some wonderful and
unique experience. It was – for him. But for the miners, whose strikes
are very rarely less than three months . . . the strike or lockout is no
exceptional thing.'[5]

Despite this fighting talk, Hodges himself was worried about the
situation in 1921; and it was Hodges, not Thomas or Bevin, who
destroyed the brittle unity. Hodges himself had really invented the proposal for a national pool. But it had now become MFGB policy, despite
opposition from Herbert Smith and other miners' leaders. Now Hodges
seemed to be using the idea for all it was worth. The Cabinet met on
12 April. The Prime Minister was 'almost entirely occupied with negotiations with regard to the industrial crisis',[6] now only three days away.
He had seen 'Mr Hodges, whose attitude indicated extremist leanings,
and who was forcing to the front the question of the national pool'.[7] He
replied that, while a national pool of profits with uniform wages in all

districts was quite out of the question, a national settlement with wages varying in different districts could not be excluded.

So a document had been prepared,[8] arguing that while a compulsory pool was impossible 'without the resumption of complete and permanent control by the State of the mining industry', a voluntary pool would break down. In any case, pooling must result in inefficient and un-economical working of the industry. National negotiations, combined with varying district rates of wages, were the only practicable method of dealing with the present difficulty. In consequence, when the triple alliance reassembled the following day, it was faced with a complete breakdown of negotiations. The miners were still demanding a national wage settlement and the pooling of a proportion of the surplus as an indispensable condition of such a settlement. The Government had clearly ranged itself alongside the owners against national settlements and in favour of district ones, while denouncing the demand for a national pool as an attempt by the miners to use industrial action to secure a political end – the nationalisation of the mining industry.

In these circumstances there seemed nothing for the triple alliance to do but reissue the strike call. The Government claimed this was really a political threat, and justified calling up the Reserve and forming the Volunteer Defence Force by 'the desperate character of the miners' policy', which revealed itself in the MFGB's refusal to give adequate guarantees about the safety workers.[9] In fact, all the miners had done was to refuse the Government's demand that the safety question must be 'disposed of'[10] before negotiations could be resumed. The safety question, like the political strike, was another Lloyd George canard, a turnip-ghost with which he hoped to terrify public opinion. Despite reports from some mineowners that 'miners were going about in gangs of 2,000 strong . . . frightening the men at the pumps',[11] the safety men worked normally almost everywhere throughout the three-month mining strike of 1921. In the same way, the support of other unions for the miners in 1921 (and later in 1925 and 1926 itself) was simply sympathetic action on a large scale, not a deliberate political threat like that in 1920 during the *Jolly George* affair. But the Government had stumbled on the 'Constitutional issue', which was used with such potent effect in 1926.

Despite this, public opinion in 1921 was clearly swinging behind the miners. The abortive negotiations had at least had the result of making the actual wage reductions which the owners were trying to impose on the miners more widely known. They were too drastic for anyone reasonably to expect that they would be accepted. Even the Minister of Labour,

T. J. Macnamara, agreed in Cabinet. 'A drop from 80s to 44s is a bit thick,' he told Chamberlain. 'Give them the hope that their case is going to be examined.'[12] Yet the Prime Minister went on talking in apocalyptic terms :

> It is plain that the executive committee of the Miners' Federation are resolved to let the mines go to destruction in the belief that they will intimidate the Government into surrender to their demands. . . . The nation is, for the first time in its history, confronted by an attempt to coerce it into capitulation by the destruction of its resources, and this menace is apparently now to be supplemented by a concerted plan to suspend the transport services which are essential to the life of the country.[13]

Lloyd George concluded, 'The cause of the present dispute is being represented in some quarters as a deliberate attack upon the wages of the worker. There is no justification of any kind for this suggestion. The Government have never pronounced any opinion, nor have we formed any, upon the rates of wages which have been offered to the miners by the coal-owners.'[14] But in private the Prime Minister was singing a different tune. Discussing the appeal for a Defence Force in Cabinet, Lloyd George told his Cabinet colleagues, 'Must be careful in saying "not out to break wages down" – sooner or later got to have wages down.'[15] Yet at the same time Lloyd George was clearly working, as only he could, for some kind of settlement. He was well aware of the doubts and divisions on the union side. 'I don't think J. H. Thomas knows where he is,' he told the Cabinet, 'or he would have been along to see me. He wants no revolution. He wants to be Prime Minister. He does not want to be a commissary for Bevin.'[16] His opinion of his fellow-Welshman was not very flattering. 'Thomas is all for peace,' he declared,[17] 'he does not want a row to please Hodges. I have complete confidence in Thomas's selfishness.'

Lloyd George's prediction proved remarkably accurate. Only two days before the strike was due to start, Thomas and Robert Williams, on behalf of the railwaymen, had written to the Prime Minister conveying their union's unanimous decision to strike on Friday, 15 April, at 10 p.m.[18] This threat stimulated an influential group of Unionist MPs, who feared the House had played too small a part in trying to resolve the crisis, to invite owners and miners to argue their case before them.

So on Thursday, 14 April, two meetings took place in the Commons. In the afternoon Evan Williams, chairman of the Mining Association, put the owners' case, but his overbearing attitude antagonised MPs. In the evening Frank Hodges put the miners' side and created a much more favourable impression.[19] Yet the crisis-point of the whole dispute was at hand – the moment when Hodges destroyed the frail unity of the triple alliance with one ill-considered reply. He had begun by stating fully, clearly and frankly the importance the miners placed on the idea of a national pool and temporary aid from the Government to support wages. A barrage of questions followed. Hodges fielded them all perfectly until about 11.30 p.m., almost at the end of the meeting. The MPs clearly had doubts about Hodges' pool. Wages, they agreed, were industrial; the pool was political. Then came the vital question. 'If we can get you a satisfactory wages settlement, will you agree to temporarily abandon your pool?' Here was the moment of truth, which Hodges afterwards believed had been carefully prepared in advance. But there was no time to prepare the answer with equal care. 'If I had said no,' Hodges later explained, 'their assumption about the pool would have been confirmed. If I said yes, it would have been entirely on my own responsibility, *and contrary to the decision of the miners' executive.*'[20]

On this last point turned everything which happened in the next twenty-four hours. 'In a moment my mind was made up,' Hodges added, 'and in the presence of my two colleagues, *and without audible opposition from them*,[21] I said "Whilst I cannot see at the moment how a satisfactory wages settlement can be arrived at in the absence of the national pool, if you can induce your Government to propose such a settlement as you suggest, I have no doubt whatsoever that such a proposition will be favourably considered by my Executive Committee".'[22] This answer torpedoed the triple alliance and transformed Hodges overnight from hero into traitor. Nevertheless, Hodges had no doubt, no uncertainty : 'It was the correct answer,' he explained later.[23] 'I have never regretted giving it. There are moments in men's lives when great events hang in the balance and quick decisions have to be taken. This was one of them. At such a moment the mind becomes extraordinarily clear and, despite the quickness of the judgment, the mind sees the whole results thereof in a startlingly clear perspective.'

Hodges saw the Government offering a settlement on wages with the pool question referred to an expert committee. After a stern struggle, the MFGB would accept. If the Government's wage offer was then unacceptable, the triple alliance would, 'like a great industrial battleship', have taken up its position and moved into action behind the miners. What happened was quite the reverse. A large part of his audience in the committee room that night believed that the wage cuts the owners were trying to impose were far too drastic. But few had any more sympathy with the idea of a pool. They felt it was an attempt to continue Government control. They were anxious, therefore, to find some way of mitigating, at least temporarily, the sweeping wage cuts without conceding the principle of financial unification of the coal industry for which the miners were fighting. Hodges' answer which, according to some reports,[24] he repeated in substance several times to incredulous MPs, without opposition or qualification from Herbert Smith or any other miners' leader present, seemed to open the way to a temporary wages settlement quite apart from the vexed question of the national pool.

If Smith and his comrades were only dimly aware of what had happened, leading Unionist MPs were not. Nor was the Prime Minister, who came down from his bedroom at 10 Downing Street in his pyjamas to meet MPs who had rushed there with the news. Lloyd George quickly collected his wits and used Hodges' off-the-cuff answer with great skill to widen the split between moderates and extremists which Jimmy Thomas had earlier revealed. Relying on his 'complete confidence in Thomas's selfishness', on Thomas's unwillingness to lead anything which looked remotely like revolution and so becoming 'a commissary for Bevin', on the fact that Thomas had let John Bromley, the locomen's leader, down 'over Ireland and had not been forgiven', and on the suspicions of Herbert Smith, many of his comrades and the Durham and Yorkshire miners about the pool and the impending strike,[25] the Prime Minister wrote a carefully phrased midnight letter to Hodges calculated to widen the rifts in the labour ranks under the camouflage of offering to reopen negotiations immediately.[26] He invited them to meet representatives of the Government and the mineowners the following day at 11 a.m.

A 9 a.m. – a few hours before the strike was due to begin – railway and transport executives met at NUR headquarters in Unity House. It was an ironic choice: unity was about to dissolve. The miners met first alone. Initially, there was optimism in the air. Hodges' bright vision the night before still seemed attainable; the potential power of the triple alliance might have done the trick, as it had in 1919. But as the minutes slipped by, optimism slowly waned and was replaced by deepening gloom. When the miners failed to reach agreement in time to meet the Government and the owners at 11 a.m., the other two unions knew they must expect the worst. It came forty-five minutes later when the crucial miners' meeting broke up angrily. Herbert Smith announced they were turning down the Prime Minister's offer to reopen negotiations and were returning to their Russell Square headquarters to draft a reply.[27] All Smith would say by way of explanation was his old favourite, 'Get on t'field. That's t' place.'

It transpired that the miners' executive had repudiated Hodges' statement of the night before – but only by a majority of one. Unity House was now in the grip of bedlam, with angry miners, railwaymen and transport workers pacing the passages shouting at each other. Hodges was slumped across a desk in tears.[28] Thomas pursued Smith across the Square, but the miners' president was past persuading. With the miners themselves so narrowly divided, the railway and transport workers' leaders, who had never been very happy about the pool or the strike, were hardly likely to strike in sympathy now. The 'great industrial battleship' Hodges had visualised moving into action the night before was now about to scuttle itself without firing a shot. The triple alliance – or 'cripple alliance' as it was now bitterly called – was quite clearly finished. Facing the divided, deserted miners, the Prime Minister passed Tom Jones a note – 'It is not good enough to have a good cause.' Jones replied 'You must have good leaders', and Lloyd George responded sanctimoniously, 'I'm not heartless enough for this sort of thing.'[29] That afternoon a semblance of calm had returned to Unity House when at 3 p.m. Thomas trotted blithely down the steps to greet eager reporters with the news 'It's all off boys'. Such was Black Friday.

Thomas knew that with the mines no longer under Government control his railwaymen and Bevin's transport workers could no longer be used to get the miners better terms. They could not coerce the mineowners as they had once coerced the Government. They could threaten the Government; and the Government could offer to mediate between owners and miners. But that was all. Thomas and Bevin had been as eager as Lloyd George for new negotiations. The refusal had come from the miners. But Thomas and Bevin knew also that the triple alliance lacked the unity to make the threatened strike a reality in April 1921; and, like Hodges, they were blamed for this realism. With their aggressively working-class manner they were sufficiently buoyant to survive the floodtide of hostility which came crashing down on them after Black Friday. Pursued at public meetings with cries of 'Jimmy's selling you', Thomas would turn to his would-be tormentors and say, with a pretence of infinite patience, 'I've tried boys, I've done my very best. *But I couldn't find a bloody buyer.*'[30]

Hodges, however, was finished as far as the British labour movement and the MFGB was concerned. The miners struck alone and stayed out for more than three months before they were forced to accept terms worse than they could have had in April. After a brief spell in Parliament, Hodges became secretary of the miners' international organisation, but lost all influence at home. He compounded the sin of 1921 by supporting the company union and class collaborationist ideas of the miners' MP George Spencer in 1926. Later Hodges received a sinecure on the Central Electricity Generating Board, became director of several coal, iron and steel companies and left more than £100,000 when he died in 1947 – 'an interesting example', as the historian A. J. P. Taylor puts it, 'of how THE THING, as Cobbett called the entrenched English system, looks after its own. What discredited Hodges with the miners was his making in other circles.'[31]

Although this is a familiar story, several key questions have not been asked, much less answered, in most of the accounts of this episode. Who asked that crucial question at the meeting of Unionist MPs which elicited the fatal answer from Hodges? If, as Hodges later concluded, the question was carefully prepared, who took part in the preparations? Bevin and Thomas? Lloyd George? Or all three together? Or did Hodges himself plant the question to make possible a last-minute change of policy? Since a question about a wages settlement on district lines without the national pool was a most likely outcome of the meeting, why had Hodges and Smith not prepared an agreed answer? And if Hodges' reply that night was such a repudiation of agreed MFGB policy, why did Smith and the other miners' representatives present at the meeting not repudiate Hodges? In the end came the extraordinary spectacle of Hodges undermining his own policy on the pool and Smith, who had always opposed the idea of the pool, defending it to the bitter end.

The view of Black Friday as a date of shame was romantic – understandable, in view of the desertion of the miners, but romantic all the same. In reality, Black Friday marked the clash of two kinds of labour strategy – the one strategy of class war, harsh and implacable, fought without quarter; and another strategy of compromise and even partnership. Robert Smillie, perhaps the outstanding representative of the MFGB's pre-war leadership and a militant socialist, resigned abruptly as union president in March 1921 because he disagreed profoundly with the no-compromise policy, and was replaced by Herbert Smith.

Smith and A. J. Cook, Hodges' successor as MFGB secretary, who were both intransigents, had won a victory, although a Pyrrhic one. The only remnant of Government concern they salvaged from the wreck was a subsidy of £10 million, which lapsed in September before it had all been spent. Average pay in the mines fell by more than 30 per cent between the first and fourth quarter of 1921.[32] The coal industry was now firmly back in private hands. For the moment the miners had been crushed. But what they wanted above all was a triumphant display of solidarity to atone for the shame of Black Friday. And with men like Smith and Cook leading them there was little doubt that at some time in the future another strike would have to be fought.

Chapter Nine

Depression

Black Friday, the disintegration of the triple alliance, and the defeat of the miners in 1921 had an immediate impact on wage workers as a whole. The following year 260,000 engineering workers were driven back to work after a thirteen-week lock out. The 'employers' offensive', which began with the collapse of the triple alliance, continued in the years ahead. Wages fell steeply in every industry, sometimes after a strike, sometimes without one. Shipbuilding, printing, cotton, railways and the docks were all hit, so that by the end of 1922 *The Economist* calculated that workers had lost three-quarters of the pay increases they had won during the war. And it was no accident that mining, shipbuilding and engineering bore the brunt of this employers' offensive. These industries, the basis of British industrial supremacy a generation and more earlier, had been hardest hit by post-war changes in the terms of trade. In the 1920s it became clear that these changes in the world economy had left British capitalism in a position of serious disadvantage – as one historian puts it, they had put 'the world's workshop on short time'.[1] This problem had become accentuated by the obsolete economic structure of such traditional industries as engineering and, above all, coal mining.

As the 1920s progressed, the real economic picture began to emerge more clearly. By 1925 imports were 10 per cent greater in volume than they had been in 1913. Clearly, home consumption had recovered. Yet exports were trailing far behind – 25 per cent down on the 1913 figure.[2] For a trading nation this was an ominous picture. In 1921 the unprecedented figure of two million unemployed had been taken as the short-term symptom of the worst trade depression since the industrial revolution. Cyclical unemployment was, after all, familiar enough. And in some ways the general economic trend after 1921 seemed promising. Soon trading picked up again and economic activity became buoyant once more. By 1924, total industrial production had regained the level of 1913; by 1925 it was 10 per cent higher. Some kind of economic recovery had occurred. Yet there were still more than a million unemployed – and there were never less than a million out of work before 1940. Thus at all times, until Government mobilisation of national resources during the Second World War, one out of every ten insured workers was out of a job. In seven of these years at least three out of every twenty were jobless, and in the worst years – 1929 until 1932 – one out of every five.[3]

These crude figures were alarming enough – but they hid even more frightening facts about structural unemployment. Three-quarters of the jobless were in the old, staple industries like shipbuilding, textile manufacture, engineering and coal mining. Here as many as 20 or 30 per cent of the insured workers were permanently unemployed. A skilled craftsman could literally go for years without touching the tools of his trade. In many historic towns in Scotland, Tyneside, Lancashire and South Wales, with names which conjured up memories of Britain's industrial greatness, more than half the insured population was out of work between the wars. The reasons for this new spectre of permanent mass unemployment at a time of buoyant economic activity eluded almost everyone at the time. They seem clearer today. The export trades were producing goods for which demand was not expanding. Primary producers round the world could not buy these goods, even if they wanted them, because the terms of trade had changed so drastically in the post-war era. While the rise in the volume of imports seemed to show that the home market had recovered, British exporters were actually selling less abroad at a time when world trade was expanding quite fast.

Something deep, something elusive, was wrong. Yet in the 1920s most observers could see no further than the decline in exports. They did not believe in further developing the home market, dealing with deficient domestic demand by raising wages. They thought Britain's problems stemmed solely from the fact that she was not paying her way in the world – the cardinal sin for a capitalist nation. Unemployment could only be reduced by raising exports; exports could only be raised by lowering prices; and prices could only be lowered by cutting wages. Today this logic – based on the premise that the only way to cut costs is to cut wages – seems less compelling. Wages were already lowest in the export industries. Further reductions, by reducing demand in the home market, would tend to create more unemployment rather than less. But the conventional wisdom of the 1920s was quite clear : the working class must accept less pay to help put the country back on its feet.

This doctrine of salvation through self-sacrifice seemed to apply with special force to the coal industry. For mining was one of the industries hardest hit by the post-war change in the terms of trade. Traditionally it had been an export industry. Of the record tonnage mined in Britain in 1913, over one-third had been sold abroad. The war had destroyed many of its richest markets; and after the war the industry found that its dreams of a post-war boom were illusory. Coal production fell from its peak figure of 287 million tons in 1913 to 243 million in 1930 and 207 million in 1933 – the lowest figure of the century except for 1921 and 1926, the years of the great mining strikes.

By 1939 it had risen again to 231 million tons; but coal exports fell from 98 million tons in 1913 to 81 million in 1924, 70 million in 1930 and 46 million in 1939.[4] In the 1920s the proportion of coal exported fell from 32 per cent of the total to 28 per cent; and while the value of all other exports increased between 1913 and 1929, coal alone declined in both value and volume.[5] The value of coal produced in 1923, the best post-war year, was £259 million. In 1933 it had slumped to £134 million, while unemployment in the mines alone varied between 300,000 and 400,000.[6] Such was the sorry story of Britain's once mighty mining industry in the post-war years – a story, by and large, of falling demand, falling profits, falling wages and rising unemployment.

Average earnings in the mining industry had reached a post-war peak in the first quarter of 1921. After Black Friday they fell from nearly £4 10s per week to less than £3 in the fourth quarter of 1921.[7] The highest pay was 68s 9d in the East Federation; the lowest 38s 3d in the Forest of Dean. The downward trend in wages continued; and by 1925 Government figures revealed that the average pay of miners was only 48s 6d a week – or lower than the pay of workers in the most depressed industries, such as textiles and shipbuilding. True, wages in some areas actually went up – in the Forest of Dean, for example, by 1s 4d to 39s 7d a week and even more steeply in Kent, where they rose from 51s 9d to 65s 6d a week. But they had fallen in others, like the East Federation, over the same period from 68s 9d a week to 49s 2d.[8] Average earnings per shift from mid-1921 until March 1925 varied from 9s 4d to 12s 8d across the country as a whole.

The complexity of wage structure in the coal mining industry, where most miners were paid piece rates rather than day rates, and where miners or coal-face workers in abnormal or difficult places could earn far more than labourers, is perhaps best illustrated by evidence which Herbert Smith gave a commission of inquiry in 1924.[9] On the week ending 1 April 1924, Smith said, a collier named W. White at the Burbank and Gower Company Ltd, in Scotland, cut fifteen tons of coal and earned £3 16s 6d. With extra work, repairing and so on, he made this up to £4 2s 10d. Deductions of £1 2s 8d for explosives (coal-face workers had to buy their own) and other deductions of 2s 7d made his net pay £2 17s 7d. The next week he earned £3 15s gross, with similar deductions. He was allowed a ton of coal at a special price of £1. Another miner at the same pit filled twelve tons that week for a gross rate of £3 9s 8d. He paid 3d to the blacksmith, 1s 2d insurance, 5d for the pit medical scheme, 3d to a collection, 1s to the checkweigher and 19s 11d for explosives, leaving £2 8s 8d net take-home pay.

Taking the industry as a whole, it was clear that miners' wages had fallen faster between 1921 and 1924 than those of any other group of workers. Smith produced figures to show that 31,716 miners earned between 35s and £2 a week, 46,304 between £2 and 45s, 66,777 between 45s and 50s, 58,087 between 50 and 55s, 61,275 between 55s and £3, 56,238 between £3 and 65s, 45,713 between 65s and 70s, 42,312 between 70s and 75s, 12,700 between £5 and £5 5s and some 2,000-odd earned more than £8 a week. Smith argued that these figures revealed a decline in take-home pay, and an even steeper decline in real wages given the rising cost of living, unparalleled in any other industry. For the owners, Evan Williams argued that Smith's figures did not discriminate sufficiently between the earnings of men, apprentices and boys, and that his argument that coal company profits were running at record levels in 1923 and 1924 of £27 million, or 2s 6d a ton, was equally misleading. Many of the smaller companies, Williams suggested, were making record losses and 'it would be just as much to the point in my opinion for me to try to base a case on the 2,000-odd men who earned over £8 a week last year as it is for Mr Smith to try to base his case upon the number of certain collieries who made big profits . . .'.[10]

As a British economist has explained, 'A crucial point about the period 1919 to 1921 is that money wages rose and then fell with prices, partly as a result of the automatic link between wages and the cost of living index. *The 1920–21 period is the one and only period in our history when money wages really fell at all fast.*'[11] Since the collapse of the post-war boom during that period was not permanent, industries producing for the domestic market quickly recovered. Wages may have fallen, but so too did prices – though perhaps more slowly and gradually – with the result that real wages rose too. Thus, despite popular belief at the time, Black Friday did not set the pattern for the 1920s as a whole. Though it had been a devastating defeat for organised labour, and was followed by the fastest fall in money wages in British history, *real* wages actually *rose* during the next ten years – perhaps by a fifth, perhaps by more – because the cost of living fell. This after all was what deflation meant – and ultimately the cost of living fell more than earnings.[12] Of course, severe deflation also meant mass unemployment. But falling prices and rising real wages were a highly mitigating factor of deflation for those fortunate enough to enjoy regular work.

Thus in 1924 real wages for those in employment were by some estimates 11 per cent above pre-war, or 5 per cent if unemployment is taken into account.[13] The average man on full-time work in 1914 earned 32s a week; in 1924 he earned 60s a week. But although the average earnings of all wage workers for a full working week may have increased 94 per cent between 1914 and 1924, while the cost of living rose only 75 per cent, real average earnings were vitiated by higher unemployment. In consequence, working-class households were hardly better off than before, which was really the crux of the problem.[14] Yet women and un-skilled workers had made substantial advances in real wages; and the great majority of skilled workers made at least as much, allowing for changes in price levels, in 1924 as in 1911.[15]

For what most people noticed between the wars was the steady fall in prices. Cheaper world commodities meant cheaper imported raw materials and food. New techniques of mass production reduced the cost of manu-factured goods. Housing cost less. All this, coupled with the end of war-time controls, resulted in a 28 per cent reduction in the cost of living between 1918 and 1939. But though most people may have become better off during this period, they did so at the expense of a sizeable minority who remained in poverty. Some 20 per cent of the population lived below what Government surveys judged to be the 'human need standard'. For these, for the million or more unemployed, or for those like the miners who worked in declining industries, the fall in the cost of living brought little comfort.[16] In the attack on wages, the failure of the General Strike in 1926 was as important as the collapse of the triple alliance in 1921. If 1914 is taken as 100, money wages had risen to 170 or 175 by 1927, even after the failure of 1926, while the cost of living had risen to only 167.[17] But again these figures took no account of the much higher incidence of short-time working and unemployment.

Still, the great majority of skilled workers made at least as much in

1924 as in 1911, and they were at least as well off in 1931 as in 1921.[18] Among miners, accurate calculations are virtually impossible; but even here it was reliably reported that average earnings per shift increased from just under 6s 6d in June 1914 to just over 9s 10d a shift in July 1927, after the disaster of 1926 – an average rise of 52 per cent.[19] Once again, greater unemployment and short-time must have cut weekly pay, and, while real earnings may have risen for most workers in the 1920s, the cuts in money wages suffered by the miners were so steep that they finished worse off than before. Thus by 1928 the miner's average wage was 15 per cent lower than immediately before the General Strike and 25 per cent lower than at the peak just before Black Friday. His real earnings per shift were 8 per cent lower than in 1924, which was a good year for pay and profits. 'For many years the miners were the "forgotten men" of industry. Isolated in mining villages where there was no other form of work available to them they had to accept wages and conditions which reduced their standards almost to the level of the unemployed workers in the same community.'[20]

Moreover, falling wages were just one of the miners' burdens. Living and working conditions showed little or no improvement in the post-war period. Nothing effective had been done about the deplorable housing which the Sankey Commission had said could not be too strongly con- demned.[21] The accident rate was still appalling. In the three years 1922–4, 3,603 miners were killed and 597,198 injured – and an injury which did not keep a man away from work for a least seven days was not recorded.[22] In 1923 alone, 212,256 miners were injured and 1,297 killed. This meant that every working day 5 miners were killed; every hour 32 were injured.[23] Or, as Vernon Hartshorn, who for years had been a South Wales MFGB official, told the Sankey commission hearing, 'one out of every six . . . of all men and boys employed in the industry . . . get injured . . . for at least seven days . . . a large number are totally . . . disabled . . . about four men are killed every 24 hours'.[24] A miners' agent in West Wales told a story which dramatised the tragedy of mining life. A football team was chosen to represent the pit in championship matches – 'strong young men at the peak of their strength, skill and fitness. Thirteen years later one of them was dead, seven were totally incapacitated, two partially incapacitated and one was able to perform only light work on the surface. None was fully fit for work; silicosis and accidents had taken a heavy toll; and yet the oldest of the group was only 42.'[25]

After the catastrophe of Black Friday the miners were powerless for a time and their position grew steadily worse. The collapse of the triple alliance, the deepening trade depression of 1921, and the consequent rapid rise in unemployment hit the whole of organised labour. From being a rapidly expanding and increasingly militant movement, which labour had been since around 1910, it became an increasingly declining and defensive movement. Trade union membership fell from its peak of 8·5 million in 1920 to 5·5 million in 1924.[26] With the death of the triple alliance, however, the way was open for a new body which could reverse this trend and claim to speak for the mass of trade unionists once more. So the general council of the TUC began to take on new authority. Ernest Bevin, leader of the transport workers, was suspicious of the general council's increasing importance, especially as he was not yet a member and the leadership seemed to be falling into the hands of the Left. Bevin tried instead to revive the triple alliance under the new title of 'industrial alliance', but his schemes were unsuccessful.

With the moderate wing of the movement discredited, the way was also open for more militant action groups, not least within the MFGB. The Communist Party was strong in some mining areas, especially in South Wales. Encouraged by the Moscow-based Red International of Labour Unions, left-wing activists in the South Wales mining communities, like Noah Ablett, A. J. Cook and S. O. Davies, began to organise the Miners' Minority Movement to revive the MFGB, and, through the miners, the entire trade union movement.[27] The unity of the Left was still comparatively intact, at least by comparison with the divisions caused by Stalinism in the 1930s. The *Jolly George* affair had shown the power of organised labour and the threat of a general strike when aimed at the right target. The trick was to make the threat as effective when the objective was internal revolution rather than peace abroad. And whatever happened there could be no repetition of Black Friday.

Chapter Ten

The Vicissitudes of Politics

The miners felt they had been fooled over the Sankey commission and betrayed on Black Friday. The illusionist behind both tricks had been Lloyd George. But after Black Friday he lost the last vestiges of the magic he had exercised over the working class since the days of his 'soak the rich' Budget in 1909. His concern with welfare was not merely rhetorical. He had made significant advances, not least in housing and extended unemployment insurance.[1] This unemployment relief – the dole – came in the nick of time to alleviate the apparently insoluble problem of permanent unemployment. No one had foreseen that this would run, year in year out, at 10 per cent of the insured population. Everyone believed the depression of 1921 was an unusually severe dose of an old, familiar complaint. When the truth became apparent, attempts to stop the dole were too late. It was often the difference between life and death for the chronic jobless, and no Government could stop paying it.

Yet despite his very real legacy, Lloyd George had become a fraud and a sham for the working class. By the end of 1921 he was losing his hold over the Tories too. Bonar Law and Baldwin feared he would destroy the Conservative Party as he had already destroyed the Liberals. The Irish treaty of 1921, Lloyd George's finest piece of statecraft, was anathema to many Irish Republicans because it denied them the six counties of Ulster, and to Tory Unionists because it destroyed the historic Union with Ireland. It became increasingly clear throughout 1922 that Unionist sentiment was uncompromisingly opposed to Lloyd George, and that without Unionist support his Coalition would crumble. The Prime Minister's policy during the Chanak crisis, which brought Britain to the brink of war for the Greeks against the Turks, and the growth of die-hard Unionist power in the summer of 1922, finally brought him down. On 19 October 1922 a dramatic meeting of Conservative MPs at the Carlton Club decided by 187 votes to 87 to fight the next election as an independent party once more.[2] Lloyd George resigned, and, though he remained in Parliament until his death in 1945, he was never to hold office again.

Lloyd George was succeeded by Bonar Law, 'the Unknown Prime Minister', as Asquith called him.[3] The dynamic era was over; the Irish treaty signed; the unions apparently crushed. Bonar Law promised tranquillity. At first politics seemed more turbulent than ever. Three general elections in less than two years, and the arrival of the first Labour Government, seemed anything but tranquil. But this was caused by a shift in the prevailing political current. Labour had replaced the Liberals, but the Liberals refused to die. British one-member parliamentary constituencies, designed to deal with a two-party system, were ill-adapted to cope with three. So Labour, Liberal and Conservative parties, jockeying to achieve parliamentary majorities, succeeded only by accident and rarely maintained them for long. This caused choppy waves on the surface of politics. Underneath there was a new calm.

Bonar Law had been the strong-man in Lloyd George's Coalition and his premiership, though brief, marked a decisive shift in the direction of events. Within a month he had put the Lloyd George Coalition Liberals to the sword at a general election and given the Tories a majority of 77 over all parties combined.[4] But within six months illness forced him to resign and by December 1923 he was dead. His surprise successor was Stanley Baldwin, 'a person of the utmost unimportance', in the regally dismissive phrase of Lord Curzon, who had confidently expected the job himself. Baldwin had spent just six months in high office and was still relatively unknown; but it was his speech which had destroyed Lloyd George at the Carlton Club meeting the year before.

Bonar Law's premiership served as an *entr'acte* between two distinct periods – the Age of Lloyd George and the Age of Baldwin. After eight years of upheaval it was time for things to settle down again and find their own level. Industrial unrest subsided. The Republicans had accepted the treaty and partition. With Lloyd George's fall, and the death of Bonar Law, affairs passed into the hands of Stanley Baldwin and Ramsay MacDonald – rival party leaders but both masters of the kind of low-temperature politics the times seemed to demand.

Baldwin's great instinctive sense of public opinion did not reveal itself at once. He had inherited a solid majority and an improving economy.

Yet in October he suddenly decided to hold an election because he wished to introduce Protection, which meant imposing tariffs on imported food. He defended his decision by arguing that Protection was essential to end unemployment. But it seems more likely that the real reason was his overpowering desire to inflict another major defeat on Lloyd George, who inspired almost pathological fear and hatred in Baldwin, and who was out of the country at the time. If this was the case, Baldwin's snap election backfired badly. The popular vote remained much the same as it had been the year before. But thanks to the vicissitudes of the electoral system the Conservatives lost more than 90 seats, the Liberals gained 40 and Labour 50. A Tory majority of 77 over both parties had been converted into a situation where Liberal and Labour together had 92 seats more than the Conservatives, but no party had a clear majority.

Labour, with 191 seats against the Liberals' 159, had to be given a chance to form a Government. So on 22 January 1924 Ramsay MacDonald became Britain's first Labour Prime Minister. His charisma is something historians cannot really recapture. Robbed of his handsome presence and magnificent Scots voice, his speeches seem boring and second-hand. But he was the outstanding figure in the Labour Party of the 1920s. For years he had balanced with great skill between the various party factions, and with Baldwin he was now to set the parameters of inter-war politics. Both men held the premiership alternately until 1937, serving in the same Coalition Government between 1931 and 1935. Both believed in the politics of consensus, which they played with matchless skill. MacDonald wanted Labour to replace the Liberals as the predominant party of the Left by learning to play by the rules of the parliamentary game. Baldwin wanted to moderate and perhaps democratise the Tories. Both opposed extremism. Neither was encumbered by ideological baggage or fixed political principles. MacDonald was probably better than Baldwin at taking decisions and certainly better at foreign affairs, of which Baldwin knew nothing and cared less. Each reached the heights of popular and party esteem, only to fall rapidly to the lowest depths.

Such impact as MacDonald had on the trade unions was mainly accidental. In 1918 they had still dominated the Parliamentary Labour Party. By 1924 they constituted a bare majority. But the departure of labour leaders to the Government left Gaps in the industrial ranks which militant left-wingers were eager to occupy, and the political see-saw in Parliament in 1922–4 was paralleled at the TUC. Frank Hodges resigned as MFGB secretary to enter Parliament and become Civil Lord of the

Admiralty in the new Government. The other villain of Black Friday, J. H. Thomas of the railwaymen, became Colonial Secretary. J. R. Clynes, of the general workers, became Lord Privy Seal, Tom Shaw, of the textile workers, became Minister of Labour, and Margaret Bondfield, also of the general workers, held a junior post. These right-wingers were replaced on the general council of the TUC by representatives of the militant Left: A. J. Swales, of the engineers, A. A. Purcell, of the furnishing trades, George Hicks, of the building workers, and Ben Tillet, of the transport workers, leader of the great pre-war transport strikes. Their membership of the general council of the TUC marked an unplanned, and unexpected, swing to the left in 1924–5.

More important than this new direction at the TUC was a change in the leadership of the MFGB. One of the miners' MPs, Vernon Hartshorn, was made Postmaster-General. His place on the national executive of the union was taken by another South Wales miner, A. J. Cook, who was also elected to succeed Hodges as secretary of the MFGB. This was a decisive shift in leadership. Hodges had been pliable, willing to compromise, a politician's politician. Cook, a left-wing militant who hated compromise, was the direct opposite of Hodges in almost every way. Where Hodges had tried to persuade, cajole or outflank the rank-and-file, Cook interpreted his duties in a democratic way: refuse all concessions, and stick out for the best terms possible as the miners wanted. Herbert Smith had found a perfect lieutenant. Born of a military family in Somerset, but brought up in the South Wales coalfield, Cook – slim, fair, impulsive, sincere – was the Billy Sunday of the British mineworkers. Deeply influenced in his youth by the great Welsh Evangelical Revival of 1904, he was an inspired orator who could bring tears to the eyes of hardened journalists and lawyers at commissions of inquiry when describing the sufferings of the mining communities.[5] A graduate of the left-wing Central Labour College, Cook had begun to influence mineworkers' politics after the minimum wage strike in 1912 when he had collaborated with Noah Ablett in writing the celebrated syndicalist pamphlet *The Miners' Next Step*.

He had joined the Communist Party in 1920, but quit because he had advocated an early return to work after Black Friday. By 1924 he was a leading member of the Communist-inspired National Minority Movement, which was influential among South Wales miners, and apparently owed his election to Arthur Horner and the South Wales Communists.[6] A doughty class warrior, he was hated and feared as well as loved; but none could doubt the searing honesty of his beliefs. What worried many people was the way he expressed them. Beatrice Webb called him 'an inspired idiot' who did not know what he was going to say before he made a speech, did not know what he was saying while he was making it and did not know what he had said when he had made it.[7] 'An epileptic dialectician,' is one historian's verdict.[8] 'The trouble was,' said W. A. Lee, who as secretary of the Mining Association often found himself on the receiving end of one of Cook's diatribes, 'that he was so largely a creature of impulse. He responded in a personal meeting to a reasonable argument, but it left no lasting impression. He was essentially a demagogue. . . .'[9]

Though it is easy to criticise him, Cook undoubtedly expressed the deepest sentiments of a majority of the miners he represented. Arthur Horner, then a young Communist miners' organiser in South Wales, wondered why thousands of miners would wait in the pouring rain to hear him speak. 'He wasn't a logical thinker,' Horner recalled. 'He wasn't a good negotiator. He was absolutely undisciplined. Then it hit me. He's not talking *to* these people. He's talking *for* these people. . . . He was the voice of the miners.'[10] He both inspired and reflected their passionate demand for justice. Yet despite this, and despite his comparative youth (he was only thirty-nine at the time of his election as secretary of the MFGB), Cook was essentially a figure from the past. *The Miners' Next Step* was after all twelve years old in 1924, and belonged to an age which had vanished in August 1914. He was also in many ways a tragic figure who worked himself into an early grave for the miners, dying in 1931 aged only forty-six. But for the moment the future seemed to belong to him. In *The Miners' Next Step* he had called for a united industrial campaign to bring the mining industry to a halt and win the miners' demands. He was now in a position to put this policy into effect. And he could count on support from other left-wing militants, such as Swales, Purcell and Tillett, who had just been elected to the general council of the TUC.

Since Black Friday the general council had increased its authority. It offered to support the miners; but in return the miners had to allow the general council to handle negotiations. So began the strategy which led the TUC to back the miners in the General Strike, but which also led to a fatal misunderstanding between the TUC and the miners about the nature of this support. Yet in this way there was at least some hope that for the moment the TUC might get the owners and the miners to agree. In its brief tenure of office the Labour Government was able to help the miners too. Despite the familiar argument from the owners that profits in the industry did not warrant the prevailing wage rates, much less the increases for which the miners were pressing, the Minister of Mines, Emanuel Shinwell, intervened in the dispute and was able to get the owners to agree to a $13\frac{1}{2}$ per cent pay rise.[11] In fact, by 1924 French occupation of the Ruhr had cut off German coal supplies and driven British exports, for a short time, to freakish heights.[12] More important, the owners only agreed to the pay rise in such favourable circumstances as a temporary measure because the Labour Government threatened to raise miners' wages by Act of Parliament, and it would have taken another Act of Parliament to lower them.

MacDonald's first Labour Government lasted less than a year. The outcry over recognition of Soviet Rusia and the attempt to settle debts and negotiate a treaty had been a foretaste of things to come. The Campbell case finally brought the Government down;[13] and, in the subsequent election, the use of the celebrated forgery, the Zinoviev Letter, stampeded the anti-Socialist part of the electorate into the Conservative ranks in search of stability and safety first.[14] Though the Labour vote went up by a million, they lost forty seats.[15] By ruthlessly running against all Liberals, even friendly ones, Labour hoped to destroy the party. True, the Liberals were the real losers in 1924, dropping a hundred seats, mostly to Tories. For this, Labour lost Liberal support and gained nothing in exchange. The Conservatives, with 419 MPs out of 615, had won the most crushing Tory victory since 1874. Baldwin, scorned for giving Labour power in 1923, returned in triumph; and it was to prove a lasting victory. For all but nine of the next forty years the Tories either ruled alone or dominated Coalition Governments. A new Golden Age of Conservativism seemed at hand.

Chapter Eleven

The Golden Road to Wage Cuts

After all the upheaval of post-war politics, the nation needed a breathing space by the end of 1924. Baldwin promised this. Ireland was settled, Indian and industrial unrest had subsided. The economy was picking up, the Government had a comfortable majority, the outlook seemed set fair. More important, perhaps, as a stabilising factor was the falling birthrate and the consequent shrinkage in family size. The birthrate fell to about sixteen per thousand in the 1920s, to under fifteen per thousand in the 1930s, and never rose above twenty per thousand until after 1945. Strangely, and perhaps significantly from the point of view of class-conflict, miners and aristocrats were exceptions to the trend and continued to breed large families. But for the nation as a whole, the population increased at the sluggish rate of less than 0·5 per cent a year. The number of children under fifteen in 1921 was about the same as it had been in 1891, though the population was about ten million more.[1] In 1934 there were fewer children under five than there had been in 1871, though the population was about twenty million more.[2]

Apart from this underlying demographic trend, mass unemployment had broken the spirit of many, while falling prices and rising real wages signalled limited economic recovery and brought fresh hope to others. In this sense, the General Strike flew completely in the face of a deeper underlying pattern of Conservative stability.[3] The chief architect of the new Golden Age was to be Baldwin himself. He now occupied an un-assailable position at the centre of power which he clearly knew how to exploit. 'The most formidable antagonist whom I ever encountered,'[4] Lloyd George called him – a sincere tribute, since Baldwin did more than anyone to keep Lloyd George out of office for the rest of his life. Baldwin's bluff and apparently simple exterior hid a complicated, nervous and highly-strung personality which combined a shrewd tactical brain with great personal insight into the deepest desires of the nation. His leisure-class background at Harrow and Cambridge (where he was a poor scholar), his drift into politics via the family seat, his failure to make a mark in Parliament, did not seem to have prepared him for the titanic struggles ahead, or give any hint of his skill in dealing with them.

He had only become financial secretary to the Treasury – his first Government post – in 1917 because he was rich enough to do the Treasury entertaining his unsociable chief Bonar Law (a friend of Baldwin's father) so disliked.[5] After the war he had climbed so stealthily up the foothills of power that his appearance at the summit on Bonar Law's death in 1923 had been a real shock to many, not least to Curzon and Austen Chamberlain, who each hoped to become Prime Minister. Baldwin's family were iron masters : labour relations in the iron and steel trade were traditionally paternalistic and very different from those in coal mining or British industry as a whole in the early 1920s. Baldwin apparently aspired to recreate the harmony of the steel industry he remembered from his youth within British industry as a whole.[6] Already he had given some indication of his unorthodox and devious methods, by devoting £120,000, or about one-fifth (in real terms three-fifths)[7] of his private fortune, to buying War Loan and then handing it over to the Exchequer for cancellation. Seemingly he hoped that if other rich men followed his example the national debt would soon be extinguished. Few did – it seemed a futile hope – and having made a gesture which satisfied his streak of romantic patriotism, he won political credit from his secret and ostensibly disinterested act by carefully making it public.[8]

Soon Baldwin was to give further testimony of his ability to make the most of every situation. Despite his massive majority he had no real desire, at this stage at least, to continue the class war and satisfy the demands of his back-benchers for blood. He did not want to teach Labour a lesson and put it in its place. He sensed the deep public desire for peace. After all the upheaval of the last decade—the war, Ireland, India, industry, three general elections in less than two years, fierce political in-fighting – the nation wanted a breathing space in which tempers could cool. Baldwin – good-natured, easy-going, the maestro of political tactics – was just the kind of safe, unexciting family doctor whose soothing syrup and bedside manner would lower the temperature.[9] 'The art of statesmanship,' he once confided in a revealing phrase, 'is to postpone issues until they are no longer relevant.' His main ambition seemed to be to prevent the class war from becoming a reality and so shattering the peaceful, harmonious world in which he had grown and prospered.[10] As Prime Minister he now had the chance to translate his dream into hard fact.

Not all Conservatives were like their leader. The vicious political in-fighting of the past few years had left its mark on the party. The three great figures of the party, Balfour, Birkenhead and Austen Chamberlain, had all rejected the choice of Bonar Law. When Bonar Law died, and Baldwin succeeded him as Prime Minister, he had separated those Unionists who supported Protection, like Chamberlain, from Lloyd George by declaring the Conservative Party in favour of tariffs in 1923. By declaring against them in 1924, he won over opponents of Protection, like Churchill. But when the prodigals returned, Baldwin punished the repentant Coalitionists by giving them posts unsuited to their talents. Balfour, Prime Minister years before Baldwin even entered Parliament, got nothing.[11] Birkenhead, a former Lord Chancellor, was made Secretary for India.[12] Austen Chamberlain, a Protectionist and financial expert, went to the Foreign Office. Churchill, a Free Trader and economic tyro, was given the Exchequer.

The striking thing about Baldwin's team was its lack of experience. Only Chamberlain and Churchill had sat in Cabinet before 1914; only six had even served before 1922 – and service for Lloyd George was clearly *not* an advantage. Yet Baldwin did not set the style of his Govern-ment alone. Austen Chamberlain's half-brother Neville and, less con-sistently, Birkenhead and Churchill, were his strong men. Like his leader, Neville Chamberlain had had a meteoric rise to power. He had not even entered Parliament until 1918. By then he was fifty and, despite stalwart service in Birmingham local government, tainted with failure. Harsher, more abrasive and impatient of advice or criticism than either Baldwin or his own half-brother, he was not an attractive personality. Remote and lonely, he antagonised where Baldwin conciliated. He managed to seem mean even when he was being generous.[13] Bound to Baldwin by mutual hatred of Lloyd George[14] and a shared determination to keep him out of office, he became a notable Minister of Health and 'the most effective social reformer of the inter-war years'.[15]

Party activists often tried to replace Baldwin with Chamberlain: to no avail. Chamberlain was 'a man of No Luck'.[16] So he remained Baldwin's heir apparent until 1937 – when he succeeded him as Prime Minister and replaced Baldwin's supine foreign policy with his own even more disastrous policy of Appeasement.[17] Like Baldwin, Chamberlain personified the new

D*

type of Tory Government. The old-style country landowners, who usually characterised Conservative Cabinets, had been swept aside almost completely[18] by cultivated businessmen like Baldwin, with his distinguished literary connections, and Chamberlain, lover of music and wildlife. When the showdown came between capital and labour in 1925–6, it seemed fitting that the Government should be controlled by capitalists.

Birkenhead and Churchill, if not capitalists, were certainly men for a showdown. They were old cronies, larger-than-life figures who relished a good scrap. Birkenhead, great-grandson of a Yorkshire coal miner and champion bare-knuckle prize fighter, was born F. E. Smith in 1874 in modest circumstances. He followed a brilliant career at Oxford with equally dazzling success at the Bar and in politics. His brains, arrogance, sarcastic wit and devastating oratory made him a powerful figure in the Unionist party before the First World War and Lord Chancellor in Lloyd George's Coalition after it. Unashamedly a man-on-the-make, he had played a crucial role in the negotiations with Michael Collins over the Irish treaty in 1921, and was to play an equally important part in the events leading up to the General Strike. But he burned himself out and died at the early age of fifty-six in 1930.

Churchill, with a longer and more distinguished career in front of him, also had a more chequered past. Though born into a noble family in the same year as Birkenhead, and familiar since youth with the most influential political figures in the land, Churchill had always been a maverick and an outsider. Essentially a romantic, he saw every issue in terms of military conflict – a trait which enlivened his speeches and prose, but often had disastrous effects on his policies. After a brief but glamorous military career, he had entered Parliament as a Unionist in 1900, aged twenty-six, then switched to the Liberals four years later over the tariff issue and earned the undying hatred of true Tories. As Asquith's President of the Board of Trade between 1908 and 1910 he had introduced the first Labour Exchanges and helped lay the foundations of the modern welfare state. But as Home Secretary after 1910 Churchill won a reputation for reckless use of force to deal with strikes during the years of labour unrest, which destroyed his credit with the working class. His apparent responsibility as First Lord of the Admiralty for the disastrous Dardenelles expedition in 1915 similarly hurt his standing with the ruling class, and seemed to confirm his reputation for rash aggression. After the war, as Lloyd George's War Secretary in 1919–20, he had been the most vociferous advocate of British intervention against the Bolsheviks in Russia. Defeated in the general election of 1922, Churchill saw that the Liberal

Party was finished and when Baldwin reversed his policy and committed the Tories against Protection in 1924, there seemed nothing to stop a Free Trader like Churchill from returning to the Conservative fold.

As with men, so with policies – Baldwin was able to use events in several ways to suit whatever direction he wished to take at a given moment. To start with, he gave a widely publicised demonstration of his desire for peaceful industrial policies and refusal to gain cheap political advantage from his temporary position of power. There was great Conservative backbench pressure to use the large Tory majority to deal the Labour Party a crippling blow.[19] One of them, Frederick Macquisten, introduced a private members' Bill which would have drastically reduced the trade union political levy[20] – the main source of party funds – thus hitting Labour crudely but effectively. Baldwin would have none of it; and on 6 March 1925 he opposed the Bill in a decisive speech which was his personal favourite. He began by recalling the old industrial order he had known as a young man, with the patriarchal relationship between masters and men in his family firm. Now this had been replaced by mighty associations of employers and workers. There was nothing wrong in this; but such organisations had to use their power responsibly.

> We find ourselves [he concluded] in possession of perhaps the greatest majority our party has ever had. . . . Now how did we get there? It was not by promising to bring this Bill in; it was because, rightly or wrongly, we succeeded in creating the impression . . . that we stood for stable Government and for peace in the country between all classes. . . . I want my party today to make a gesture to the country and say to them : 'We have our majority; we believe in the justice of the Bill . . . but we are going to withdraw our hand, and we are not going to push our political advantage home at a moment like this. . . .' Although I know that there are those who work for different ends from most of us in this House, yet there are many in all ranks and all parties who will re-echo my prayer : 'Give peace in our time, O Lord'.[21]

With this one speech Baldwin killed Macquisten's Bill. But what was his real purpose? Was it simply a cunning method of buying time until he could fight Labour from a position of strength? The fact that Baldwin revived the Bill and incorporated it into the Trade Disputes Act of 1927 after the defeat of the General Strike makes this explanation plausible. But then his position at the head of an invincible Tory majority in March 1925 was surely strong enough to do whatever he wanted. For although this celebrated speech now sounds hypocritical, it is possible that Baldwin really believed he could revive in the nation at large the kind of patriarchal paternalism he recalled so warmly from the family firm in his youth.

After all, Labour was not entirely unresponsive. The appeal of G. A. Spencer's breakaway miners' union, based on class-collaboration, after the failure of the General Strike, and the conclusion of the Mond-Turner talks on cooperation between capital and labour in 1928, showed the latent attraction of such ideas in some quarters. As early as 1923, MacDonald had said of Baldwin, 'In all essentials, his outlook is very close to ours'.[22] Or as Clement Attlee, a future Labour Prime Minister, put it, 'He always seemed more at home with our people, particularly the older trade union people, than with his own lot'.[23] Baldwin was a calculating but not a diabolical character, who preferred postponing trouble and liked avoiding it best of all.

The real clue to Baldwin's policy was that it lacked fixity of purpose beyond an intense desire to make every issue work both ways and pay the highest possible dividend, as when he gave part of his fortune to pay off the national debt, and then leaked the news when others failed to follow suit. He campaigned for Protection in 1923, to win back the Coalition Tories like Chamberlain, and for Free Trade in 1924, to win over Coalition Liberals like Churchill. He refused to fight the class war in 1925 and then fought the General Strike in 1926. He killed Macquisten's Bill in 1925 and then used Labour's defeat to punish both the party and the unions in 1927. Thus Baldwin's devious policies undoubtedly played a major part in precipitating the General Strike, the greatest crisis of the post-war years.

Yet, at the same time, Baldwin's second administration still reflected the underlying stability of the times. However, his policies after 1925 were only possible because 1921 had marked a decisive turning-point. The collapse of the triple alliance, the defeat of the miners, the success of the employers' offensive in reducing wages, the Irish treaty and the general desire for peace were the factors which shaped the history of the 1920s. By 1925 the economy seemed reasonably buoyant: total industrial production was 10 per cent higher than in 1913. The time seemed ripe to fulfil the overriding objective of the financial world – a return to the gold standard.[24] This was one of the crucial decisions of the 1920s. It did more perhaps than any other single step to precipitate the confrontation of 1926 and had grave long-term economic repercussions. Ultimately, the decision was Baldwin's; but in characteristic fashion he left responsibility to his surprise choice as Chancellor.[25]

Churchill's talents were wasted at the Treasury; and he was about to make a policy decision which he long regretted. Now that Baldwin had abandoned his attempt to restore Protection, which had proved so disastrous in 1923, the Conservatives were merely offering the old pre-war policies. And the means of restoring pre-war stability was to be the return to the gold standard at the pre-war parity of the pound to the dollar. This symbolised the subordination of industry to finance, so perpetuating and deepening mass unemployment. In particular, it worsened the mining crisis and led directly to the General Strike. Churchill's reputation as a fighter, and his pugnacity in 1926, led to the belief that he deliberately precipitated this showdown by returning to the gold standard. Yet it is now clear that he foresaw these consequences and fought against the decision to return to gold. He felt it was wrong instinctively, and was finally worn down by the insistent technical arguments of Treasury and Bank officials. So he ended 'the prisoner of the orthodox finance that brought ruin to millions'.[26]

Of course, Churchill was in any case not in a very strong position to resist the arguments of orthodox finance. He had just returned to the Conservative Party – and to Parliament – and was still working his passage. Baldwin had taken a great gamble when he made him Chancellor. The entire business and financial community had been expecting a return to gold since the war. The deflationary policy of successive Governments had been aimed at the rapid return to pre-war parity. Black Friday had given the opening. By 1925 the moment seemed to have come. Wages had fallen and prices had followed. Stability seemed to be back. Given the unanimity of informed business, financial, and political opinion, any decision not to return to gold could only have been taken at great political cost. Neither Churchill nor Baldwin was prepared to pay that price.

So by returning to gold Churchill in 1925 for once accepted the conventional wisdom of the times, rather than flying in the face of it. Yet the final decision was not sudden. It was much discussed in Churchill's circle of advisers, with Churchill himself displaying all his formidable powers of advocacy against the step. His chief protagonists were Montagu Norman, Governor of the Bank of England and one of the most influential figures in the inter-war English establishment, and Lord Bradbury and Sir Otto Niemeyer, two top officials at the Treasury. The decision was urgent because the 1920 Act prohibiting the export of gold would expire at the end of 1925 and a choice would then have to be made whether or not to renew it. Lord Bradbury headed a committee which had investigated the whole problem, and its report provided the evidence and analysis on which this decision was based. Yet despite its momentous importance, the affair was badly mismanaged. The committee asked the wrong questions. Moreover, it did not put any of its questions in advance to its expert witnesses so that they could make considered replies. It took all its evidence *orally*, so missing the chance to receive well-argued expositions of points expert witnesses deemed important. It did not even tell witnesses in advance what its scope was, using the committee's title – *On the Currency and Bank of England Note Issues* – as a smoke-screen to hide its real purpose because of the danger of rumour and speculation. It made virtually no attempt to be quantitative about anything, notably in its analysis of the current situation as a guide to the appropriate exchange rate.[27]

Even so, when the committee reported in September 1924, with the exchange rate of the pound to the dollar standing at $4·40, it could hardly recommend an immediate return to the pre-war parity of $4·86 – though it insisted that 'a speedy return to the gold standard is highly desirable'.[28] Suddenly, the situation changed. Labour left office and the Conservatives returned with a thumping majority. Speculative pressure, anticipating the 'speedy return' which the report had recommended, drove the pound up to $4·79 – very close to the parity which had prevailed, with minor aberrations, for more than two hundred years.[29] With the gap now so narrow, the pressure to return was almost irresistible. Nevertheless, Churchill tried to resist – partly because he relished a fight and his polemical instincts drove him to play devil's advocate.

He asked his principal advisers if there was not some connection between the unique British phenomenon of chronic unemployment and the long, resolute consistency of the Treasury's particular financial policy.[30] Churchill was good at putting the right questions. Unfortunately, he was rather too easily satisfied with the answers which Norman, Niemeyer and Bradbury gave him even when they begged all the important points. Niemeyer, for example, did not feel he actually had to argue the case for return to pre-war parity, since the 'best opinion' was so overwhelmingly in favour of it. He denied that Treasury policy was the cause of unemployment, which he blamed on 'maladjustment of labour supplies'. The idea of stabilising at $4·40, which probably represented the correct value of the pound, was beneath contempt. So ignoring the need to justify a return at $4·86, Niemeyer concentrated solely on proving that the precise moment for return had arrived. His chief argument was that since British and American prices were now 'within $4\frac{1}{2}$ per cent of each other' the 'extra sacrifice' needed to achieve par would be 'negligible'.[31] This meant lower wages and possibly higher unemployment. But the gold lobby never talked about the level of wages and employment but solely of *prices*. Moreover, there was no real attempt to look at the *speed* of movement which was essential if the return was to be successful.[32] Wages extremely rarely fell by more than 1 per cent per year – even in the 'great depression' between 1875 and 1900. Over-impressed by the rapidity with which wages had fallen in 1920–1, men like Niemeyer imagined they could repeat that pattern in 1925–6 without ever asking how this could be achieved.

To politicians like Churchill, however, such considerations were of paramount importance. Yet after nearly three months of fighting his advisers, Churchill was being worn down by their insistent arguments that a return to gold would be a return to reality, demanding genuine competitive effort from British industry and a switch from basic industries, which had lost their competitive edge in export markets, to other means of earning. With British and American prices so close to each other, now was the time to return.

On this score the economist J. M. Keynes was quite clear. The real discrepancy between British and American prices was not $4\frac{1}{2}$ per cent, as Niemeyer said, nor $2\frac{1}{2}$ per cent, as others estimated, but nearer 10 per cent. If Britain returned to gold at the pre-war parity it would be necessary to deflate domestic prices by 10 per cent – at the cost of rising unemployment and bitter strikes. Reginald McKenna, Asquith's Protectionist Chancellor in 1915–16, who had been offered the Exchequer by Baldwin in 1923, when pressed for political advice, agreed with Keynes's analysis but not his conclusion. 'There is no escape,' he said. 'You will have to go back. But it will be hell.'[33]

So, in his Budget speech on 28 April 1925 – in which he also brought in contributory old-age pensions, doubling the income of the elderly poor[34] – Churchill announced that the Government had decided to allow the 1920 Act prohibiting the export of gold to lapse. This crucial decision had not been discussed in Cabinet, except as part of the Budget preview the day before the speech.[35] Afterwards, critics complained that the return to gold would make the City of London subservient to Wall Street.[36] But that was the whole point of the policy. As Keynes pointed out, 'A gold standard means, in practice, nothing but to have the same price level and the same money rates as in the United States. The whole object is to link rigidly the City and Wall Street.'[37] Since Britain was the weaker partner, and since the United States now held most of the world's gold reserves, this would mean enslavement to New York. Niemeyer met Keynes's argument by asserting that the return to gold would strengthen

London's position *vis-à-vis* New York, improve Britain's economic performance by expanding world trade, and thus enable her to withstand the pressure of dear money and deflation.[38]

In fact, the decision to return to gold at the pre-war parity of $4·86 was a colossal and unnecessary gamble on a rise in American prices. It took no account of prices in any other country. Yet in judging Britain's competitive position, it was obviously necessary to take account of the French franc and the German mark. Indeed, the trouble in the coal industry after 1925 was a direct result of the high exchange rate of the pound in relation to the mark, not the dollar. But no such calculations had been made.[39]

With the return to gold, Britain made a last attempt to apply simple, conventional principles to financial and economic problems which lasted until the economic crisis of 1931. Keynes predicted the results in a brilliant polemical pamphlet, *The Economic Consequence of Mr Churchill*. Why was unemployment so high in Britain, Keynes asked, when world trade was reasonably good? Because the pound had been over-valued by 10 per cent abroad. Now, one of two things would happen. Either exports would fall, and the consequent balance-of-payments deficit would be filled by shipments of gold from Britain which would imperil the maintenance of parity, or wages must be forced down, either by the pressure of unemployment, or by direct Government action. Clearly, the second was the only likely policy, and direct Government action was certain if wages were to be brought down at all fast. Churchill was not heartless – his new pensions policy showed that – and he was certainly not a fool. But he was committing himself to force down wages and all money values without any idea of how it was to be done. The Government would find itself engaging in a struggle with each separate group of wage workers in turn, with no prospect that the final result would be fair.

'The working classes cannot be expected to understand, better than Cabinet Ministers, what is happening,' Keynes explained.[40] 'They are justified in defending themselves . . . they are bound to resist as long as they can; and it must be war, until those who are economically weakest are beaten into the ground.' This was a remarkably prescient forecast of what was to happen in the next eighteen months. And it was plain why the miners were to be attacked first. Wages formed two-thirds of the cost of coal production, and the secretary of the Mining Association, W. A. Lee, confirmed that going back on the gold standard put at least 1s a ton on the cost of coal.[41] The Macmillan Inquiry into the coal crisis concluded that 'the main cause of the rapid worsening of the situation in the industry from the early part of 1925 onwards' was the return to pre-war parity.[42]

The first 'adjustment' which Niemeyer and Norman demanded in order to make their gold policy work was to cut miners' wages. As a railway-men's leader put it, 'We went to the help of the miners because we believed they were in the front-line of the wages war. If the miners were defeated, we could no longer defend our own position.'[43] Or, as Keynes put it, the return to the gold standard had created 'an atmosphere favourable to the reduction of wages'. The reversion to pre-war parity created a new and more serious crisis in the mining industry. Its first test – a test which gave the unions a chance to atone for the shameful memories of Black Friday – came in July 1925. It was to be known symbolically as Red Friday.

Part Three:
The Nine Months
July 1925 - May 1926

Chapter Twelve

Red Friday

Britain's return to the gold standard in April 1925 came at the worst possible moment for the mining industry. The pound had been over-valued, perhaps by as little as $2\frac{1}{2}$ per cent or as much as 10 per cent: enough, coupled with other factors, to erode the slender profit margins in export trading. This delivered the *coup de grâce* to the nation's struggling export industries; and no industry was as certain to be hit as coal. Two lean years in the coalfields after Black Friday had been followed by an artificial boom in 1923, when French occupation of the Ruhr and strikes in the United States had cut off German and American supplies and sent British coal prices rapidly upwards once more in a seller's market. Exports had risen to an inter-war peak in 1923, while from mid-1921 until March 1925 mining profits were nearly £$58\frac{1}{2}$ million.[1] Helped by pressure from the Labour Government, the miners had won a favourable new agreement. But French withdrawal from the Ruhr (which, ironically, was MacDonald's greatest foreign policy *coup*), the negotiation of a new reparations agreement under the Dawes Plan, and increased competition from the United States and Poland, rendered this agreement out-of-date almost before the ink was dry. Just as recovery seemed possible, foreign competitors got back on their feet and began cutting British coal profits savagely.

While German coal exports soared once more, British exports slumped. The owners would now either have to sell more coal abroad, or accept lower profits, or else cut wages; and there was little doubt which they would choose. By mid-1925 a crisis was clearly at hand. The industry was losing £1 million a month, while some 400 collieries – more than a tenth of the total – had been forced to close. Between May and July 1925 nine colliery districts were making a loss, eight of them of more than the 1s a ton W. A. Lee of the Mining Association had predicted.[2] Within five months of the 1924 agreement every district except the profitable South Yorkshire coalfield, which sold on the easy home market, was paying a bare minimum wage; by July 1925 even South Yorkshire was reduced to paying the minimum.[3] From now until the General Strike the owners became obsessed with the problems of wage rates, profits and exports – above all, exports. This preoccupation has a familiar ring to anyone who lived through the perennial British balance-of-payments crisis of the 1950s and 1960s. In this later period the problem seemed to be that while exports rose, Britain's share of world trade declined from about 25 per cent in 1951 to 10 per cent in 1972. In the 1920s the problem was similar, with exports declining ominously in industries like coal where Britain had been traditionally pre-eminent.

On 30 June 1925 the owners reacted to this major crisis. They announced they would end the 1924 agreement, cut wages, abolish the national minimum and maintain standard profits however low wages fell – though they added that they could offer better terms if the miners would be willing to revert to the pre-Sankey situation and work an eight-hour day. This new agreement would take effect on 1 August. These new terms were a declaration of war, and, not unnaturally, the miners refused even to consider them. What the owners' proposals meant for them was that the minimum wage be abolished, the principle of the national minimum percentage abandoned, and no limit set on wage reductions. The subsistence allowance for the lowest paid miner would thus be borne by the highest paid. At the same time, with no minimum wage, profits would remain secure and guaranteed at no less than £13 out of every £100 of divisible proceeds. If these proceeds were insufficient to provide a decent national minimum wage, the MFGB argued, the difference should be made good from the mining profits of earlier years and then paid back later.[4] But once again the pressure on the Mining Association was coming from the smaller, less profitable pits, and from the hard-hit export regions like Durham and South Wales.

If the miners were adamant about wages, they were equally intransigent over the owners' hint about working an eight-hour day instead of the existing seven hours. The miners' leaders quoted figures which showed that a higher proportion of accidents occurred during the final hour of work, when miners were tired and less attentive. Refusal to accept the new terms would mean a lock-out. But the miners would fight. The question was: would they have to fight alone again, as they had after Black

Friday four years before? The answer to this question depended on the reactions of the TUC and the Government.

Black Friday had in fact accelerated the rise of the general council of the TUC. The collapse of the triple alliance had left a vacuum which had to be filled by another body claiming to coordinate the activities of individual trade unions. Yet despite much discussion no such body had clearly emerged by mid-1925. True, the general council had a mandate to act in trade union disputes. During MacDonald's Labour Government they had acted on the miners' behalf with Cabinet cooperation. But there was no chance of similar collaboration with Baldwin's Cabinet. And, moreover, it was far from certain that the bigger unions would now accept the general council's authority. The railwaymen and the transport workers had already made it clear that they were becoming a little tired of always having to come to the aid of the miners. But in the crunch of 1926, events showed that the miners were unwilling to hand over all their real authority to the TUC during the General Strike. Bevin, soon to play a crucial part on the general council, did not altogether like the idea of such a central authority, and tried to organise an industrial alliance, which would have revived the triple alliance in a new form.[5] These arguments were still continuing when the mining crisis broke in 1925 and demanded action.

This policy debate was sharpened by political changes in the composition of the general council. The TUC, traditionally the conservative wing of the British Labour movement, had been travelling Left in the period 1924–5. Despite the revolutionary atmosphere in the immediate post-war period, the TUC had shown little interest on the return of its delegation from the Soviet Union in 1920 or the Russian experiment in Communism. By 1924, however, interest was aroused by the Labour Government's negotiations over the abortive Anglo-Russian treaties. From within, left-wing supporters of the National Minority Movement prodded the TUC towards the Left. The resignation of such prominent right-wingers as Thomas, Hodges and Clynes to serve in MacDonald's Government in 1924 had, as we have seen, made more room for the Left. Cook had replaced Hodges as secretary of the MFGB while a left-wing group had formed behind the new chairman of the TUC general council, A. A. Purcell, an organiser of the furnishing trade workers and Labour MP for Coventry from 1923–4.

Purcell, highly critical of the reformist tendencies of MacDonald's Government and attracted by Communism, took the lead during his year as chairman of the general council of the TUC in 1924–5.[6] The new mood of left-wing militancy was apparent at the TUC conference at Hull in

September 1924 with men like Hicks, Swales and the Communist engineer Harry Pollitt prominent. The meeting gave a warm welcome to the Soviet trade union leader Tomsky, a fraternal delegate speaking in Russian. The following month, the TUC sent a delegation to Russia, led by Purcell, which included Herbert Smith, Ben Tillett, hero of the transport workers' pre-war strikes, John Bromley, a moderate locoman, and Fred Bramley, secretary of the TUC. Despite difficulties, the delegation appeared to have improved relationships between British and Russian trade union movements. A 'Red Dawn' seemed to be breaking as the industrial crisis developed in mid-1925.

Yet this move to the Left was far from universal. Some labour leaders, even right-wingers like Thomas, were prepared to use the threat of concerted action to try to win concessions from the mineowners and the Government. Others genuinely feared the consequences of another head-on clash such as had been threatened in 1921. If it failed, Labour would suffer another devastating reverse, which it might take years to overcome. If it succeeded, moderate Labour leaders might suddenly find themselves cast adrift on some kind of anarcho-syndicalist ocean of revolution with no charts to guide them. Nevertheless, on 10 July 1925, the general council of the TUC met the MFGB executive and promised to support them in their fight to preserve 'the standard of life of their members'. Everything seemed set for a showdown. On 25 July, less than a week before the mineowners' notices were due to expire, the national executives of the railway, transport and seamen's unions met to coordinate their plans. Though deadlock was never far away, the general council managed to persuade all factions to agree, and the three unions instructed their members to place a complete embargo on coal from midnight on 31 July.

Faced with this situation, the Government reacted equivocally. When the mining industry had been taken under Government control in 1917, it had been possible for the trade union movement to use the threat of concerted action to try to force the Government to intervene directly in a dispute. But once the mines were returned to private hands in 1921 this was no longer possible. The TUC's attempts to get the Labour Government to impose a solution on owners and miners alike in 1924 had met with only limited success. And neither Labour nor Conservative Governments had been able to solve the problems of the mining industry. True, Lloyd George's Government had agreed to pay the mineowners a short-term subsidy to protect pay and profits in 1921; but Baldwin's Government in 1925 ruled out a similar subsidy. However, Baldwin did agree to set up a court of inquiry, under Hugh Macmillan, MacDonald's

Scottish Lord Advocate and chairman of several influential inter-war committees, to investigate the coal industry for the second time in a year.[7]

The Government now seemed ready for anything. The Emergency Powers Act of 1920 gave them all the authority they needed to deal with the threatened national embargo on coal, to which had been added the danger of a major strike in the woollen industry.[8] The preparations in 1921 had seemed ominously effective; and since then the machinery had been overhauled and improved by the Civil Service under both Conservative and Labour Governments.[9] But in 1925 the Government was clearly divided about whether or not to use this machinery. The hawks were Chamberlain, Birkenhead, Churchill and the Home Secretary, Sir William Joynson-Hicks. 'Jix', as he was known, a 'Reds-under-the-beds' alarmist, had the job of reviewing the emergency preparations, and he reported to the Cabinet on 14 July. He concluded that Government plans were, for the most part, ready but that only a nucleus of an organisation existed. Volunteers could not be recruited in sufficient numbers to operate the arrangements which had been made to provide food, transport, fuel and power, communications and so on during a national strike without the declaration of a State of Emergency. It was hoped to complete the transport arrangements 'before the end of July' and the Post Office was still making arrangements for communications. Despite this apparent urgency, the Cabinet did not discuss the report until 23 July, barely a week before the mineowners' notices expired.[10]

On the union side, divisions were also clearly apparent as the 31 July deadline drew nearer. Moderates in the TUC pressed strongly that the lock-out notices be postponed while the Macmillan court of inquiry looked for a solution. When Citrine made this suggestion at a preliminary meeting with the miners before meeting the Prime Minister on 27 July, George Hicks told him, 'Walter, you're too far ahead. Don't worry. Let the thing develop.'[11] But if Hicks was not worried, Baldwin was sufficiently alarmed to have been forced to enter negotiations personally with the TUC. Swales, the left-wing engineer, told the Prime Minister, 'We are out to back the miners and we mean to support them'. The more moderate Citrine added that they could not allow the miners to be beaten on this issue, and appealed to Baldwin to ask the owners to withdraw the notices.[12] The owners refused; and Citrine noted in his diary, 'Looking at the Government side, I could not see any sign of fear of anything we were going to do. They seemed perfectly calm about it.'[13]

Not everyone was calm on the union side. Cook, the miners' secretary, refused to see George V to talk about the impending crisis. 'Why the hell should I go to see the King?' he indignantly asked Citrine. 'I'll show them they've got a different man from Frank Hodges to deal with now.' Later he added, 'I'm going to fight these people. I believe a fight is certain. There may be a postponement, but a fight is certain.' Citrine advised him to make sure he was fighting with discretion, and Cook replied with a sudden burst of emotion that he had something to pay back. Six years before he had been led in handcuffs from one end of the train to the other at Swansea and Cardiff stations.[14]

On 29 July – almost the eve of the expiration of the owners' notices – the Macmillan court of inquiry published its report. This was a decisive moment in the 1925 crisis. Though the MFGB had refused to give any evidence to an inquiry which even *considered* lower wages and longer hours, the court came down strongly in favour of the miners. It recommended a fixed minimum wage and sharply criticised the way the industry was organised and managed.[15] *The Times* greeted this news with a prim leader which argued that the owners now had no choice but to suspend the notices and withdraw their proposal for lower wages and protected profits.[16] The furious owners flatly refused, and passed a resolution saying they would not accept the report. Baldwin was aghast. When he resumed discussions on 30 July – the day before the notices were due to expire – it was in the full knowledge that the mineowners, whom he had trusted as his friends, had put themselves completely out of court in the eyes of public opinion by this petulant refusal to accept the findings of an impartial inquiry. Sir Arthur Steel-Maitland, the Minister of Labour, was equally angry, and told the Cabinet that the owners' action had been most ill-considered and had put the whole future of negotiations in jeopardy.[17]

Shuttling between miners and owners, the Prime Minister must have felt he was on shifting sand. He offered the miners another exhaustive inquiry into the industry with which they agreed to cooperate. But they refused to give anything else in return; and Baldwin for his part still refused to consider the question of a subsidy. In the afternoon, Baldwin persuaded the owners to preserve the minimum wage, while the miners went to a special conference of the TUC. *There was no talk of a General Strike*,[18] but the miners secured promises of a complete embargo on coal and financial support. Thus fortified, the MFGB met the Prime Minister later in the afternoon and pressed again for a subsidy. Baldwin again refused, and instead asked Herbert Smith for concessions. Smith's reply was laconic. 'Nowt doin'. We've nowt to give.' Baldwin repeated that there could be no question of a subsidy, and urged the miners to make some contribution to solving the nation's economic difficulties. The miners' representatives pointed out indignantly that what Baldwin proposed meant wage cuts. The Prime Minister replied blandly, 'Yes. All the workers in this country have got to take reductions in wages to help put industry on its feet.'[19]

Baldwin's notorious statement about the necessity for universal wage cuts was the catalyst in the 1925 crisis. The miners took it as a declaration of war. So did the TUC. It solidified union opinion at a vital moment – at the very moment, indeed, when it had melted away in 1921. Already rumours had reached the King at Buckingham Palace that Jimmy Thomas was saying there would be no embargo on coal, that the railwaymen would refuse to support the miners.[20] At the special TUC union conference that afternoon there had been heated argument about whether the Labour Party should raise the subject in the House. Thomas was strongly in favour, Bevin, Cook and Smith strongly against. No one could forget that the disaster of 1921 had been caused by astute politicians exploiting a statement made by Hodges at a meeting in the Commons. So the matter was not raised.[21] Meanwhile, however, a decision was already being reached.

At 6.30 p.m. Baldwin met the Cabinet. It was a vital meeting. Baldwin was beaten and he knew it; the problem was to get the hawks in the Cabinet to accept his policy. The Prime Minister began by reporting on the continuous talks he had had with owners and miners during the past 48 hours and summarising the position. The owners had made some slight concessions over the minimum wage, but the miners had made none. A wide gap separated the two sides, and there was deadlock with no settlement in sight. Consequently, the lock-out would begin at midnight the following day, all trade unions would give financial support to the miners and railwaymen and transport workers in particular would refuse to handle coal.[22] Baldwin then reviewed the arrangements for meeting the emergency. By refusing to handle coal, the railwaymen were clearly in breach of contract; but sacking the defaulting railwaymen would only lead to a national railway strike, and make the situation much worse. A skeleton emergency organisation was ready, but it could not function without volunteers – and no volunteers could be called until a State of Emergency had been proclaimed, which would in itself seem provocative. Baldwin believed the Army was better placed to help than in 1921, and that there would be no need to call up the Reservists or enrol the Defence Force as before.[23] Stocks of coal and other fuel were 'unprecedentedly large'.

But despite these encouraging portents, Baldwin believed that a national strike on the scale now contemplated would hit the public services so hard that they could only be maintained at great and costly effort. The financial and economic effects of the strike would be 'extremely grave'.[24] During the Cabinet meeting a letter arrived from the MFGB confirming their support for the kind of inquiry Baldwin had mentioned in his discussions with the miners earlier that day. But the letter emphasised that the inquiry's terms of reference must be satisfactory, and that in the meantime the miners must not be asked to work at lower wages or for longer hours.[25] Steel-Maitland intervened to say that the present state of coal trade meant owners could not sustain existing pay and hours without a subsidy. On 28 July the Cabinet had agreed that a subsidy would only be considered 'in the remote contingency' that, after both parties had made the largest possible concessions, 'there was still a gap which could not be bridged, and that a subsidy for a limited term of months might provide the only means of securing a durable settlement on an economic basis'.[26] In Baldwin's view, that 'remote contingency' had now been reached. Accordingly, the Cabinet decided, but not unanimously,[27] that a subsidy would be less disastrous than a national strike, and that the Prime Minister and some of his colleagues should try to reach a settlement on the basis of a comprehensive inquiry into the mining industry. While this inquiry was taking place a subsidy should be paid, if necessary, to maintain pay and profits. The meeting also agreed that the Prime Minister should tell the Commons that talks were still in progress and that 'unostentatious preparations should continue for maintaining public services in the event of a strike'.[28]

And that was the end of the embargo threat. When the meeting ended after three hours, Baldwin, Chamberlain and Churchill went across to the Ministry of Labour to meet the miners and the owners. The Prime Minister told the miners he had decided to do what he had said repeatedly he would not do; grant a subsidy to the industry for nine months, until 1 May 1926. During that period a royal commission – the third inquiry in a year – would investigate the problems of coal mining, and the miners would be expected to honour their pledge to participate. He then met the owners and told them they must withdraw their notices. Cook reported jubilantly that the miners were getting practically everything they wanted, and Citrine noted in his diary, 'I retired at midnight with the feeling that unless something very unexpected happened, the whole business was practically settled'.[29] Talks went on after midnight and final terms were drawn up on Friday at 4 p.m. Churchill told Cook, 'It's a good job it's over, but you have done it over my bloodstained corpse. I have got to find the money for it now.' The money was more than anyone imagined. The subsidy was expected to cost about £10 million; in fact it cost £23 million. Churchill also added that some of his friends ought to be in jail – a reference, perhaps, to some of the Cabinet doves.[30] Cook sent out a terse telegram to all his MFGB branches : 'Notices suspended. Work as usual. Cook, Secretary.' Recalling the shame of 1921, the *Daily Herald* headline gave this victory the name by which it is now universally known : 'Red Friday'.

Why did Baldwin back down in July 1925? According to one of his biographers, he gave the answer himself : 'We were not ready.'[31] In view of what happened nine months later, this argument is plausible enough on the surface, and has been accepted by most historians. But there is more to the problem than that. To accept that Baldwin was simply buying time by capitulating to the miners in 1925 is rather like accepting that Chamberlain was simply buying time at Munich in 1938 when he capitulated to Hitler. In both cases the time gained did, in the end, enable the Government to survive a later challenge; but in neither case was this the object of the exercise. The Prime Minister's conduct in July must be seen against the background of his 'Give peace in our time' speech in March. Was Baldwin simply playing a cunning game and running away so that he could live to fight (and fight on much stronger ground) another day? Or was he simply postponing a direct confrontation in the hope that something would happen to dissipate trouble in the meantime?

Clearly, the argument 'We were not ready' is not in itself enough to explain Red Friday. Government machinery for dealing with industrial emergencies was in a high state of readiness. Evolved after the passing of the Emergency Powers Act in 1920, it had been used effectively in 1921 and then overhauled by senior Civil Servants such as Sir John Anderson and J. C. C. Davidson in 1923.[32] Some historians have contended that the system was allowed to run down under the Labour Government;[33] but the reverse would be more the truth. Certainly, some senior Civil Servants and Army officers had at first been chary of sharing their secrets with men like Thomas, who might well be leading the other side in the next industrial conflict. Yet the Labour Government had shown itself ready not only to review the emergency plans, but to use them against striking dockers and railwaymen.[34] Though there might have been a shortage of volunteers in 1925, these could have been speedily recruited had a State of Emergency been declared. The skeleton organisation was ready; and the Army was certainly better placed to deal with industrial trouble than it had been in 1921, when the Irish troubles had meant troops had to be stationed there.

Of course, the owners' decision to withdraw the 1924 agreement, which had precipitated the 1925 crisis, had been sudden and had given the Government only a month to decide on policy and make its dispositions. By contrast, in 1921 and again in 1926 the Government had several months' warning of impending confrontation. More important, perhaps, was the fact that in 1925 an impartial inquiry had just come down strongly in favour of the miners, while in 1926 another inquiry was to issue findings which were far less favourable in the short run. With public opinion behind the miners in 1925, Baldwin did not feel justified in risking a national stoppage, with all its grave economic and financial consequences.

Some idea of the kind of pressures that influenced Baldwin's decision can be gleaned from a confidential memorandum he received from Finlay Gibson, secretary of the South Wales Coalowners' Association in May 1925. Gibson argued that while the short-term prospects in coal-exporting regions like South Wales might be bad until about August 1925, within six months South Wales could be producing fifty million tons a year and by the end of 1926 unemployment there could be ended. The coal industry in South Wales might employ 230,000 men directly, *but the key to this was the reduction of working costs by 2s 6d a ton.*[35] This in turn depended on the acceptance by the miners of lower wages, and by the railway companies of more expensive steam coal. Owners like Gibson expected the miners to agree to less pay and the customers to agree to higher prices so that their working costs could be reduced while mining profits remained sacrosanct. They showed an equally obstinate belief in the efficacy of increasing the miners' hours from seven to eight a day, when the problem was *selling* the coal already mined. Gibson also had strong objections to any idea of a subsidy for the industry and resisted any attempt at Government intervention.[36]

Another rationalisation of Red Friday came from Arthur Griffiths-Boscawen, a former Tory Minister of Health and Agriculture and an old crony of Baldwin's. He told the Prime Minister :

I hate the idea of seeming to capitulate to trade union threats to hold up the community, but under the circumstances I am sure you were right to stop an immediate strike, the consequences of which no one could foresee, to gain time which may bring a solution. . . . The time gained may enable things to come right, since I am sure the railwaymen are not Bolshies (though some of their leaders are), but there was the real fear that every trade would demand a reduction in wages in turn. Hence the determination to stand together.[37]

So despite protests from the King's private secretary, Lord Stamford-ham, 'Jix', the coalowners and Conservative backbenchers, a small but influential group of Tories – including hawks like Birkenhead, Chamber-lain and Churchill – backed Baldwin.[38] No doubt the hawks thought in terms of an inevitable showdown at some later date, when the Government would fight from better prepared positions. Churchill, for example, defended the Government's policy on 10 December 1925 when he said, 'We decided to postpone the crisis in the hope of averting it, or, if not averting it, of coping effectually with it when the time came'.[39] But Baldwin was more equivocal. He hoped that if the crisis were postponed it might not recur. The inquiry might actually find a solution acceptable to all parties; Labour solidarity might dissolve again; prosperity might return in the coal export trade; the problem might just go away. The object of statesmanship, after all, was to postpone dealing with issues until they were no longer relevant. By this definition, far from being the 'sell-out to syndicalism' its right-wing critics claimed, Red Friday was the apotheosis of Baldwinian statecraft.

Chapter Thirteen

The Government Prepares

Not all the opposition to the Red Friday settlement came from Tory backbenchers. Much the most lucid statement of right-wing reaction came from within the Cabinet. Lord Salisbury, the Lord Privy Seal and an influential figure in Conservative circles, wrote a forthright memorandum, dated 4 August, in which he argued that the mining subsidy would have to be continued until such reorganisation which the inquiry might recommend had taken place. This could well be several years; and after eighteen months or two years its temporary character would be forgotten. Moreover, with so much public money committed to the subsidy, the Government would have to exercise a measure of control. The next logical step would be nationalisation. Salisbury continued:

> I need not say that, to a Government pledged as we are, this conclusion is absolutely unacceptable, even if such a policy were feasible. But it is not feasible, because obviously the coal industry cannot be treated, even if our pledges allowed it, as exceptional. What should we have to say to steel, or shipbuilding, or agriculture? . . .
>
> If our present policy leads to nationalisation, and this is unacceptable, at what point are we going to draw the line? Is there any ground on which, in our retreat, we could hope to make a stand: and if there be such ground, which I do not perceive, have we the strength to hold it? . . . For good reason or bad we have retreated because we did not venture to fight. We have not only thought it right to give way to force, but we have condoned the breaking of their contracts by the allied unions in their threatened sympathetic strike and we have actually agreed to pay a large sum for the arrangement. Whatever our ultimate

5a. Philip Snowden seems to be bracing himself to take the burden of office. He served under Ramsey MacDonald in 1924 and 1929–35 and was the Treasury's favourite Chancellor.

5b. Ramsay MacDonald (right) and Arthur Henderson call on Prime Minister Baldwin during the 1923 political crisis.

6a. Stanley Baldwin, who was Prime Minister during the General Strike.

6b. Winston Churchill, Baldwin's controversial choice as Chancellor of the Exchequer.

intentions may be, there is no doubt that this is how the trade unions themselves and the world regard the event. Who will believe us, after the experience of the last few days, when we say we will die in some ill-defined ditch, rather than accept the nationalisation of the coal industry, and inferentially, the nationalisation of every other industry? I shall be glad if my confidence can be restored, but the moral basis of the Government seems to have dropped out.[1]

Salisbury's fears that Red Friday marked the start of the slippery slope to socialism were ill-founded. His confidence in the Government must have been quickly restored. For it began immediately to draw up plans for dealing with a General Strike. The royal commission under the former Liberal Minister and Governor of Palestine, Sir Herbert Samuel, was soon constituted.[2] Efforts to influence membership of the commission included pressure from Frank Hodges on behalf of Sir Charles Markham, an enlightened owner.[3] Churchill offered to set up the commission while Baldwin was on holiday as usual at Aix, and also suggested he take over direction of the Mines Department, since 'Now that we are paying the subsidy I shall in any case have to give a good deal of time to coal'.[4] But what if it should fail to solve the problems of the mining industry? By 5 August, the Cabinet had met to discuss a 'more effective scheme . . . than at present exists for maintaining vital national services in the event of a strike'.[5] The Home Secretary, Joynson-Hicks, reported on the existing emergency organisation in a manner which made it clear that it could have gone into action on 31 July.[6] He emphasised that the primary responsibility for combating a General Strike rested with the Cabinet Supply and Transport Committee, of which he was chairman. In addition, other sub-committees dealing with food and fuel, protection, communications, finance, publicity and other matters had been established. 'The underlying principle,' Jix wrote, 'is that each of the Government Departments must be responsible . . . for seeing that such arrangements as are possible are made for dealing with the emergency.'[7]

He added that to stimulate local activity, especially recruitment of volunteers, the country had been divided into ten districts, each under the control of a Civil Commissioner, and that for the purpose of recruiting labour the country had been divided into eighty-eight areas, each under the chairmanship of an influential local person. Jix went on to discuss the role of the police, the Army, special constables and reserve forces, noting that 'movement of troops . . . might . . . in some quarters be regarded as provocative', but adding that 'on some occasions it has been

E

useful . . . to send a warship to a port where disturbances are threatened'.[8] Straight after the Cabinet meeting, Jix told his Northampton constituents, 'Sooner or later this question has to be fought out. . . . Is England to be governed by Parliament and by the Cabinet or by a handful of trade union leaders?'[9] The report concluded, 'The most difficult as well as perhaps the most important aspect of the problem . . . [is] the protection of workers of all kinds who are prepared to continue at work, whether at docks, power stations, on transport services, telegraphs, telephones or whatever it may be.' Jix felt it might be necessary to call up the Defence Force, which had been used so effectively in 1921.[10]

Accordingly, the emergency machinery was quickly overhauled and streamlined. The Cabinet agreed to the Home Secretary's recommendations to make proper arrangements for a national strike. Further to dividing the country into districts, arrangements had to be made for staff, communications and transport, and accordingly £10,000 was allocated to be spent on these services. A further report would be made in October.[11] By October each of the ten districts had its own headquarters and staff. Few county boroughs as yet had a Labour majority, so the Government could use the town clerk as their local agent without offending the council. Staff meetings had been held, and the Civil Commissioners had spent some time in their own areas. Already four-fifths of the emergency manpower had been appointed, with the final fifth in readiness. At fortnightly conferences, officials from Government departments had worked out such details as the best emergency routes for food and transport, the allocation of qualified volunteers to man key positions in power stations, and the security of arms and explosives. There were plenty of motor vehicles; petrol stocks were good; and food supplies more than adequate. By February 1926 Jix could tell the Cabinet that 'little remained to be done' to deal with a possible General Strike.[12]

The Government's formal, and secret, plans for dealing with any future industrial emergency were augmented by the informal, but more public, activities of the Organisation for the Maintenance of Supplies. The OMS was an unofficial body and was supposed to employ nobody in Government service : so the Government could not be accused of acting provocatively. But the OMS had been set up, after statements and letters in the Press, and was headed by such solid figures as Lord Hardinge, a former Viceroy of India, and Lord Jellicoe, who had commanded the British Fleet at the Battle of Jutland in 1916, when the whole fate of the Empire had seemed to hang in the balance. These men clearly belonged to the Establishment and their names were obviously meant to inspire public confidence. As the Home Secretary, Joynson-Hicks, put it, 'The time has come when publicity must be risked in order to make proper arrangements for dealing with a General Strike'.[13]

So the OMS came into existence in the early autumn of 1925 to recruit, train and organise, in the Government's words, 'those citizens who would be prepared to volunteer to maintain supplies and services in the event of a General Strike'. The OMS was defined as 'an association of loyal citizens organised in the public interest to provide the Government in times of emergency with classified lists of those who will assist in maintaining essential public services . . . food, water, light, fuel, power and transport, and who, when called upon by the constitutional authority, will cooperate in upholding law and order'.[14] Its purpose, in short, was to fill those gaps in Government preparations revealed by Red Friday and put some flesh on the skeleton of the official organisation without having to declare a State of Emergency.

Volunteers were called upon to act as special constables, public service workers, clerical workers, dispatch riders and drivers – especially lorry drivers.[15] Joynson-Hicks admitted,

> I have known of the inauguration of this body for many weeks past; in fact, the promoters consulted me as to their desire to form some such organisation. . . . My plans have been long since made, and have been approved by the Government as a whole. We have not thought it necessary or desirable to make a public parade of our willingness and ability to do that which is our duty, nor have we desired to assume what might be considered a provocative attitude by enrolling several hundred thousand men.[16]

From the beginning it was 'clearly understood' that if an emergency arose, the OMS organisation would disappear and hand over its lists to the Government,[17] and when the General Strike began the OMS dropped all pretence of independence and immediately merged with the Government organisation.

Yet the OMS suffered serious internal administrative problems. The question of how to ensure that the OMS organisation would merge painlessly with the Government when the time came caused Home Office officials much anxiety. Since volunteers agreed only to work under the direction of the OMS, what 'guarantee have we', asked the Chief Civil Service Commissioner, Sir William Mitchell-Thomson, 'that recruits who have registered with the OMS will transfer their services to the Government organisation?'[18] Sir William mentioned rumours that itinerant OMS agents were telling local authorities that in the event of an emergency the OMS would be in charge of transport, food arrangements and the like. 'Statements of this kind, even if they are only the indiscretions of youth, cause us a great deal of trouble.'[19] Just how much trouble had been revealed at the end of November, when rumours reached the Home Office that in parts of North Wales the Ministry of Health was setting up its own OMS organisation.[20]

The Home Office tried to reaffirm 'the doctrine that OMS is complementary to the Government organisation but it is prepared to hand over its records . . . on the outbreak of an emergency'. But an internal memo pointed out tartly that 'the attitude adopted by subordinate officials of the OMS rather weakens this'.[21] Eventually, the incident was found to be based on a misunderstanding; but the whole episode gave rise to some anxiety about the bureaucracy of the OMS. 'Is the organisation set up by the Ministry of Health supreme in its own area,' asked an official somewhat plaintively, 'or is this overlapping to continue?' The official insisted that he must have 'a definite, clear answer',[22] but none exists in the Home Office files, and there is every reason to believe that OMS organisation remained inefficient. Such problems as overlapping, communication, training, insurance and recruiting reliable special constables were raised and recognised. But according to Home Office files there is no evidence they were ever solved satisfactorily.

While these internal problems were wracking the OMS, serious criticisms were being voiced in public and in Parliament. Following noisy protests against the use of Hampstead Town Hall in London as a recruiting office for OMS volunteers, special articles appeared in Labour newspapers such as the *Daily Herald*.[23] Questions were asked in the House, and Joynson-Hicks answered by saying that he welcomed the help which the OMS was offering but had no control over the way local authorities spent their money or used their town halls or offices.[24] This answer was somewhat less than frank : the OMS had been set up on Government initiative and Joynson-Hicks certainly had close control over its activities. In a series of internal memos, Home Office officials had to agree that the objections made by the demonstrators and the *Daily Herald* had some validity and could not be quietened by the kind of bromide the Minister was offering.[25] Despite all these difficulties, internal and external, the OMS managed to register about 100,000 volunteers in the nine months between Red Friday and the start of the General Strike.[26]

Yet the OMS was not particularly effective in helping to break the strike. It lacked equipment for training recruits properly and, by and large, it tended to appeal to middle-class and white-collar people who, in the scornful words of C. T. Cramp of the railwaymen, had 'never worked in their lives' and certainly would be unused to loading and unloading heavy cargoes from ships or driving railway locomotives pulling massive goods trains. The OMS also tended to appeal to extreme right-wing elements, like the British Fascists. The Fascists, followers of Mussolini, had earlier won some lurid publicity by raiding the headquarters of the British Communist Party and kidnapping one of its leaders, Harry Pollitt. Now Fascists began to embarrass the authorities by volunteering *en masse* as special constables.[27] Liverpool decided to cancel these arrangements, while Wolverhampton said it would only recognise Fascists as individuals, not as members of an organisation.[28] Nevertheless, during the General Strike the Fascists merged with the OMS and the Government organisation, and, though they played no decisive role in events, they controlled the distribution and unloading of supplies in some areas. But even if the OMS failed to provide any really effective training, it was significant because it began to rally public opinion behind the Government.

Chapter Fourteen

Union Disunion

In contrast to these careful preparations on the Government side, the trade unions made virtually no effective plans for mounting a future general strike. This failure has never been satisfactorily explained. Red Friday had looked like a triumphant vindication of TUC policy and of left-wingers like Swales, Hicks and Purcell at the TUC, and of Smith and Cook among the miners. But the MFGB was in no mood for self-congratulation. What had been the practical result of Red Friday? Simply that there had been no reduction in wages. But the owners were not paying a living wage. Had Cook asked for an increase? What sort of 'victory' was that? Smith had no illusions. 'We have no need to glorify about a victory,' he said. 'It is only an armistice.'[1]

The armistice would end when the Government subsidy expired in nine months' time on 1 May 1926. The unions knew this as well as the Government, and knew that fresh fighting would break out again. Why then did they not prepare for it? Part of the answer lies in internal union politics. The TUC conference at Scarborough which followed Red Friday in September 1925, for all its class-conscious, Marxist phrase-making, marked the end, rather than the beginning, of left-wing influence. Faced with a motion empowering the TUC to call a General Strike to assist the miners, the conference merely referred the whole question to the general council. Such prominent right-wingers as Thomas, Bevin and Clynes had persuaded the TUC to strengthen the general council's growing power and influence, anticipating events the following year when the trade union movement gave the TUC full power to conduct the General Strike.[2] This decision took on a new significance because the three new members whom the conference elected to the general council were all well-known moderates : Jimmy Thomas and Margaret Bondfield, reclaiming the old seats they had relinquished to enter the Labour Government the year before, and a crucially important newcomer, Ernest Bevin, the transport workers' leader. The new president, Arthur Pugh, who succeeded the left-winger Swales, a moderate from the Iron and Steel Trades Confederation, 'might have made a fortune as a chartered accountant',[3] and was an advocate of the paternalistic labour relations admired by Baldwin. Then came another crucial change : the general secretary of the TUC, Fred Bramley, died in October 1925, and his successor, Walter Citrine, like Bevin, personified the new, cautious, efficient, moderate and non-doctrinaire bureaucracy of the trade union movement.

With the restoration of right-wing influence, the general council was occupied with preparations for the coming crisis. The problem seemed intractable. How was the TUC to act? It could no longer hope to use concerted pressure to force the Government to intervene directly, as it had before the return of the coal industry to private hands in 1921. Under the Labour Government the TUC had been able to play a more active role, with Cabinet support. Yet the solution which the Government had imposed in 1924 had been acceptable only to the miners, not the owners, and under a Conservative Government the TUC would not be allowed to act on the miners' behalf in the same way. Nor could they expect a repetition of Red Friday when the subsidy expired. But what could they expect, and how should they prepare for it?

Lack of planning on the union side can also partially be explained by the fact that it was much more difficult for the TUC to emulate Government preparations. The unions did not have the Government's money, or its ability to activate in secret Civil Service machinery which had existed since 1920 or earlier. Any preparations they made might be regarded as provocative – and the Government's successful prosecution of Harry Pollitt and eleven other leading Communists in October 1925 for incitement to mutiny showed the danger of this. Still, it is surprising that the TUC did not try to work out more detailed plans with such organisations as the Co-operative Wholesale Society for helping the unions in any future industrial conflict.

The Co-operative Movement's role in the great railway strike of 1919, when it used a voucher system to supply food to the strikers and loaned £500,000 strike pay, had not been forgotten. Cook described it as 'the victualling movement for the fighting forces of labour'. But by 1925 the Co-op movement was being run by moderate-minded men who were angered by Cook's remarks and refused to make any arrangements about future strikes.[4] Cook's own conception of preparations seems to have been more primitive. Dismissing the threat of troops – 'bayonets can't cut coal' – he assured a cheering audience that 'We have already beaten, not only the employers, but the strongest Government in modern times', and added that they had to get ready for the next round. 'My own mother-in-law has been taking in an extra tin of salmon for weeks past,' he explained, prompting Jimmy Thomas to explode: 'By God! A British revolution based on a tin of salmon.'[5]

Though some of the militant Left was eager for revolution, it showed little grasp of what was necessary in terms of practical organisation, and practical advice and proposals came largely from the moderates. Thus in January 1926 Walter Citrine, the new acting-secretary of the TUC, drew up a characteristically clear-headed memorandum which asked some pointed questions about policy and preparations.[6] Citrine had held several posts with the Electrical Trades Union and then joined the TUC as assistant secretary in 1924. At thirty-nine he was one of the youngest labour leaders, but on the brink of discovering his true role. His cool, pragmatic approach and outstanding administrative abilities, which included immaculate shorthand, made him Bramley's obvious successor when the TUC secretary died in 1925. Citrine, who, in Beatrice Webb's words, was 'an intellectual . . . intent on real power',[7] held office until 1946 and so became, with Bevin, one of the most influential figures in British trade union history at a decisive period.

Citrine did not share the jubilation felt by most trade unionists after Red Friday. 'Everyone who thought at all must have realised that the subsidy would last only until 1 May 1926, and could not possibly be enough to transform the finances of the industry,' he explained.[8] The problem facing the Samuel commission on the mining industry was how soon they could get any of their recommendations into operation. 'I didn't see the owners acting speedily on anything except issuing notices to the miners,' he commented.[9] He added,

At the end of 1925 I began to get more and more uneasy at the lack of preparation on our side for the trial of strength which I felt lay ahead. The Samuel commission was hard at work. The Government were going ahead with recruitment for an organisation for maintaining supplies, and there wasn't the slightest doubt that they would be far better equipped to face any emergency in 1926 than they had been in 1925. On our side the only preparations were the speeches of Arthur Cook and a few others, including myself. . . .[10]

Citrine had already written several articles in which he tried to puncture this euphoria. Now he drafted a report to the TUC's Special Industrial Committee stressing the need for centralised authority, the development of proper administrative machinery for handling an emergency and the evolution of some kind of coordinated policy between member unions for conducting the dispute. Red Friday, he believed, had been just a pre-liminary skirmish. 'It is certain the Government will not allow a similar situation to arise without seeking to establish methods whereby trade unions can be combated. . . .'[11] Next time, the Government would be prepared to force matters to a conclusion on ground of its own choosing. The Citrine report echoed Lord Salisbury's Cabinet memorandum by emphasising that any recommendations the Samuel commission might make about reorganising the industry would take time to implement.

The real problem, therefore, was what would happen when the subsidy lapsed; for, without it, the owners would try again to cut wages at once and fresh trouble would start. Citrine felt the Government would have to subsidise the industry for another year at least, and possibly longer, until progress had been made in reorganising the mines. Nevertheless, the TUC must prepare for a possible confrontation along the lines he had suggested. He urged consultation with the Labour Party, the MFGB, the Co-opera-tive Union and other interested parties to create machinery comparable to the Government's for dealing with an emergency and 'to force the Government to a favourable decision'.[12] He also stressed the need to create good publicity and so win public opinion over to the side of the miners and the unions in general. He drew up a separate memorandum dealing with this problem, but made an addendum to the main report urging that, in the event of a crisis, member unions should vest power for calling, conducting, and concluding a General Strike in the hands of the general council of the TUC.[13] Once again, Citrine had hit on a crucial point, one which was to play a decisive part in the events of May 1926. But for the moment the TUC's Industrial Committee rejected the report as being too extremist, and it was buried with a few kind words from Smith and Cook.

The need for unity was made more urgent by the deep divisions on the union side. Wherever Thomas spoke, the miners were immediately on the alert, and Cook said that 'Thomas was completely distrusted'.[14] Even within the miners' own ranks there was tension. Thus Frank Varley, a miners' MP from Nottinghamshire who was also on the MFGB executive, complained that Smith contradicted anything he said, merely because he had said it.[15] By the start of 1926 it was clear to Citrine that

E*

the miners 'did not want to face the issues raised by my memorandum and would do anything to put off a decision. . . . The miners were divided amongst themselves and terribly suspicious . . . of one another.'[16]

Nor did the miners, any more than the mineowners, want to face up to the issues raised by the crisis in the coal industry. Since the return of private ownership in 1921 it had become clear that any spark of hope which the Sankey report may have ignited in 1919 had long since been extinguished. The subsidies paid by the Government to protect pay and profits in 1921 and 1925, and the artificial prosperity of 1923–4, had helped disguise the profound problems facing the industry. Neither Lloyd George's Coalition, nor subsequent Labour and Conservative Governments, had been able to solve these problems. Everyone talked about the urgent need for reorganisation. Salisbury in his memorandum to the Cabinet, and Citrine in his memorandum to the TUC, had both stressed this. It has been argued that while everyone talked about the need for reorganisation, few cared to spell out in any detail that its implications would be painful for all concerned, miners and mineowners alike.[17] In fact, evidence from the Baldwin Papers made recently available makes it clear that much more detailed exploration of this kind was taking place than historians had suspected.

For owners like Lord Londonderry, the question seemed simple. 'Why are wages per ton double what they were in 1913?' he asked Baldwin somewhat wistfully. 'Are wages too high, hours too short or are there too many mines?'[18] Londonderry then launched into an irrational attack on high wages, quoting figures from his own pits to show that at Christmas-time miners pushed up their output so that they could earn between £5 and £12 a week. Other owners like Cunliffe-Lister, from Yorkshire, were more reasonable and defended the principle of the national minimum.[19] The real problem was to put the coal crisis into a wider perspective. Lord Aberconway, chairman of John Brown Ltd, the great steel and shipbuilding firm of Sheffield and Clydebank, argued that the Government should establish selling committees to buy up coal and sell it at prices below British competitors in the Mediterranean, Baltic and South American ports, which had been British preserves. They could guarantee a subsidy of 1s a ton up to a maximum of twenty million tons, which would only cost the Treasury £1 million a year.[20] Other suggestions included a proposal that the Government lend money to the owners to pay for reorganisation and improvements at below the market rate and that they should compensate owners who were forced to close. This argument included job protection, retraining, and regrading of posts in an effort to encourage the miners to feel they too had a stake in the prosperity of the industry. Emigration to other parts of the Empire was to be encouraged for those miners thrown out of work.[21]

Sir Alfred Mond, one of the great industrialists of the 1920s, submitted a long written report on the coal position to the Samuel commission on 21 January 1926. Mond's report was a lucid statement of the problem and possible solutions, including the abolition of wayleaves, the payment of royalties by the thickness of coal seams rather than by the ton, and the working of longer hours for three years. Attempts to increase the tonnage of coal raised per man shift should include the extensive regrading of jobs underground, the regrouping and reorganisation of coalfields and pits and greater use of modern techniques such as electrification. But Mond always argued that the subsidy should be ended. He estimated that the industry's output would probably have to be reduced by 20 per cent, and that 100,000 miners would have to be laid off permanently and given priority in other jobs on the land, in road construction and public works.[22]

Lord Weir believed that an inquiry into mining *by itself* could only be futile. Apart from hours, the main remedies for coal were outside the industry itself and not dependent on the efforts of owners or miners. The only useful inquiry, he told Baldwin as he was setting up the Samuel commission, would be one with a much broader frame of reference than coal alone, or alternatively one with a broader reference plus an auxiliary reference to coal.[23] Opposite fears had been expressed by Sir Ernest Gowers, permanent under-secretary at the Mines Department: 'Samuel's intensely orderly mind,' he wrote, 'and Beveridge's passion for information for its own sake were diverting the royal commission from its task of concentrating on a few points to surveying the whole problem of the industry once again.'[24] These few points were becoming painfully clear. Reorganisation would mean closing many uneconomic pits and drastically reducing the number of miners employed. And until the industry was thoroughly reorganised it would never be able to pay proper wages or declare decent profits.

This was also the general conclusion of the long-awaited report of the Samuel commission, published on 6 March 1926. Though it had heard evidence from nearly eighty witnesses representing both sides of the coal industry,[25] neither miners nor mineowners had been invited to serve on the commission, because Baldwin had wanted 'fresh minds' to examine the problem. Their absence had caused some derision. 'What would they say,' Cook had asked indignantly, 'if *I* appointed a commission on the Stock Exchange out of a plate-layer, a shop assistant and an engine driver?'[26]

Despite Cook's sarcasm, the Samuel report should have brought more satisfaction to the miners than it did to the mineowners. The commission emphasised that the depression in the coal trade was caused by the collapse of the export market. Sales abroad had slumped from 98 million tons in 1913 to only 68 million tons in 1925. 'Our share of the world's consumption,' the report explained, 'in 1909–13 amounted to 9·8 per cent; it had fallen to 8·4 per cent in 1924 and to about 7·0 per cent in 1925.'[27]

But the report refused to accept the mineowners' contention that the burden of solving the problem be shifted onto the backs of the miners. Longer hours, it sensibly said, would in the current state of trade simply mean piling up bigger stocks of coal which could not be sold. Lower wages, the owners' other favourite panacea, could only be a temporary expedient. Moreover, the commission was 'strongly of the opinion that national wage agreements should continue'.[28] The real solution to coal mining's problems, the report suggested, was root-and-branch reorganisation of the whole industry. 'We cannot agree with the mineowners,' it concluded, 'that little can be done to improve the organisation of the industry . . . large changes are necessary . . . and large progress is possible.'[29]

Detailed proposals as to exactly what form these 'large changes' should take then followed. The Samuel report made a reasoned rejection of state ownership of the mining industry. It recommended instead nationalisation of royalties: this meant, in effect, public ownership of coal but not the coal mines. On the structure of the mining industry, the report argued that, although private ownership should remain, existing units were too small and amalgamation was desirable. However, the Government should only foster those amalgamations for which there seemed to be some spontaneous desire, rather than seek to impose them from outside.[30] The report also recommended spending more money on scientific research into the use of coal through new processes, like smokeless fuel, and urged the coordination of the electrical, gas and coal industries through a national fuel and power committee. Further recommendations included improved methods of transporting and selling coal; the continuation of the 'valuable work now being done on safety and health'; a series of reforms to improve living and working conditions and the general welfare of miners, such as pit-head baths; a system of compulsory profit-sharing; and the creation of a national wages board.[31]

But all this was in the future, as more far-sighted observers like Citrine had predicted before the commission issued its report. The immediate recommendations were less palatable to the MFGB. True, on the question of national wage agreements, the report came down completely on their side. But the question of the subsidy to the mining industry was, as Citrine had foreseen, the really crucial point. Here the report was quite unequivocal. The subsidy 'should stop at its authorised term and never be repeated'. Continuation would be 'indefensible'.[32] Wage reductions might only be a temporary expedient; but since the Government subsidy could not be extended beyond 1 May, the report's only immediate proposal on what to do while the industry was being reorganised was a steep pay cut.

Present wage rates had been fixed during the artificial prosperity of 1924. Without the subsidy, about half Britain's coal was being mined at a loss; and wages made up 75 per cent of the cost of coal. Without subsidy, and without a reduction of wages below the 1924 level, many mines would be forced to close. 'What the commission propose, put bluntly and briefly,' the Minister of Mines, G. R. Lane-Fox, explained, 'is that the subsidy should in no circumstances be continued and that wages should be reduced . . . that the minimum percentage of $13\frac{1}{2}$ on standard agreed in 1924 should go. This . . . does not mean a return in all districts to the previous minimum of 20 per cent (on standard). In some districts less may be needed, in other districts more. But in all districts the present wages are too high as a minimum.'[33]

What was becoming increasingly apparent was that questions of wages and hours were not the real issue. The Government subsidy had protected pay and profits and kept coal cheap both at home and in the export markets. Figures could be quoted in a district to show losses or microscopic profits per ton. The point was that the actual results obtained by individual enterprises revealed a very different picture. The margin between the modern economic collieries and the old unecomonic ones, in cost of production, was so large that when the subsidy ended unprofitable pits would be forced to raise prices. Moreover, a wage cut in *all* pits would not improve the competitive position of low-productivity pits against high ones, though it would make British coal more competitive in foreign markets. As Mond told Baldwin, 'It is not clear how either increased outputs or lowered wages would, in themselves, alter this state of affairs.' He suggested that the solution lay in the use of a national sales policy abroad, like the Germans used. Mond estimated that at current wage rates 50 per cent of Britain's total coal output was actually mined at a loss.[34] The real problem was that this percentage was not spread evenly: losses were heaviest in South Wales, Durham and Scotland and lightest in Nottinghamshire and Yorkshire.

In such a situation the tactics likely to be pursued by both sides were clear. The owners would press for a speedy return to district settlements; the miners would defend national agreements and urge that the most profitable pits should help keep the worst wage rates higher. Baldwin could not effectively budge the owners, but he felt there was some give on the miners' side. By February, at any rate, the Government believed the MFGB had abandoned its claim that the settlement on Red Friday in July 1925 had meant that the basic rate could not be altered. But the Mining Association still refused to sign a national agreement covering the subsidy period,[35] and, unless each side was prepared to give a little, conflict seemed inevitable.

Chapter Fifteen

Samuel Comes to Judgement

The Samuel report is crucial to understanding the events of 1926. It dominated all the discussions of the problems of the mining industry. While the initial response of miners and owners to the commission findings was clearly of the utmost importance, the Government attitude was decisive. The Government, after all, had brought the 'four wise men' together. As one historian has put it, 'With judgment pronounced they [could] go back to their own concerns, to cotton or banking or economics or the construction of a system of belief. . . . The deliberations of the Liberal doubter in search of a philosophy, and his fellow-commissioners, could elicit nothing new. It was the philosophy of the Government that decided the fate of the mines.'[1] *The Times* urged the Government to give a lead and strike the right note of unity by accepting everything in the report; and this policy was strongly advocated by some members of the Cabinet when it considered the commission's proposals.[2]

But such acceptance was clearly difficult for other members of the Cabinet. As early as 28 July 1925 – before Red Friday – the Cabinet had set up a committee to investigate the question of State purchase and State control of mining royalties. Churchill had been in the chair, and the committee's members included Lane-Fox, the Minister of Mines.[3] Strongly influenced by Churchill, this committee had decided against nationalisation; and now Churchill, as Chancellor, circulated a confidential note to all his Cabinet colleagues criticising the Samuel commission's case for nationalising mining royalties. The cost would be prohibitive, he contended, and (echoing the kind of arguments Niemeyer and Norman had used against him over the Gold Standard decision) would render it impossible for him to achieve 'the great object of financial policy in the next few years' – namely the reduction of interest on War debt. 'From the standpoint of general public finance,' Churchill warned sombrely, 'there is, therefore, everything to be said against acquiring mining royalties at this juncture.'[4]

Lane-Fox agreed that the Samuel report's recommendation on nationalising royalties should be rejected, while his own department was 'in emphatic disagreement' with some of the other proposals.[5] On the question of ending the subsidy there was firm agreement. 'Given the will,' Lane-Fox concluded, 'a new wages agreement could be made in six weeks; if the will is not there, six months would be insufficient; and if the subsidy is continued the will would certainly not be there.'[6] Despite his disagreement, he stressed the need for the Government to accept the report unreservedly, emphasising that the immediate wage cut recommended by the commission depended 'upon the acceptance by all parties of such measures of reorganisation as will secure to the industry a new lease of prosperity leading to higher wages'.[7]

Lane-Fox then revealed that ambiguity which, emanating from Government, owners and miners alike, was to make such a powerful contribution to the misunderstandings of the next few weeks. ' "Acceptance" by the Government at this stage,' he added, 'does not, of course, mean an undertaking to give effect to all the recommendations in all eventualities; it merely means the Government will not, of their own motion, refuse to take the steps the commission have recommended they should take. How far they may actually be called upon to do so must depend largely upon the attitude of the other parties.'[8] Clearly, those Cabinet members who had urged the Government to accept the Samuel report in full and without conditions had been defeated; and on 24 March, more than two weeks after the report was published, Baldwin told the House, 'The conclusions reached by the commission do not in all respects accord with the views held by the Government and some of the recommendations contain proposals to which . . . the Government are known to be opposed.' However, the Government was willing to accept these, provided that the owners and miners also accepted the report as a whole.[9] This may have sounded reasonable; but it was in effect an abdication of responsibility. Both owners and miners had shown over the years a total obstinacy, inability to compromise and unwillingness to accept new ideas. There was no chance of either side accepting the report as a whole – and Baldwin knew it.[10]

So instead of making agreement a precondition of Government action, or taking the initiative in providing the basis for agreement, Baldwin tacitly invited owners or miners to veto the report. Both sides seized the opportunity with alacrity. The owners now showed that, like the Bourbons, they had learned nothing and forgotten nothing since 1919. They felt they had Government backing and were determined to make the miners taste defeat so that they could really drive their wages down. Even hawks, like Chamberlain, found it hard to be kind to them. 'Not a prepossessing crowd,' he observed tersely, while J. L. Garvin, the editor of the *Observer*, remarked that they had 'been tactless and irritating to the last degree'.[11] Tom Jones was more personal in his criticism.

> Evan Williams, who for the last seven years has been putting the owners' case, is an insignificant little man. One hardly realises the gravity of the issues at stake. What he lacks in emphasis, however, is promptly supplied by Sir Adam Nimmo . . . chairman of the Fife Coal Company and . . . also, I believe, a local preacher. . . . The coal owners have always gone to the utmost limit of self-sacrifice, the question in debate . . . is always fundamental and always involves a vital principle on which the owners cannot possibly carry compromise an inch further. He is one of the greatest stumbling blocks on the path of peace. Among the thirty or forty others there is hardly an outstanding personality.[12]

Pressed by the least profitable pits, the owners wanted lower wages, district instead of national settlements, and talk of better terms only if the miners would agree to an eight-hour day. This last point inevitably involved the Government, since miners' hours were fixed by Act of Parliament. Existing agreement ended on 30 April 1926, and the cuts would vary from district to district. The position was relatively easy in the Eastern Division and in Lancashire, Cheshire and North Staffordshire, serious in Scotland and very serious in Northumberland, Durham and South Wales. As Lane-Fox put it, 'The miners in the exporting districts . . . must . . . suffer substantial reductions; the owners . . . will on average still have a loss of face; and it is inevitable that a certain number of collieries must close.'[13]

Herbert Smith reckoned that without the subsidy there would be wage reductions of 7d a shift in the Eastern Area, 1s 6d in Lancashire, Cheshire and North Staffordshire, 1s 8d in the Forest of Dean, 1s 9d in South Staffordshire and Shropshire, 2s 7d in Scotland and North Wales, 3s 2d in Northumberland, 3s 5d in South Wales, 3s 6d in Cumberland and 3s 8d in Durham.[14] The Durham miner would lose 18s 4d a week; a face-worker in South Wales would have his weekly earnings cut from 78s to 45s 10d.[15] The rates almost everywhere would be back to the low point at the end of 1921, and in Durham and South Wales lower than those of 1914. The miners simply would not look at such reductions, even as a preliminary to the kind of reorganisation the report had promised. That was much too vague. As Smith put it, 'I want to see the horse I am going to mount', while Cook kept repeating that the Prime Minister was asking the miners 'to buy a pig in a poke'.[16] The miners now based their case on three points: national agreements; a seven-hour day; no pay cuts. The Samuel report had supported them in the first two. But on the one that mattered most immediately to the miners, namely no pay cuts, it had come out against them. When a friend told Cook the report had given the miners two-thirds of what they wanted, Cook replied 'It gives us three-quarters, and we can't accept it'. Then he summarised the miners' demands in the irresistible slogan, 'Not a penny off the pay, not a second on the day'.[17]

The immediate threat to their living standards, and Cook's demagogic appeal, unified the miners and hid important incipient divisions within their ranks, which were to become more important as time passed. The rivalry between Varley, Smith and Cook, for example, was based on deeper regional differences, which in turn reflected the contrast between the state of the home and export trade in coal. The bitterest battles between miners and owners in the 1920s took place, for the most part, in those regions, like the North-East and South Wales, which produced coal for export and had been hardest hit by the collapse of the export markets. South Wales steam coal was the finest in the world. But narrow seams – in places only twelve to eighteen inches high – made it difficult and therefore expensive to mine. The Yorkshire, Derbyshire and Notting-hamshire coalfields, on the other hand, which were newer and more up-to-date, were centres where coal was mined for the softer home market. Easier and cheaper to cut, it was sold on the domestic market with an assured sale and steady profits. Moreover, these coalfields were, on the whole, better as far as housing and general working conditions were concerned. Compared with Durham or South Wales, which were always hot-beds of militancy, industrial relations here were much more peaceful. Indeed, after the failure of the General Strike, a breakaway union, the Miners' Industrial Union, founded by the Midland miners' MP G. A. Spencer, flourished there for a time in the late 1920s and early 1930s, advocating a policy of cooperation with the coalowners.[18]

Similar divisions split the mineowners. Those from the more profitable regions were more willing to compromise than those from regions produc-ing coal for export. Even within regions there were sharp differences of opinion and policy. Thus David Davies, a Welsh landowner, mineowner, Liberal MP and Parliamentary Private Secretary to Lloyd George, was scathing in his criticism of the evidence Evan Williams had given to the Samuel commission. He regarded it as 'more stupid than one could possibly have anticipated. He has done his best to rile the miners. There is not a note of conciliation in the whole evidence. He has put the railwaymen on their guard, and cemented the alliance between them and the miners. He has boosted the royalty owners when there was not the slightest justification or reason for doing so, and he has not made a single constructive contribution towards the solution of the problem.' Davies himself tried to influence his fellow directors of the Ocean Coal Company, and through them the Mining Association, towards a constructive contribution, but with little success. He was opposed to the owners' obstinate insistence on repealing the seven-hour day, arguing that 'unfair European competition' was the real problem and that the answer was not to make the miners work a longer shift, but to take up the unfair competition with the International Labour Organisation. Davies also wanted a permanent, independent tribunal set up to arbitrate coal disputes.[19]

The attitude of men like Davies led Tom Jones to remark that 'there are some decent and progressive coalowners ready to move forward'. Other owners pursued different policies. 'The Powell Duffryn Company,' Jones reported, 'have been screwing the men down mercilessly for a long time.' George Hall, the Labour MP for the mining seat of Aberdare, predicted 'grave trouble owing to the prevailing bitterness' there if the men came out on strike. Hall wanted the subsidy for exporting districts continued for at least six months. Yet only a few miles away, in the Glamorganshire pits owned by Sir David Llewellyn and his brother William, feeling among the miners was much better, because the owners moved among the men and took the trouble to get to know them personally.[20] Sir Alfred Cope, managing director of the Amalgamated Anthracite Collieries, used all his influence to try to delay the South Wales owners posting up lists of the wage reductions they wanted, and to moderate terms which he regarded as quite unacceptable, but without success.

Negotiations dragged on in futile fashion throughout April. Owners and miners met separately and together, the TUC tried to mediate, appeals were made by all three to the Government. The debate rapidly became bogged down amidst proposals for new district minima, percentages above standard and guaranteed weeks. In some ways it was 1925 all over again; but this time the Government was ready for trouble and refused obstinately either to act on the Samuel report itself or to put pressure on either side to accept it. When the owners met the miners on 13 April, Evan Williams insisted that national agreements were no longer possible, while Smith refused to continue the talks unless the owners agreed to discuss the minimum wage nationally.[21] Nor would Smith or Cook consider lengthening the working day, either directly or by 'redistribution' over the week to a maximum of 48 hours. They strongly denied that the subsidy was a means of maintaining unrealistic wages, arguing quite logically that it was equally a subsidy in support of profits. 'Some of the owners have got substantial profits upon it,' Cook pointed out. 'The quarterly statement proves that.' But Williams refused to discuss the question of profits, or even consider it 'pertinent to the issue we are discussing at the moment'.[22]

The problem of profits – of cutting profits as well as pay when the mining industry ran into difficulties – received surprisingly little attention from the non-socialists who wished to reform the industry. The Liberal prejudices of the Samuel commission, especially of Samuel and Beveridge, shone clearly through the prose of their report. But on the question of profits the report had been strangely silent. Profits, of course, were sacrosanct. So long as the industry remained in private hands it would have to maximise profits. The only way it could pay for the sweeping reorganisation suggested in the Samuel report was by attracting fresh capital investment on the free market by maximising profits.

Moreover, though the industry's gross profits in good years – like 1923–4 – looked good on paper, and indeed the industry's whole performance since 1914 was not unimpressive,[23] the detailed picture was very different. In many regions, or at many pits within regions, conditions varied enormously. While some pits might be profitable, at others the difference between profit and loss was extremely narrow. When profits for the industry as a whole might still look comfortable, at least half the coal companies in the country might find themselves working at a loss, or very close to it. The divisions within the ranks of owners and miners alike usually closely followed the relative profitability of their pits.

For the moment it looked as if the discussion was becoming preoccupied once more in the details of wage scales and balance sheets. But Smith raised another sore point when he told a meeting of owners, miners and Government representatives on 23 April that, 'It is a bigger dispute than wages because they are attacking our customs that have been built up in the districts for years'.[24] In South Wales, for example, the old custom of giving six shifts for five, which had been established for thirty or forty years, was to be ended, and in Yorkshire and elsewhere similar local practices seemed at risk. Nevertheless, despite the solidarity of the districts in defence of local custom, 'save the national minimum' was the MFGB's real rallying cry. 'In Yorkshire,' Smith told the owners and the Government, 'with the subsidy, the owners have been getting profits of over 2s a ton . . . if anybody thinks they can buy industrial peace and see the owners getting that and the miners getting lower wages they are mis-understanding us. While we are out for peace, we are not out for peace at any price.'[25] But Yorkshire was a profitable area. The real problem was what to do about export areas, like Durham and South Wales. If the trouble was caused by over-valuation of the pound, an export subsidy would solve it. At the start of the current crisis Baldwin had noted, 'we do not rule out the possibility of giving those districts some further assistance for a period of two or three months, on a tapering basis', to mitigate the miners' sacrifices, but such a subsidy would be dependent upon a firm agreement ensuring peace in the industry 'for a substantial period'.[26]

Chapter Sixteen

Signs of a Settlement

If renewal of the subsidy for a short period might provide the basis for a settlement it was clearly worth pursuing. Sir Alfred Mond had earlier opposed the idea of a new subsidy. But now, as chairman of Amalgamated Anthracite Collieries, he tried to use his influence in favour of a compromise. He may have had 'immense industrial and financial interests' and 'a bias towards ruthless American business methods',[1] but this did not prevent him from having some enlightened ideas – indeed, it may have encouraged them, since it was generally the small and less profitable collieries which had intransigent owners. Using Cope, his managing director, and Tom Jones as go-betweens, he suggested to Baldwin on 17 April a plan for a selective subsidy, based on profitability. Alternatively, Mond put forward a scheme for a Government loan for mining reconstruction, particularly for companies short of capital but with geological advantages and good prospects,[2] which the Treasury refused to consider. Mond had as much trouble persuading his fellow mineowners to accept such radical ideas. He met his colleagues at the Savoy on 22 April and wrote hopefully to Baldwin that 'something can be achieved' if the Government came out strongly in favour of the Samuel report. But the Government would have to impose a settlement. 'I assure you the whole country is looking most anxiously for you to force a settlement. Among all the coalowners present last night, the opinion was that the attitude of their representatives in the negotiations was quite unreasonable.'[3] Cope confirmed this, telling Jones that Sir Adam Nimmo, chairman of the Fife Coal Company, and Wallace Thorneycroft, a Scottish mineowner and director of the Lochgelly Iron and Steel Company, were strongly opposed to Mond's scheme for a subsidy or loan, but the rest of the owners were more friendly.[4] Of course, Churchill and the Treasury regarded Mond's scheme as madness and would have absolutely nothing to do with it, as they made clear on 19 April. In any case, Evan Williams and the leaders of the Mining Association would have rejected the idea.

On the miners' side there were fleeting glimpses of a possible settlement too, which vanished almost at once. Cook told Jones privately that the owners were stiffening their side by rushing out notices of new terms and making it impossible for miners to draw unemployment benefits if they refused to accept them. 'We are economically in the weakest position we have ever been,' he confided, 'and while a lot of our chaps won't agree with me, we shall have to have a national minimum not only with pluses above it, but minuses below it.'[5] In public, Cook asserted, 'I am convinced that a settlement can be reached by a straight return to the commission's proposals, and from them to a discussion on the basis of a national agreement'.[6] But the report had said wages must come down and Cook's slogan was 'not a penny off the pay'.

Underlying disunity in the miners' ranks was revealed on 23 April when the owners offered what Williams himself admitted were 'miserable' wages for a seven-hour day, and 'reasonable' ones – 20 per cent on standard – for an eight-hour day. In reply, Smith rambled hopelessly. At one point he seemed willing to negotiate wages nationally; at another he wanted to keep wage rates exactly as they were. Humour broke the prevailing tension when both Williams and Cook interrupted at the same moment to correct Smith's figures on district wages. 'I can deal with one Welshman at a time,' he told them, 'but not two at once.'[7] When the Prime Minister confronted Smith with figures showing that, without a subsidy, existing wage scales would close nearly all the pits in the export districts and throw 200,000 miners out of work, the MFGB president replied that he would prefer to see them unemployed than accept lower wages and longer hours. Frank Varley, the Nottinghamshire miners' MP, supported him. But of course neither Varley nor Smith came from an area likely to be badly hit by unemployment if the subsidy ended while present pay scales continued.[8]

Towards the end of this meeting came what Jones called 'a significant hint from one or two of the miners'. This was that 'there should be a definite agreement to reorganise the industry, and if the subsidy were continued during the reorganisation then it might be possible to come to terms'. Sir Horace Wilson, permanent secretary of the Ministry of Labour, and Sir Ernest Gowers, permanent under-secretary for mines, were attracted to the idea. But the owners were strongly against.[9] The

differences between the two sides struck Tom Jones forcibly. The MFGB
executive members were mostly 'well under forty. . . . The PM's attitude
is always most friendly and sympathetic.' But he added :

It is impossible not to feel the contrast between the reception which
Ministers give to a body of owners and a body of miners. Ministers
are at ease with the former, they are friends, jointly exploring a situation. There was hardly any indication of opposition or censure. It was
rather a joint discussion of whether it were better to precipitate a
strike or the unemployment which would result from continuing the
present terms. The majority clearly wanted a strike and during the
strike [Sir] Adam Nimmo asked that the Government should either
repeal or suspend the Seven Hours Act.[10]

As the end of April neared, and time ran out on the mineowners'
ultimatum, it was clear the hawks had the initiative. Baldwin seemed
to accept the strike as inevitable and adopted an attitude towards negotiations which was so leisurely that it alarmed the Cabinet secretariat,
especially Hankey. He was shocked that the Prime Minister should go
away for the weekend on 24 April – Cup Final Day – and also feared
he was failing to keep the Cabinet properly informed.[11] A majority of both
owners and miners wanted a strike; an influential group in Cabinet
preferred a showdown; and even the moderates could not face a repeat
of Red Friday. Baldwin told the miners they were mistaken if they
thought he had capitulated in 1925 and granted the subsidy 'out of funk'
as he put it. 'I did it because I am a pacifist,' he explained. 'But if you
push a pacifist too far he can be very combative and obstinate.' They were
not to delude themselves into believing that 'the country's money was
going to be poured out indefinitely'.[12] But no one on the TUC general
council wanted a General Strike; and as May Day loomed, the general
council became the last best hope of avoiding a head-on collision.

The Cabinet was now convinced of this.[13] The miners, for their part,
knew that they would have to have TUC support in reaching agreement
or in fighting a strike. Observers outside the industry could see both the
vital necessity of reorganising the mining industry, and that reorganisation would mean painful readjustment. The TUC, for example, believed
that if such a reorganisation could be achieved it would mean higher wages
and better conditions for the miners in the long run. So, in the short run,
a temporary cut in miners' wages would be a price worth paying. They
also believed that, if they could get firm assurances from the Government
and the owners about when reorganisation would start, the miners might

agree to accept pay cuts. At all events the TUC general council, not the MFGB executive, would handle negotiations and, in cooperation with the Government, persuade both miners and owners to accept the kind of compromise they were incapable of reaching themselves.

There were several things wrong with this policy. None of the parties was really in the mood to compromise. The owners were unwilling to make any firm assurances about reorganisation. Even if they had, the miners would have refused to accept the kind of terms they were offering. Finally, the Government had shown no sign of wishing either to accept the Samuel report or to impose a solution. But the really fatal flaw in the TUC's strategy was that the MFGB executive never really accepted it. The miners would not agree to pay cuts or longer hours, and probably not to any reorganisation which meant miners losing their jobs. They had lost all faith in Governments, inquiries, royal commissions and the recommendations of reports. They hated the owners; and their hatred was fully reciprocated.

The trouble was, the MFGB *seemed* to have accepted the TUC's strategy; and it was this ambiguity which proved fatal. The miners needed the TUC's moral support in conducting negotiations with the Government and the owners, and its financial support in conducting a strike. Jimmy Thomas was gloomy. 'I am perfectly convinced, Walter,' he told Citrine, 'there is absolutely no hope. Stanley Baldwin talks to me like a pal. There is going to be trouble and I can see no way out of it at all.' When Citrine asked if he thought the Government would go to extremes, Thomas replied emphatically, 'Of course they will, they are bound to.' He added,

> They have tested the feelings in different parts of the country, and they have made up their minds that there will be trouble. They are going to smash it. It won't last more than a few days. A few of these people [indicating the general council and the miners] will be shot, of course, more of them will get arrested. . . . Of course, the shooting won't be done by them direct, it will be done by those damned Fascists. . . . You see Walter, they have come to the conclusion they must fight. Who is this strike against? It is not against the coalowners, it must be against the State. The money is not in the industry, so the strike is against the State. Well, Baldwin says the State must be supreme, and he is right.

He believed Churchill would be the key man, and Citrine agreed that it would depend on Churchill, Birkenhead and Joynson-Hicks.[14]

Yet all was not quite lost, and at one point something occurred which looked like a real breakthrough along the lines Tom Jones had foreseen in Baldwin's discussions with the miners. After a day negotiating with the TUC, the miners reluctantly agreed they would consider wage reductions once the Samuel scheme for reorganisation 'had been initiated by the Government'. At last Cook's rampart of 'not a penny off the pay' had been breached.[15] But any hopes which this concession raised were soon dashed by the Government's reply. The Cabinet said they were willing to initiate reorganisation only *after* the miners had accepted the principle of wage reductions. In effect, Baldwin was demanding that the miners surrender their aces before starting the card game. Thomas was aghast at such a mean response from the prophet of industrial peace. He asked Baldwin if he really meant what he said, and almost went down on his knees to get him to change his mind. 'I never begged and pleaded like I begged and pleaded all day today,' he explained.[16] The Prime Minister was unmoved. Clearly Thomas's persuasive powers were not enough. The miners must have the full authority of the TUC behind them.

So on 29 April – on the eve of the threatened lock-out – the executives of 141 trade unions met at the Memorial Hall, London. Though the meeting was long and confused, interrupted and delayed by hurried consultations and meetings between miners, owners and Government, it was a solemn occasion. The unions had to decide, for the first and so far the only time in their history, whether to hand over their autonomy completely to the general council of the TUC. Such was vesting day. The general council would handle all the last-minute negotiations on behalf of the miners; and if these failed they would empower the general council to call a *national* strike in support of the miners to begin on 3 May. The TUC never used the word 'general' in describing the stoppage. Unlike the Government, who denounced the strike as a political threat to Constitutional government, the TUC insisted it was purely sympathetic industrial action spread over the whole country.

Compared with the General Strike called by the Protestant Ulster Workers' Council in May 1974 this was true. The Ulster strike raised most important Constitutional questions and there was no industrial dispute. It was a purely political strike. Its sole object was to destroy the new Assembly and Executive, based on power-sharing with Roman Catholics, force fresh elections, which would ensure the restoration of the old Protestant ascendancy, and discredit the Sunningdale Agreement with the Dublin Government, which would have established an all-Ireland Council. After thirteen days, during which the strikers effectively ran the province, the resignation of the Unionist members of the Executive led to its collapse, the virtual dissolution of the Assembly and the re-imposition of direct rule from Westminster. The Loyalists celebrated a famous victory, but it may have been a Pyrrhic one. In the long run the strike may be seen as the episode which persuaded the British Government to abandon the Union with Northern Ireland, which the Loyalists had tried to preserve at all costs.

As delegates at the Memorial Hall meeting played cards and ate sandwiches during the endless delays and discussions, they moved slowly to their historic decision. When the roll was finally called, the first union on the list was the Asylum Workers, who voted 'Yes' amid some laughter. An atmosphere of inevitability permeated the hall. Listening to delegates cast their votes with resolve rather than fervour, C. T. Cramp, the moderate railwaymen's leader, turned to a neighbour and remarked, 'Pure fatalism. We can't win.'[17] But for the moment this prophetic remark was lost in a mounting wave of solidarity with the miners. By more than $3\frac{1}{2}$ million votes to fewer than 50,000 the unions voted 'all power to the general council of the TUC'. Delegates sang the Red Flag. And while the meeting was in progress, before the vote had been taken and long before negotiations were broken off by the Government, the King had proclaimed a State of Emergency because of an immediate threat 'to deprive the community . . . of the essentials of life'. Warrants went out; the reservists, volunteers and special constables came in. The great strike – whether National or General – came perceptibly one step closer.

The miners have been blamed for intransigence in 1926, but their apparent solidarity hid real divisions. Thus, after the voting, Herbert Smith told delegates at the Memorial Hall meeting that he was willing to go 'from page one to the end of the [Samuel] report, and go thoroughly into it and inquire into it, and accept the findings when we had gone through it'. This looked like a completely fresh undertaking from the highest authority in the MFGB to accept the report. Cook was astounded. He leapt up to repudiate his president, saying he had gone too far. The meeting was already breaking up, but other delegates came forward demanding that Smith clarify his statement. Smith, mindful no doubt of Hodges' fatal statement before Black Friday, did so. He now said he did not mean that he would accept the report without reservations, but that he would accept the conclusions they reached after going through the report page by page 'and to stand by the result of the inquiry'.[18] But had not Cook himself said in the *Daily Herald* only three days before that he was 'convinced that a settlement can be reached by a straight return to the commission's proposals'? Now that the MFGB had handed over absolute authority for conducting negotiations to the TUC general council there might still be some faint hope of reaching an eleventh-hour settlement.

Chapter Seventeen

Final Talks Fail

A settlement could now only be reached by talks between the Government, owners and TUC. For when the MFGB surrendered its responsibility to the general council in return for the promise of support it created a new tactical situation. The miners' executive may have been intransigent; the general council, which had become more moderate since the 1925 TUC Conference, was likely to be more flexible. And even the miners had given some indication of flexibility. Now the general council persuaded Baldwin to reopen talks with them. If no progress was possible on pay, what about hours? Baldwin's real hopes for peace were based on this belief. He told Tom Jones of an idea 'I have not mentioned to a soul'. If the two sides would accept his arbitration he would propose that present pay rates be maintained for two years if the miners agreed to work an eight-hour day up to a maximum of 48 hours a week.

He would also propose reorganisation of the industry, coal sales and royalties with a promise of Government help for miners thrown out of work by consequent pit closures.[1] The owners might accept such a scheme, and Jones replied that its advantage was that it did not cut the standard of living but only added to the length of the miners' working day. 'There is more sympathy for the latter than the former among the normal person,' Jones observed, and Baldwin added, 'It is the normal person we must carry with us if there is a strike.'[2] Baldwin believed there was support for such a solution among the miners too. 'I know that,' he explained, 'both from South Wales and from the Tyne.'[3]

Yet whatever slender hopes Baldwin may still have entertained of reaching a settlement were crushed on 30 April when he finally managed to persuade the owners to give him their final offer. Reluctantly, the owners agreed to maintain a national minimum. But the new minimum would rescind the 1924 pay agreement, cutting wages by $13\frac{1}{2}$ per cent and reverting to the 1921 figure of 20 per cent on 1914 standard. Nor was that all. Local customs, such as six shifts for five, were to be abolished and there was no mention of reorganisation. Yet even this offer was conditional on acceptance of an eight-hour day, which would not be reviewed until 1929.[4] It was not an offer but an ultimatum. Baldwin was shocked, and warned the owners that it would have a fatal effect on public opinion. 'You simply set the heather on fire,' Baldwin told Evan Williams. 'People do not look at the reason why these figures are published, they simply look at the figures', adding pointedly that 'a General Strike with public opinion on your side would be short and sharp; without its support, long and difficult'.[5]

The Samuel commisioners attacked the offer as 'wholly unreasonable and unjustified' and totally at variance with the spirit of their report.[6] Its content was bad enough. Its lateness made it worse. Already two-thirds of the miners were locked out, and there was no chance of getting them back on such humiliating terms.[7] Baldwin managed to keep the offer from miners and TUC for 24 hours. By then talks had begun with a general council negotiating committee which reflected its moderate position. Only Alonzo Swales was associated with the Left, while Jimmy Thomas and Arthur Pugh were men of the Right and the Centre. From now until 3 May these three men handled the important discussions with the Government.

The Cabinet team consisted of Baldwin himself, Birkenhead and the Minister of Labour, Steel-Maitland. Sir Horace Wilson, for the Government, and Walter Citrine, for the TUC, were also present to make notes and give advice.[8] In an atmosphere of mounting tension and crisis these eight men conducted hours of talks, often late at night, lacking sleep and proper meals, covering complicated and contentious ground. In a melodramatic atmosphere of hasty telephone calls, hurried taxi rides, scribbled notes and smoke-filled rooms they struggled to find a solution to the great industrial crisis. Small wonder they often became confused and irritable. Small wonder they ultimately failed.

Lord Birkenhead was the dominant personality in the strike negotiations on the Government side, and Thomas the outstanding figure on the union side. They were old sparring partners. Birkenhead had said of Thomas that he was one of the few people in the 1924 Labour Government he would trust to hire out bicycles; later, when Thomas had complained of 'an 'orrible 'eadache', Birkenhead had advised him to 'try a couple of aspirates'. Thomas was the shrewdest and most experienced negotiator on the trade union side; Birkenhead had one of the best legal brains of his generation. In Tom Jones's judgement, he 'has all the ability required to grasp the situation . . . only speaks when he has something to say, and when he speaks does so with perfect lucidity'.[9] Both Birkenhead and Thomas suffered a similar handicap : neither was completely trusted by his own side.

Thomas was very anxious to avoid a strike and secure a settlement; Birkenhead, despite his hawkish reputation, now appeared equally keen to avoid a conflict, though as anxious to avoid another Red Friday and rather dubious of achieving an honourable peace. Both men tended to eclipse their colleagues on the committee. On the Government side, Baldwin said little, mostly smoking his pipe, while Steel-Maitland, in Tom Jones's words, left a 'total impression . . . of weakness and cloudiness'.[10] On the union side, Swales said little for a man with a reputation of left-wing militancy, while Pugh seemed disconcerted by Baldwin's benevolent paternalism. The two secretaries, Wilson and Citrine, both exercised a quiet yet powerful background influence.

Final negotiations began on Saturday, 1 May – international labour day. 'What a May day!' Citrine noted in his diary.[11] Nearly a million miners were now locked out : it would be impossible to get them back to work without some firm assurance about wages. Nevertheless, the two sides met again in search of settlement. They agreed that the most hopeful line of progress was to draft heads of agreement for the proposed reorganisation, and leave the wages problem until later. It was felt a week or two should be sufficient for this. Thomas insisted that the lock-out notices must be withdrawn before negotiations could be concluded, and Pugh repeated the statements of Cook and Smith to the effect that the miners were prepared to reach a settlement 'along the lines of the report'.

After adjournments to enable both sides to consider their position, and long arguments over semantics, the following statement was drafted at 1.15 a.m. and so became known as 'the midnight memorandum'.

> The Prime Minister has satisfied himself, as a result of conversations he has had with representatives of the Trade Union Congress, that if negotiations are continued (it being understood that the notices cease to be operative) the representatives of the Trade Union Congress are confident that a settlement can be reached on the lines of the report within a fortnight.[12]

When this memorandum had been drafted, Steel-Maitland passed Birken-head a note saying, 'A taper has been lit this day in England', to which Birkenhead replied, 'If it's a taper without a wages settlement not even God's help will enable it to be put out'.

In fact, the midnight memorandum caused enormous trouble on both sides. Hankey, the Cabinet Secretary, said he had never experienced a scene like that which transpired when the memorandum was put to the Cabinet at noon on 2 May. 'All who were not present when it was agreed,' he explained, 'reacted in the same way against it, and felt it would be read by the whole country as a capitulation on the part of the Govern-ment to the threat of a General Strike.'[13] There was also some doubt about how far the memorandum committed the Government. Eventually, the Cabinet adjourned to find out what progress the TUC had made with the miners. But there was equal division and dissension on the union side. For a start, the miners' executive had all left London to rally their troops, and their secretary, Cook, refused to take the responsibility of replying to the memorandum on their behalf. This was very embarrassing for the TUC, after all they had said to the Cabinet representatives about being able to get the miners to agree. Cook consented to wire the miners' execu-tive ordering them back to London; but at the same time he angrily questioned the right of the TUC to negotiate on their behalf. The miners had never agreed to accept the Samuel report, and Cook hotly reiterated that Smith had no right to say they had.[14] 'We had visions of Black Friday on our minds,' Citrine recalled. 'The miners had expressly handed their powers over to the general council, but it would not do to attempt to force a decision upon them.'[15]

When the Cabinet learned that the miners' executive had left London it caused grave disquiet. Steel-Maitland and Wilson were now far less happy about the midnight memorandum. The TUC kept Cabinet waiting practically the whole day; and as they waited the chances of a settlement gradually slipped away. Yet a settlement was always a real enough possi-bility to persuade those who wanted a showdown to screw the crisis up to snapping-point. For example, when the Cabinet learned from the Post-master-General that the TUC had already sent out telegrams to ensure strike action on 3 May, it chose to regard this as an act of war.[16] Yet the Government knew that the scattered nature of the TUC's organisation made such precautionary telegrams essential and normal. Moreover, the Government itself had already sent round its circular about its emergency organisation and proclaimed a State of Emergency. The day before the TUC had told Baldwin that it had as yet passed no formal resolution in

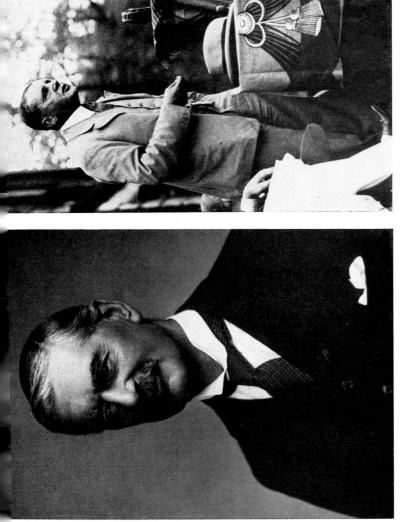

7a. Neville Chamberlain, Baldwin's Minister of Health, who said during the General Strike, 'The best and kindest thing to do now is to strike quickly and hard'.

7b. Lord Birkenhead, 'the cleverest man in the Kingdom', who headed the Government negotiating team which tried to avert a showdown in May 1926.

7c. Sir William Joynson-Hicks who, as Baldwin's Home Secretary, was responsible for preserving public order during the emergency, was a 'Reds-under-the-beds' alarmist.

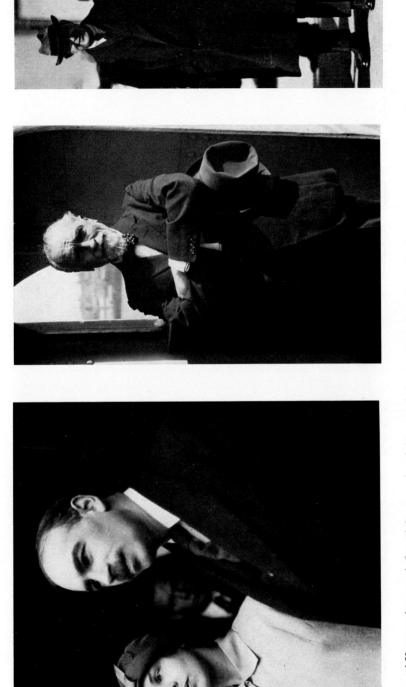

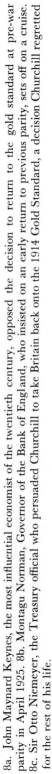

8a. John Maynard Keynes, the most influential economist of the twentieth century, opposed the decision to return to the gold standard at pre-war parity in April 1925. 8b. Montagu Norman, Governor of the Bank of England, who insisted on an early return to previous parity, sets off on a cruise. 8c. Sir Otto Niemeyer, the Treasury official who persuaded Churchill to take Britain back onto the 1914 Gold Standard, a decision Churchill regretted for the rest of his life.

favour of a General Strike, Baldwin believed the TUC was still bluffing and was really afraid of the consequences of any strike action.[17]

Nevertheless, all kinds of wild rumours were circulating in the corridors of power. For example, Baldwin's principal private secretary, Sir Ronald Waterhouse, told Tom Jones and Horace Wilson 'in great confidence' of a secret plot he claimed to have uncovered, by which Birkenhead, Beaverbrook, the owner of the *Daily Express,* Churchill and Thomas 'had all agreed to bring SB [Baldwin] down in the crisis and seize the helm themselves'.[18] Jones dismissed such rumours as 'bunkum' and Birkenhead drafted a second formula.

> We will urge the miners to authorise us to enter upon a discussion with the understanding that they and we accept the [Samuel] Report as a basis of settlement and we approach it with the knowledge that it may involve some reduction in wages.[19]

Though the last phrase about pay cuts would never have been accepted by the miners, the general impression left by this formula was one of vagueness – but a vagueness which pleased the negotiators, not least those on the union side. 'Never mind what the miners or anyone else says,' Thomas ejaculated excitedly. 'We accept it.' Of course, by 'we' he meant the TUC. Birkenhead, too, was happy with the formula. True, in a memorandum written *after* the strike had actually started, Birkenhead concluded 'that at no moment in the discussions on Saturday or Sunday were we within reach of agreement'.[20] But at the time the possibility of a settlement must have seemed real enough in those final hours to frighten the hawks who were excluded from the discussion.

At this point a joker suddenly appeared in the pack which destroyed any faint chance of a settlement and gave the game to the hawks. The Government negotiators had retired at 11.30 p.m. on 2 May to report progress to the rest of the Cabinet at 10 Downing Street. The TUC team went back next door to the official home of the Chancellor of the Exchequer. In the Cabinet room Baldwin dropped exhausted into an armchair while Birkenhead read out his latest formula. There was a clear and sharp division of opinion. 'Some of us,' wrote the Colonial Secretary, Leo Amery, 'would have been prepared to continue the negotiations so long as there was the faintest chance of an agreement.' Others were determined that no concessions of any kind should be made. The leaders of the hawks were Churchill, Neville Chamberlain and Joynson-Hicks. On the other hand, Birkenhead (despite his later memorandum) now seemed inclined towards a settlement, while Baldwin was felt by the

F

hawks to be too sympathetic to the miners. As these discussions continued, the telephone rang. The caller was the editor of the *Daily Mail*, who brought news which precipitated the General Strike.

The machine-men at the *Daily Mail* had refused to print an editorial 'For King and Country' calling on the nation to support the Government. The editor, Thomas Marlowe, was an extreme right-wing Tory, and the paper was owned by Lord Rothermere, an eccentric Conservative supporter who had a burning ambition to exercise political power himself.[21] His brother, Lord Northcliffe, had started the *Daily Mail* to promote his own political ambitions in 1896 and made it the first of the modern newspapers. He had let two men think they had been appointed editor and then left them to fight for possession of the editor's chair each day in the office itself. The winner was Marlowe, a fierce-looking Irishman now nearing retirement.[22] In 1924 the *Mail* had published the notorious Zinoviev Letter; and both the political opinions of the editor and proprietor, and their close connection with the Conservative Party, make plausible the suggestion that Marlowe wrote the provocative editorial with encouragement from inside the Cabinet itself.[23]

There certainly had been earlier signs of secret links between Press and Cabinet. The previous year the Cabinet had discussed a 'serious leakage' about Churchill's pension scheme immediately after the details had been communicated to the Cabinet. Since the pension increases had been paid for from import duties, somebody stood to gain. Another Budget item had also been published prematurely in the Press.[24] In May 1926 encouragement for Marlowe would most likely have come from Joynson-Hicks and Churchill; and Churchill had certainly called at the *Daily Mail* office earlier in the day. The Government had bought advertising space in all newspapers to appeal for volunteers to break the impending strike. Other editors got this past the printers on the grounds that there could be no tampering with advertising. Marlowe alone, after Churchill's visit, decided to write a stiff leader supporting the advertisement.[25]

If a plot did exist, its objective must have been to provoke a showdown between Government and TUC; and this certainly transpired. Coupled with the fact that the TUC had already sent out telegrams calling member unions out on strike at midnight on 2 May, the *Daily Mail* incident was enough to persuade the doves that the Cabinet must break off negotiations. When Birkenhead heard the news he growled 'Hear hear!' and 'Bloody good show', only to be reproved for flippancy. Then Waterhouse, Baldwin's PPS, got the King's assistant private secretary, Eric Wigram, out of bed to tell him the news by phone. 'The situation is ambiguous,' he told him. 'The *Daily Mail* has ceased to function.' Wigram was obviously still befuddled by sleep, and this message had to be repeated several times. 'Tell His Majesty not to go off the deep end,' Waterhouse said reassuringly. Wigram finally realised the point, and then responded with unintentional humour. 'That's alright. We don't take the *Daily Mail*. Or the *Daily Express*.'[26]

But if Wigram failed to grasp the significance of the *Daily Mail* incident, the hawks in the Cabinet certainly grasped it. And they used it to convince their wavering colleagues that it raised profound Constitutional issues about the freedom of the Press which made it imperative for the Government to break off negotiations immediately. When the TUC negotiators returned to meet the Prime Minister at 12.45 a.m. they were astounded to find the atmosphere completely changed. Baldwin solemnly announced that the Government faced 'a direct challenge' and that 'these negotiations cannot continue'. He then handed them a note and showed them to the door. The TUC delegation, completely nonplussed, shook hands limply with the Prime Minister. 'Goodbye, Mr Pugh,' he told the leader of the negotiating committee. 'You have been a brick with me, and I hope when we meet again we will meet with as friendly a spirit as we are leaving now.'[27] When the negotiators met their TUC colleagues next door at 11 Downing Street they crowded round eagerly while Thomas read the note aloud. It referred to certain 'overt acts' (the sending of the telegrams and the refusal to set the *Daily Mail* leader) which had forced the Government to break off negotiations with the TUC, and demanded that the TUC withdraw the notices calling for a General Strike before they could be resumed. 'That settles it,' Purcell exclaimed. 'We will fight them.' Thomas growled agreement, 'War has been declared'.[28] Later, the TUC learned that the letter had been handed to the Press before it reached them and suspected that it had been written before the meeting at which Birkenhead had evolved the second formula for settlement.

In fact, a letter breaking off negotiations had been drafted *before* Marlowe's telephone call telling the Cabinet about the printer's strike at the *Daily Mail*. Marlowe's message was like a *deus ex machina* for the hawks; and in Hankey's words, 'The document approved at the previous meeting was accordingly re-drafted to meet the new situation'.[29] No wonder, as Birkenhead said in the memo he wrote after the strike, no settlement was ever in sight. Nevertheless, the letter called specifically for a reply;[30] and Baldwin could not be certain what that reply would be. Yet when the TUC went next door to 10 Downing Street at about 1 a.m.

to hand their answer to the Prime Minister they were again astounded. Baldwin had gone to bed. 'Is it true,' a friend asked Baldwin, 'that you went to bed to avoid receiving their surrender?' Baldwin's reply was characteristic. 'No. I had done all I could and there was nowhere else to go.'[31]

When Baldwin went to bed after the *Daily Mail* incident it effectively brought negotiations to a halt. Yet nearly 24 hours remained before the strike deadline. This feature of the crisis has caused little comment from historians. But it is highly unusual in a crisis of this kind for talks not to carry on until the very last minute. Instead, everything was suspended for a full day. It was as if events had finally crashed over a steep precipice and were now in free fall. The TUC negotiating committee drafted a reply to the Prime Minister's letter. Citrine expressed 'surprise and regret' that the conversations had been broken off without warning and with no specific reasons given. The general council had been 'astounded' because the 'overt acts' were things the TUC knew nothing about and could not be held responsible for in any way. They were simply 'an excuse for breaking off peace discussions'.[32]

The TUC and the miners' leaders continued to discuss plans for a National Mining Board on which miners, owners and Government would be equally represented, to supervise reorganisation and wage cuts. But the miners refused to accept Bevin's idea that they might have to accept *a* national minimum rather than *the* national minimum, while Ramsay MacDonald protested that if all three sides were represented on the Board it would never agree. Horace Wilson finally torpedoed the plan when he told Bevin that unless the TUC was prepared, on the miners' behalf, to accept immediate pay cuts the Government was not interested. The Commons debate on 3 May saw Baldwin stressing the threat to Constitutional liberty and a free Press, MacDonald assuring the House that he respected the Constitution as much as Sir Robert Horne and Thomas asserting that they had been within an inch of agreement on Sunday but that 'In a challenge to the Constitution, God help us unless the Government won.'

Immediately after the debate MacDonald, and his deputy Arthur Henderson, went to Baldwin, Churchill and Steel-Maitland for one last appeal to reason. 'Have you come to say that the strike notices are withdrawn?' Churchill demanded. MacDonald shook his head, and Churchill continued brusquely, 'Then there is no reason to continue this discussion. You tried it in Italy and failed, and you are not going to be successful in Great Britain.' Churchill's opponents wondered if he was casting himself in the role of Mussolini as the saviour of the social order from

Bolshevism, and Henderson wondered more mildly if Winston 'was trying to give us a dose of Sidney Street'.[33] Steel-Maitland retorted that it was about time the Labour Party and its friends were put in their place, and Churchill concluded the discussion with the words, 'You will be better prepared to talk to us in two or three weeks'.[34]

In a sense, of course, Baldwin's action in breaking off the talks helped the TUC to avoid making, for nine days at least, the awkward choice they had set themselves during the mining crisis. They had hoped, right up to the last minute, to force a settlement which the miners would accept. Red Friday had shown in 1925 that the Government *could* be forced to intervene in a dispute between owners and miners and impose terms on both sides. The TUC's whole policy of backing the miners in 1926 was based on this belief. So too, in a way, was the miners' decision to vest all authority for conducting negotiations with the TUC. If 1925 was the guide, no General Strike would be necessary. But, of course, when the Government refused to give way and spoke instead of threats to Constitutional freedom, the TUC were impaled on the horns of a dilemma. They could either back down and be humiliated; or they could stand up, accept the Government's challenge and embark on a struggle for which they were totally unprepared, for which they had no stomach, and which had no clear end in sight. In the words of one historian, 'A short General Strike, called off as soon as could decently be done, was a kind of ironic compromise'.[35] Ironic compromise or not, the nation awoke on 4 May to find itself facing the gravest domestic crisis between the wars.

Part Four:
The Nine Days
3-12 May 1926

Chapter Eighteen

Overview

The British labour movement responded to the strike call with a solidarity which surprised the TUC almost as much as it did the Government. 'What loyalty!' exclaimed Cook, 'What loyalty!' As the historian Alan Bullock reminds us, 'It is easy to underestimate what this meant'. A trade union is not an army which obeys orders without question. Hundreds of thousands of strikers were risking secure jobs at a time of mass unemployment, pensions for which they had been paying all their working lives. 'The response to the call for a national strike was a remarkable demonstration of working-class unity and of unselfish support for the miners.'[1] Only the 'first line' workers employed in transport, the railways, printing, iron and steel, metal and chemical industries, building and power stations were called out. The 'second line' workers in such industries as engineering, shipbuilding, textiles, woodworking, the Post Office and distributive trades, were instructed by the TUC to remain at work for the time being.

At all events, the unaccustomed stillness of the first day or two of the strike seemed ominous: the Government feared it might have to quell a revolution and the TUC that it might have to lead it. Informed opinion on both sides believed that if the strike lasted much longer than a week bloodshed was likely to occur somewhere. These fears proved illusory. There were many sharp clashes all over the country and thousands of arrests. But miraculously there were no deaths or widespread destruction of property. The anxiety of both Government and TUC was groundless. Beatrice Webb was nearer the mark when she wrote on the second day of the strike, 'For the British trade union movement I see a day of terrible disillusionment. The failure of the General Strike of 1926 will be one of the most significant landmarks in the history of the

British working class.' It would signify, she added, the death of 'the pernicious doctrines of workers' control and direct action'.[2]

In a sense, of course, Beatrice Webb was right. Yet the doctrines of workers' control and direct action were not effectively tried out during the strike. Government preparations for the emergency were far superior to those made by the unions. As we have seen, these emergency preparations had first been drawn up as early as 1920, and the Government's plans augmented by the creation of the Organisation for the Maintenance of Supplies in 1925. When the strike started, the OMS, having served its purpose of recruiting and training men for the emergency, quietly merged with the local committees of the Government's organisation. Undergraduates from Oxford and Cambridge enjoyed a week's holiday blacklegging with college approval, though a few University men like the future Labour Party leader Hugh Gaitskell, the Socialist historian and philosopher G. D. H. Cole, and the poet W. H. Auden, supported the strike, while students at Ruskin College, Oxford, the trade union educational institute which had experienced the celebrated student strike in 1909, helped the strikers.

The Government possessed a well-oiled machine by 1926, though it would not have worked without volunteers. In contrast, the strikers depended almost completely on instant improvisation. They had not made any detailed plans before the strike, partly because the TUC feared this would be provocative, but mainly because most of the leaders of the TUC were not really committed to the idea of a General Strike. The extremists, like the miners' secretary, A. J. Cook, seemed to have a very hazy notion of what it would entail in terms of organisation. Only Ernest Bevin and Walter Citrine, who opposed the idea of striking, had tried in the weeks beforehand to make detailed contingency plans, though without much success.

The story of the strike is familiar in outline. The picture has yet to be presented properly from the local point of view. Councils of Action, which had first appeared during the *Jolly George* affair in 1920, were resurrected again and worked with varying degrees of efficiency. In the mining districts in the North-East and South Wales, in London and Liverpool, they worked well on the whole. Elsewhere organisation was patchy. The crucial question was usually how much help the local branches of the Co-operative Wholesale Society were prepared to give strikers over food, supplies, transport, use of halls and buildings and so on. Since the Co-operative Movement shared the moderate Labour movement's disapproval of the General Strike, this support varied greatly from place to place. Indeed, the Co-ops were often angered by strike committees who picketed local stores and stopped supplies, which led to much bad feeling.

But although much of the activity took place in the provinces, London remained the real centre of power. TUC headquarters was run effectively by Citrine and Bevin, who made their names by their handling of the nine-day emergency. They took the important decision to refuse money from Russia, to cancel all permits for the special delivery of supplies, and to call out the 'second line' unions on 11 May. The strikers had vested 'all power to the general council', and the TUC also undertook the vitally important task of publishing the TUC newspaper the *British Worker* as a counterblast to the Government's *British Gazette*. Finally, the general council made one other crucial move : calling the strike off on 12 May.[3]

This final decision is even more puzzling because only the day before, the general council, apparently despairing of the secret negotiations it had been conducting with Sir Herbert Samuel, had called out the second line unions, which seemed to widen and strengthen the strike. But the decision to call out the second line men on 11 May widened but probably weakened the strike. Workers were already beginning to drift back, especially on the railways. Fear and suspicion among the railway unions is the key to the collapse of the General Strike and helps to explain why the TUC failed to receive any guarantees from the Government about the miners. Government plans were working effectively. Its propaganda had hit home and the public was rallying behind it on the Constitutional question. The General Strike was arguably won and lost on the Constitutional issue. Yet this only really emerged once the strike had started. Of course it had always been implicit in the situation, at least in the minds of the moderates in the TUC. As early as 1919 Lloyd George had warned union leaders, 'I feel bound to tell you that in our opinion we are at your mercy . . . if a force arises in the State which is stronger than the State itself, then it must be ready to take on the functions of the State, or withdraw. . . . Gentlemen, have you considered, and if you have, are you ready?'[4]

The union leaders had not been ready in 1919, when the general situation was much more favourable, and they were certainly not ready in 1926. Jimmy Thomas never disguised his support for the Government in a confrontation of this kind. Yet the Constitutional question, on which the General Strike seemed to turn, was in many ways a non-issue. Many Unionists, notably Bonar Law, who later became Prime Minister, and Joynson-Hicks and Birkenhead, who were now in Baldwin's Cabinet, had advocated unconstitutional resistance in Ulster to the Home Rule Act of 1914. Moreover, though each side in 1926 denounced the other for their extremism, they treated each other for the most part like reasonable and moderate-minded men. On both sides good organisation depended on the maintenance of proper communications. Government and unions took it for granted that they would be able to telephone and telegraph during the strike. The general council assumed they would be able to draw strike pay from banks. Moreover, each side was in reality accepting the other's case without realising or admitting it. The TUC was not fighting the owners. It was trying to force the Government to take part in negotiations and put pressure on them. This was a political threat. But the Government said that the mining dispute was really a question for owners and pitmen, and nothing to do with them. So the TUC's support for the miners was not really a Constitutional threat at all but purely a sympathetic strike.

Of course, no one saw these paradoxical points at the time, and few have discussed them since. Instead, Churchill appeared to grant the Army *carte blanche* to do anything they wished to break the strike, which made violence more likely. Moreover, though the notorious *ex cathedra* statement of Sir John Simon, and Mr Justice Astbury's judgement that the strike was illegal and all strikers were liable to punitive damages (which really had no legal foundation),[5] probably did nothing to rattle the TUC, the strong rumours that the Government planned to arrest the general council of the TUC and members of local strike committees, impound union funds and call up the Army reserve was enough, coupled with other factors, to persuade the TUC general council to call off the strike.

Perhaps Baldwin's most potent weapon was the power of public opinion. Millions of people who were not on strike had sympathised with the miners. But once they came to believe the General Strike was a threat to Government they rallied behind the Prime Minister. Baldwin, suddenly revealing himself to be a natural master of the new art of radio broadcasting, persuaded the public that the Constitution was indeed at risk in a series of brilliantly effective, short, low-key fireside chats. The number of people volunteering to break the strike increased steadily throughout the nine days. Despite traditional views, many of these strikebreakers came from the ranks of the working class, from other trades hit by the strike call, or from unemployed men. And just as radio broadcasting helped the Government when the strikers stopped the Press, so trucks, lorries and private cars showed that a complete stoppage of the railways, which would have brought the life of the nation to a standstill a generation earlier, was no longer so effective.

The radio and the motor car, which were to prove so effective in defeating the strike, had great symbolic importance too. Both belonged to the new age, struggling painfully to be born in the 1920s. The General Strike, like the gold standard, pre-Keynesian economics and the head-on class conflict within the mining industry, which did so much to create the crisis, were soon discredited. When the strike started many feared, or hoped, that its dramatic failure signalled the end of a generation of bitter industrial struggle. In 1912, for example, 38 million working days had been lost in strikes, while in 1926 the figure was 162 million. In the three years 1919–21 the average number of workers involved in strikes and lock-outs was 2·1 million; in 1926 it rose to 2·75 million; in each of the thirteen years 1927–40 it fell dramatically to 0·3 million. Ironically, it took the return of war, and the full employment it created, to repair the damaged morale which organised labour suffered as a result of the failure of the General Strike.

Chapter Nineteen

Shutdown

Baldwin woke on Tuesday, 4 May, to a world of hard reality. Downing Street is normally a secluded cul-de-sac; but even the Prime Minister, in common with millions of other people in cities all over the country, must have noticed the eerie quiet of that first morning of the strike. A fog settled on London, and 'the darkness was symbolical', Sir Samuel Hoare, a member of Baldwin's Cabinet, recalled, 'People were in a complete mental fog.' Had Baldwin lived in a great industrial city, or near a large railway marshalling yard, the silence would have seemed even more oppressive. No trains were running, no trams or buses taking people to work, no mines or steel works or blast furnaces operating. Factories which depended on electric power were hit. Manufacturing towns were silent and the air was unusually clear. In London the fog soon lifted. And just as in the great crisis of 1940, what everyone remembered afterwards about the General Strike was that it was fought in beautiful summer weather. Of course, not everyone realised at first the gravity of the situation. Hamilton Fyfe, the editor of the socialist *Daily Herald*, recalled that when his wife mentioned the strike to her milkman, he replied with scornful certainty, 'But that's nowhere near London. It's the miners. Nothing to do with us.'[1]

Yet the stillness at the start did not last long. By the time the army of office workers were ready to go to work, the streets of every large city were filled with cars, lorries, bicycles and improvised vehicles of all sorts. Lifts were freely sought and given,[2] and the prettier secretaries and shop girls had an advantage. The congestion in London was worse than anywhere. As Hamilton Fyfe put it,

I found the streets filled – and frequently blocked – by more continuous streams of traffic than I had ever seen in any city before. I think there was a vague idea that when the omnibuses were taken off, the roads would be strangely clear. [In fact it] was the signal for every sort and condition of motor car to come out. Traffic was far more tangled . . . than usual. . . . Thousands of bicycles added to the confusion. . . . Carts and lorries filled with lucky clerks and typists . . . rumbled along. . . . Taxi cabs were still plying. . . .[3]

The streets near Regent's Park and Portland Road Station were blocked, traffic in the West End moved at only a few yards an hour, the Embankment was blocked solid from Blackfriars to Westminster.

The overwhelming solidarity of the union response to the strike call surprised Government and TUC alike. The general council's instructions had not been for a universal stoppage. Notices had gone out only to workers in what were designated 'first line' industries. Transport and railwaymen – the core of the old triple alliance – dockers, printing workers, iron and steel, metal trades, chemical industries and power plants were affected. Together with the million miners who had been locked out this meant that over three million workers were involved – more than half the country's trade unionists.[4] Messages from all over the country poured into TUC headquarters, showing that the response had been virtually unanimous. This is unusual. Even strikes in single industries generally have a weakness somewhere. This strike, which involved many industries and had been poorly planned, should have been patchy from the very start. Instead it was solid. In a situation of mass unemployment, millions of men were prepared to put their jobs and pension rights at risk, not in their own cause, but in support of the miners. It was a remarkable demonstration of working-class solidarity.

Yet the TUC denied it was a General Strike, preferring to call it a 'national' strike;[5] and, of course, many unions still remained at work. Engineering and shipbuilding workers, textile and woodworkers, postmen and the distributive and allied trades had not been asked to strike. By holding back these 'second line' unions the TUC was keeping some of its forces in reserve. A few unions – Havelock Wilson's right-wing seamen's union, the National Union of Journalists, an electrical power engineers' association – refused to strike. In addition, millions of non-unionists – white-collar workers and women – were unaffected. The strike depended on organisers being able to send telegrams and draw strike pay from banks. Both Government and TUC expected to be able to send telegrams and make telephone calls. The general council of the TUC also faced the problem of what to do about essential services. It had decided, on humanitarian grounds, that these should be maintained in certain circumstances. Special 'permits' stated that electricity should be provided for lighting, but not for power; that hospitals, the old, the sick and children should not be hit. The trouble with these permits[6] was not just that they weakened the impact of the strike, but that they were unworkable. The Cabinet brusquely rejected the TUC's offer to cooperate with the Government in maintaining essential supplies.[7] More important, it proved impossible to separate electric lighting from power in the way the general council had instructed. So the TUC's orders about electricity supplies became so vague that local strike committees had to send puzzled or angry letters, and even delegations, to London, to try to find out what they meant. 'Will you give us a clear definition on this matter?' asked Burnley strike committee. Similar difficulties arose over permits in other industries. What exactly constituted 'essential' building, 'essential' supplies? The whole question of issuing permits to allow certain work and supplies to continue was fraught with trouble from the start.[8]

These difficulties revealed the TUC's great organisational problems. The general council had never really wanted the strike. It was not equipped to lead such a strike. It had not made proper preparations beforehand for fear that the Government and public opinion would denounce them as provocative. Now, with over three million of its members out on strike, it had to improvise. The general council met each day, morning and evening, at its headquarters in Ecclestone Square – a house which, ironically, had once been owned by Winston Churchill, now the scourge of the unions. 'Most TUC conferences during the strike,' Jimmy Thomas recalled, 'took place in a room that Winston had used as a dining room.'[9] While the general council decided policy here, detailed day-to-day decisions were taken by committees. The most important of these was the Strike Organisation Committee. Bevin appointed himself head of this, despite scornful opposition from Thomas and other older and more moderate members.[10] So Bevin and Citrine, now acting general secretary, held the key posts in the TUC organisation during the strike. Other committees included Intelligence, Publicity, General Purposes, Propaganda and the Political Committee, headed by Thomas and Arthur Henderson, secretary of the Labour Party.[11]

Once the strike had started, the general council really had little to do in London except negotiate the terms, when the time came, on which the strike would be ended.[12] Telegrams and despatch riders might fly back and forth between London and regional strike headquarters, but much of this bustling activity was to keep up morale rather than achieve any tangible objective. Right at the very beginning the general council had decided not to allow local trades councils to set up their own local strike committees – a decision which many of the TUC, notably Citrine, strongly opposed. But Bevin insisted on forcing it through because he believed unions would refuse to hand over their functions to trades councils.[13] The General Strike was fought under the slogan 'All power to the general council of the TUC'; but in fact the general council spent a lot of its time trying to control provincial activities. The actual calling out of workers had been left to individual unions.[14] Councils of Action, a revival of the organisations which had appeared during the *Jolly George* affair six years earlier, were springing up all over the country, and the TUC feared that in many areas these would fall under Communist or left-wing control. 'What I dreaded about this strike more than anything else was this,' Thomas confessed. 'If by any chance it should have got out of the hands of those who would be able to exercise some control, every sane man knows what would have happened.'[15] In general, the TUC's strike organisation showed 'all the defects of . . . rigid centralisation, blended as it was with the decision to permit each union to call out its own members'.[16]

More serious than this failure of organisation was the failure of communication between the TUC and the miners, which had been apparent even before the strike started. At the dramatic vesting day conference in Memorial Hall at the end of April, the MFGB, in common with a majority of the unions, had agreed to give the TUC full conduct of negotiations with the Government before, during and after the General Strike. But did this mandate given to the general council mean the power to resume negotiations at any time, without consulting the miners? Or was it only a mandate to fight the strike to a successful conclusion? This was the crucial point; for when the general council later opened negotiations with the Government on the miners' behalf, the MFGB accused them bitterly of acting in bad faith and in effect betraying them and all the other unions. As A. J. Cook put it, 'the decision of 1 May was to stand against the miners having a reduction in wages. I repeat that we had nothing to negotiate on.'[17] The general council, of course, rejected this charge with equal vehemence. 'We may have made all the mistakes in the world,' Bevin told Cook and the miners, 'but that does not affect the question of whether or not we had the power to do what we did do.'[18]

Ultimately, the whole fate of the General Strike was to turn on this point. The preparations on the union side, for all their magnificent spirit of improvisation, were thus crippled from the outset by this flaw. But in the beginning few saw this, just as few saw the dangerous lack of communications between the labour movement and the Labour Party. Instead, everyone was carried away by the heady atmosphere of working-class solidarity and loyalty to the embattled miners. But the coal crisis was the core of the dispute, and the failure of communications between the leaders of the miners and the TUC was one of the reasons for its ultimate collapse. And there was a more practical reason for doubting the long-term strength of the miners' position. The coal trade had been remark-ably buoyant since Red Friday. The boom since November 1925 was not far below the record two years before when France had occupied the Ruhr.[19] By cutting so much coal, in this way, the miners had contributed to their own downfall. The mineowners had been deliberately stock-piling against a possible stoppage in May, public service and utilities had large reserves of coal, and in addition stocks of fuel oil were 'unprecedentedly large'.[20] The position was better than it had been in 1921. More than $10\frac{1}{4}$ million tons of coal were stockpiled, enough for eight to ten weeks' supply for power plants and five weeks' for the railways.[21] In addition, the Government was making secret plans to buy large amounts of coal from Germany, the United States and elsewhere. The TUC knew about these secret plans but were afraid they could not stop the coal eventually being distributed in Britain.[22] An embargo on the movement of coal by dockers and railwaymen, such as had been threatened in 1925, might have been more effective than a strike.

Despite the incipient weakness of the miners' position, the General Strike was of course initially more solid in the mining regions than any-where else. Reports streaming into the general council of the TUC showed dramatically how well the improvised strike machinery was working. From Tredegar, in South Wales, for example, came a message from the Trades and Labour Council saying 'Everything very satisfactory in Tre-degar. The whole of the trade unions are on stop. Everyone surprised at the response to the call of the TUC.'[23]

The message was signed by Aneurin Bevan, then an unknown rank-and-file agitator, later architect of the National Health Service and one of the outstanding figures in the Parliamentary Labour Party. Bevan was undisputed choice as chairman of the Tredegar Council of Action on 3 May 1926, and for the next nine days the Council sat in permanent session at the Workman's Institute, with Bevan effectively ruling the town. Every trade unionist for miles around answered the call to strike and for a while the workers used the industrial weapon with apparently dazzling success. Despite some verbal clashes with the police, there were no incidents and law and order was maintained. Later Bevan's Council of Action collaborated with the local miners' union lodge to organise relief, recreation, concerts and so on during the six-month agony of the lock-out.[24]

Elsewhere the pattern was similar. The Mines Department learned at the start of the General Strike that 'All pits have stopped work'.[25] In Scotland there was a complete shutdown, and the same was true in North Wales, Lancashire, the South Midlands and South Wales. There were a few isolated reports of weakness on the strikers' side. Thus in the Northern Division the Minister learned that 'It is probable that the small land sale collieries not in the Owners' Association have continued work and will endeavour to continue working'.[26] In the North Midlands the report added that 'All work is stopped except at about six outcrop pits near Chesterfield'; but at some of these the owners' notices did not expire until 6 May, and at others those still at work were mostly safety men. Indeed, the safety men remained at work throughout the strike, in contrast to the situation reported by Lloyd George during the Yorkshire coal strike in 1920 or the national strike in 1921.[27] The mere threat that the safety men might be withdrawn, which could do irreparable damage to the pits, especially those liable to flooding, was enough to persuade the police in Tredegar to leave the strikers alone.[28] Of the 818 men reported to be still at work in the Chesterfield area, some were safety men, such as 'datallers and repairers', while 'deputies are still at work and although some pits were picketed no trouble has yet arisen'. In fact, joint committees had been appointed at several pits to allocate work to safety men 'and this is likely to become general'. All safety men were at work in the Swansea Valley except at one small colliery at Ystalyfera, where six stokers, who belonged to a tiny union outside the MFGB, had refused to go down. 'The owners can, if necessary, manage without these stokers,' the report assured the Minister. Hints of trouble appeared in Yorkshire, however. 'Generally speaking' all pits had stopped, 'but there may be some trouble later owing to safety men being asked to work outside their normal duties. . . .'[29]

Perhaps the most impressive demonstration of the extent of the strike, at least as far as the general public was concerned, was the almost complete shutdown of the nation's transport industry. Despite the difficulty of picketing railway yards effectively, the train service virtually stopped. As a report to the Minister of Transport put it rather plaintively, 'Only three men reported for duty at Paddington Station and very few elsewhere. One passenger train has started for Oxford.'[30] Another ran from the north of

England to the south, stopping at every station on a circuitous route. The traffic figures speak for themselves. On the first day of the strike only 3–5 per cent of the nation's passenger trains were running, and far fewer goods trains. Even at the end of the strike, when passenger services rose in some cases to nearly 20 per cent of normal, goods remained at 2–3 per cent, and sidings were choked with loaded trains left there on 3 May. Though the railwaymen were probably risking more than any other group of industrial wage workers in terms of lost security and pension rights, they struck almost to a man. For example, on the London, Midland and Scottish – largest of the four main networks – only 207 out of more than 15,000 engine drivers reported for work, only 62 out of more than 14,000 firemen, only 153 out of nearly 10,000 guards.[31] Nearly 90 per cent of the wages staff and more than 40 per cent of the salaried staff were out at the start of the strike, despite intense pressure from the companies. Even such key men as station masters came out – a totally unexpected blow.[32] And the railwaymen remained solid. Such improvement as there was in rail traffic – and there was very little – came about as a result of volunteer labour and strikebreaking. For more than a week men in all walks of life suddenly had the chance to achieve their boyhood ambitions and become railway drivers.

This failure of volunteer labour to sustain adequate railway services was really one of the most obvious lessons of the strike. Yet it did not prevent the growth of a deeply rooted and much-cherished myth. For as Julian Symons has noted, 'No aspect of the strike took a deeper hold on the middle-class imagination than . . . grimy men standing at the footplate, waving happily and triumphantly at the end of a journey . . . signalmen in Fair Isle jerseys and plus fours, volunteers tuning a locomotive, checking points, cleaning the Flying Scotsman . . . fulfilling childhood dreams of adventure. . . .'[33] But whatever the therapeutic effects of such activities may have been for the individual volunteers, their impact on the railway system was slight. The companies' dependence on highly skilled workmen was clearly shown. Strike bulletins, issued by most councils of action, were especially scathing among railway workers, pouring scorn on the inefficient pretensions of the volunteers. One reported, 'We understand that luncheon cars are to be put on trains running between Westminster and Blackfriars'[34] (white-collar districts of London about a mile apart), while another drew attention to 'Notices posted on cemetery walls at Highgate and Finchley calling for Volunteers. We suggest it should be picketed by Underground men.'[35]

Transport within towns and cities – by bus and tram – was equally hard hit at first. On the opening day of the strike not one of London's 3,300 buses moved. On the last day, despite the fact that it was easier to teach blacklegs to drive buses than to drive trains, only just over 500 buses were in operation, and many of these were 'pirate' vehicles rather than company ones. Fewer than 100 London trams ever got on the roads on any one day during the strike. Perhaps the strikebreakers' greatest success came on the London underground railway system, where 71 out of a total of 315 trains were running half-way through the strike and about double that number by the end,[36] one of them carrying Winston Churchill. 'He knows nothing of the life of ordinary people,' his wife Clementine confessed. 'He's never been on a bus, and only once on the Underground. This was during the General Strike, when I deposited him at South Kensington. He went round and round [on the Circle Line] not knowing where to get out and had to be rescued eventually.'[37]

The transport picture in other urban centres was mixed. In Oxford and Bristol, for example, the regular bus service ran virtually without interruption throughout the strike, while in Cardiff, Grimsby, Chatham, Southampton and Portsmouth services were quickly restored to something like normal. On the other hand, in such important cities as Manchester, Newcastle and Hull, and in the North and the North-East in general, pickets put up strong and, on the whole, successful resistance to attempts by volunteers to operate regular city transport.

Of course, few of these strikebreaking activities would have been possible had power supplies been cut off more effectively by the strike. The whole London underground railway system, automatic signalling, cranes and power equipment at the docks were just three of the things completely dependent on electricity. How did the Government manage to maintain these services? Partly because of the ambiguous instructions issued by the general council of the TUC about 'essential' supplies. Thus, for example, electrical power workers at Stepney Power Station shut down all supplies at the start of the strike and refused to transmit power even to London Hospital.[38] On the other hand, power workers in the north-west area agreed to keep the power stations going for essential supplies and even to supervise non-union labour which might be engaged to do purely physical work.[39] However, at Lots Road Power Station, which supplied the London underground, there were no firemen or switchboard staff, the uniformed railway staff were also on strike and services were completely suspended. They were restored only when Naval ratings had been sent to Lots Road and Shepherd's Bush power stations. By 5 May 270 Naval ratings and 182 civilian volunteers were at work in various power stations in the

London area, and later the number of civilians rose to 311 working at 16 generating plants. 'Generally speaking,' the Minister learned, 'it would appear that so far as the ETU [Electrical Trades Union] are concerned the strike is spreading and there are very few stations where employees of this Union are at work.'[40]

Such services that were maintained during the strike often depended on electric power, and power in turn depended on supplies of coal. Stocks of coal and fuel oil were unusually high; but this fuel had to be transported to power stations, just as food had to be shifted from country to town. How was this achieved without a railway system? Part of the answer lies in road transport – the strikers' Achilles Heel. The General Strike showed that the railways could not be operated without skilled labour. The actual driving of an engine was not difficult : it was the reading of signals, taking the proper line, keeping up steam on gradients and nursing and responding to the sounds of the steam locomotive which took a lifetime's experience. Road transport was different. If one could drive a car one could drive a truck, a lorry, a tanker or a bus with minimal training, ride a motor cycle and act as a despatch rider. Here what the strikers derisively called the 'plus-fours brigade' came into their own. Comparatively little skill was needed; but with the railway system paralysed it was needed desperately. The Government had long foreseen this and their preparations had been more complete than anyone outside the inner circle of decision-making had imagined.

Yet road transport on its own would not have been enough. The ultimate importance of sea transport, especially for really heavy loads which would normally have travelled in long goods trains, has only recently been recognised. But without the use of ships, road transport alone would not have been sufficient to prevent paralysis. As J. C. C. Davidson, a key figure in Government counter-strike strategy, explained, Britain is a small island with many good ports and harbours.[41] Nowhere is further than ninety miles from the sea. Supplies could thus be sent by ship, unloaded at convenient harbours and then transported by road to distribution points. The importance of this sea strategy has been neglected, despite the fact that the determined opposition of Havelock Wilson's right-wing seamen's union to the strike helped Davidson's plan. Yet he clearly exaggerates its importance, since with the dockers on strike few ships could be unloaded. The real answer was that power stations and warehouses had more than nine days' supplies in hand when the strike started.

Chapter Twenty

Emergency Machine

The first reports of the strike's overwhelming success dramatised the gravity of the situation and seemed to rattle the Government. Baldwin believed the nation was nearer civil war than it had been for hundreds of years.[1] The Cabinet met at 11 a.m. on 4 May and thereafter at least once a day until the strike was settled. For nine days it discussed only one item – the General Strike. The eyes of the nation, and indeed the whole world,[2] were focused on the unfolding drama. On the union side a vast industrial army had entered battle with high spirits and incomparable *élan*. The trouble was that this mighty army, for all its high morale, was largely leaderless. As Bevin put it when he placed himself at the head of the TUC strike organisation on the first day of the strike, 'Now we've got to appoint generals'.[3] On the Government side, however, the problem was the reverse. A powerful leadership existed, but its task was to recruit an army. The generals were all ready, in the Cabinet or in Whitehall, at the head of an official war machine and a staff of Civil Servants.

The strike at last tested Government plans for dealing with such an emergency which had been in preparation for six years. The OMS had suffered some teething troubles, not least over publicity, the limits of its authority, and how it would be integrated with official Government organisations if the General Strike started. But the Government's responsibility was far wider in scope than the OMS. It stemmed from the Emergency Powers of 1920, which gave it full authority to deal with any activity 'calculated to deprive any substantial proportion of the country of the essentials of life'. Local Government authorities had already been briefed, as long ago as 20 November, in the crucial circular 636, about what to do to activate the Government's plans. All that was needed was the pre-arranged signal. In the early hours of 3 May, Whitehall sent the one-word telegram : 'Action'.[4]

This dramatic message breathed life into an organisation which had been gestating slowly since the end of the war, and more rapidly during the previous nine months. Based on wartime contingency planning, it had first been tried out during the 1919 railway strike. Lloyd George had then emphasised the need to divide the country into divisional areas, each with its own civil commissioners and staff, ready to act at a moment's notice in the event of a general strike. The plan had remained essentially unchanged in the next seven years while its details had been slowly perfected. Although Government secrecy was probably less marked in 1926 than in 1919 or 1921, and hints about preparations had appeared in the Press from time to time, few Labour leaders had any idea of what would confront them when the General Strike started.

The object of all the Government's planning was principally to maintain law and order, transport and supplies. Under the direction of a special Cabinet committee, the Supply and Transport Committee, each civil service department was to be responsible for a particular activity. Thus the Board of Trade was to secure stockpiles of food, fuel and other necessities, and arrange their local distribution. London's Hyde Park was barricaded off and transformed into a huge storage centre for supplies. The Ministry of Transport was to arrange long-distance distribution and the supply of electrical power. The Home Office was to take charge of the potentially explosive area of law and order, including the crucially important problem of how best to protect the Government plans for transport and supply. The country had been mapped out in ten areas, each with a commissioner, a junior member of the Government and a Ministry of Health Inspector as staff officer to stimulate local activity. This local activity was in turn supervised by eighty-eight so-called voluntary service committees headed by locally prominent or influential figures.[5]

It was natural, but not without a certain ominous significance, that the regional commissioners were all military men, including such figures as Sir Phillip Sassoon, Earl Winterton, Lord Clarendon, and Captain Douglas King. Sir William Mitchell-Thompson was first commissioner at the Home Office. Each regional commissioner had a departmental staff for finance, food, coal, transport, postal work and shipping, as well as a police officer and military liaison officer. These officers had received preliminary instructions and briefing from their departments, but were now entirely at the disposal of their respective commissioners, who in the event of serious disorder or violence exercised all powers of Government. Fourteen departments were represented on the central coordinating committee, though it was understood that if the crisis became acute the whole organisation would have to be simplified so that it functioned merely to provide food, fuel, transport, communications, finance and publicity.[6] Powers existed for the requisitioning of motor and other vehicles, and a complete system of road transport had been organised.

In fact, no attempt was made to requisition vehicles. Instead, the hauliers organised themselves on a voluntary basis and road transport was carried out by 150 haulage committees. All printed matter – priority orders, instructions and so on – had been prepared and circulated months in advance. The ten regional emergency divisions each had a road commissioner and the services of 150 road officers, stationed at selected local centres within each division. They were assisted by the local haulage committees, composed of men connected with transport undertakings. Special organisations were necessary for dealing with the docks and with greater centres of population, especially London. As a shrewd observer in the TUC camp put it, 'Government "strikebreaking" has become a very definite function, and . . . an effective technique has been evolved by the highly intelligent men who run the Civil Service'.[7]

Certainly, the greatest single success story of the Government's preparations for the General Strike was in road transport. Before the advent of the internal combustion engine a national railway stoppage could paralyse the nation. But by 1926, as the General Strike showed, road transport could be used to maintain essential supplies and keep the life of the nation alive, especially if ships could be used to carry supplies to ports and harbours. The TUC reported on the second day of the strike that 'All essential industries and all transport services have been brought to a standstill', but added significantly, 'The only exception is that the distribution of milk and food has been permitted to continue'.[8] Once the strikers had to start making exceptions and allow some Government road transport to pass their picket lines, it became harder to stop non-essential supplies. Milk was never a problem. A ban on cheese-making produced a surplus of milk, and daily supplies were brought to towns on milk trains – virtually the only trains to run regularly throughout the nine days. The biggest single burden on the system was the transportation of potatoes. Yet road transport did all that was expected of it and more – and remarkably cheaply too.[9] For the whole system was based on voluntary labour – in particular, the volunteers recruited by the OMS.

The importance of the OMS has been the subject of great controversy, both at the time and subsequently by historians. Sir John Anderson, permanent under-secretary at the Home Office, tried to play down its contribution. 'The OMS was a useful lightning conductor before the strike,' he wrote, 'but apart from the fact that it trained a few drivers its practical utility was almost nil.'[10] Yet during the nine days, driving became *the* essential skill in maintaining or breaking the strike. Both sides were dependent on road transport, the strikers the more so since the picketing of harbours, docks, power plants and railway yards depended on good transport to move the pickets around. Anderson, of course, took a dislike to the OMS because of the difficulties it had caused him and the Civil Service. These problems had arisen over structure.[11] They had cost Sir John and his Civil Service colleagues some time and trouble; but eventually he and the Home Office had persuaded the OMS to amend their recruiting cards so that the pledge recruits made on enrolment was *not* made specifically to the OMS but in such a vague way that it could be transferred to the Government.[12]

From the very beginning it had been the Government's intention that the OMS should be merged with the Government's emergency machine if a General Strike began. Certain organisers of the OMS had wanted to act independently. But ultimately, on 3 May, the OMS handed over about 100,000 volunteers to be controlled by the Government.[13] Few of these recruits had any special skills. The total included more than 1,300 lorry drivers trained at special OMS 'schools', a similar number of car drivers, 144 bus drivers and 351 mechanics. The OMS lacked the proper training equipment; nevertheless, it was able to produce nearly 1,200 skilled, semi-skilled and unskilled engineers for the Electricity Commission and 250 Ford van drivers for the General Post Office. The OMS also handed over 640 railwaymen, 116 inland waterway workers and 91 tram workers.[14]

The purpose of the OMS organisation was to provide a cadre of key men without whose services no emergency organisation could function. Joynson-Hicks was clear about this point. 'The most important of such key men I consider are locomotive drivers and other workers on the railway, electricity workers and motor drivers.' Jix said the railway companies could get strikebreakers themselves, drivers were not too difficult to come by, while 'the Electricity Commissioners have an up-to-date and detailed list of skilled electrical workers'.[15] This letter reveals an important point about the people who broke the strike. Not all the OMS recruits came from 'the plus-fours brigade'.

True, most of the OMS volunteers lived in the south and east of the country, which had large middle-class regions. The City of Westminster

– not the most solidly proletarian borough in Britain – provided the highest number of volunteers, more than 7,700. Leeds, on the other hand, in the gritty heartland of industrial Yorkshire, provided only 400, while such important urban centres as Manchester and Liverpool did not appear on the OMS lists at all.[16] Everyone knows that undergraduates from Oxford and Cambridge drove buses during the strike, that volunteer drivers for trains and lorries and special constables were recruited from ex-officers and from the universities. As the historian A. J. P. Taylor has put it, 'This was class war, in polite form'.[17] It may have been class war, but it was not always polite – witness the violence and thousands of arrests in London, Glasgow, the mining areas and industrial regions around the country.[18]

Nor was it simply a war fought *between* the classes: there were important defections from both sides. Some middle-class people supported the strike. Moreover, the colourful, and more usual, activities of undergraduates and the middle class in trying to break the strike have also helped obscure the fact that an important source of strikebreakers, taking the country as a whole, was the working class – unemployed men glad of the chance to regain some tattered traces of self-respect with a few days' work, strikers from one trade ready to work at another job in another town for a change, working men who, when the crunch came, feared the power of organised labour and rallied to the Government side. Without them it is doubtful if the General Strike could have been broken as quickly as it was. Without volunteers, the Government's plans to beat the strike would almost certainly have failed.

The recruitment of these 'loyal subjects', as the civil commissioners called the strikebreakers, was left to voluntary organisations such as the OMS. The Ministry of Labour, concerned solely with the task of conciliation and the search for a settlement, would have nothing to do with recruitment. But the Government recognised that it had a responsibility for 'the protection of loyal subjects'.[19] Throughout the strike the Cabinet was constantly occupied with how best to maintain public order while supplying public services. Ugly struggles between pickets and strikebreakers at bus garages, tram depots, docks and power stations around the country emphasised the importance of public order and how best to protect those who were working to maintain essential services.[20] By 7 May the Cabinet decided 'in view of the intimidation already carried out and threatened' that the 'first essential in the present situation' was that 'forces available for this purpose should be expanded on a considerable scale'. Police should be used in the first instance, aided by special constables, with troops only used as a last resort. Tear gas would only be detonated when the alternative seemed to be firearms, and the regular army reserve and territorials were not to be used.[21]

The Government's machinery worked with some efficiency and precision throughout the strike. The Supply and Transport Committee functioned to all intents and purposes as the Government strike committee. It met every day, usually with Joynson-Hicks in the chair. More significant for the conduct of the strike, the three strong-men in the Cabinet – Birkenhead, Chamberlain and Churchill – attended all the meetings. They had not done so before the strike, and they stopped attending once the strike was over. But during the nine days the Supply and Transport Committee was really the focus of power within the nation, and the three hawks were determined to play a crucial role in shaping that power. On the face of things their influence would seem to have been increased by the surprising fact that the Prime Minister himself was not a member of the Cabinet strike committee and never even attended a single meeting.[22] But he remained more influential than anyone, managing to keep his hands free to balance between all the factions in Government and among miners, owners and the TUC. The strike committee became bogged down in detail, while Baldwin and trusted aides such as J. C. C. Davidson really shaped events.

Chapter Twenty-one

The Press Appears

The newspaper industry had been the first casualty of the strike. Indeed, the Government had used the *Daily Mail* incident as a pretext for breaking off talks with the TUC. There is some evidence to suggest that Churchill might have deliberately precipitated this.[1] Yet the disappearance of the Press created a problem. Rumours could spread alarm and lead to disorder. Moreover, the Government had no means of spreading its own propaganda. Control of the Press was thus of crucial importance. Before the strike began it had been clear that it might stop all national and most provincial newspapers. But no one could be sure how badly the industry might be hit. Though the printing unions had stopped work, the National Union of Journalists had voted against the strike; and there was a chance that enough key production men might be available to print at least one national newspaper to spread Government propaganda.

With this in mind, Baldwin appointed J. C. C. Davidson, his former PPS and one of his closest personal friends,[2] deputy chief Civil Commissioner, 'the member of the Government,' as Davidson himself put it, 'responsible for publicity . . . collector and distributor of Government news, censored when necessary but undoctored.'[3] On 2 May, Lord Burnham and the Newspaper Proprietors' Association told Davidson that they would not themselves pool resources to produce a joint newspaper during the emergency, but would help the Government produce daily news bulletins which could be displayed at town halls, post offices and other public buildings throughout the country. Davidson was clearly not satisfied with this solution. What the Government wanted was to produce its own newspaper. 'I wrote a private note to the Editor of the *Morning Post*,' Davidson explained, 'urging him to point out to his colleagues that they, being experts, must help and not be helpless in the face of the General Strike.'⁴

When the strike began, therefore, the Government was faced with the urgent necessity of creating an organisation for the production and distribution of a daily newspaper which the best opinion in the business said was quite impossible. This heavy responsibility rested on Davidson's shoulders; and much of the credit for Government propaganda activities during the next nine days should go to him. On the eve of the strike he called a meeting in Churchill's room at the House of Commons. Here details of the operation were finally hammered out by Churchill, Davidson, Sir Malcolm Fraser and officials from Davidson's staff and His Majesty's Stationery Office. The Stationery Office, which published all Government documents, white papers, and so on, would also be publishing the projected newspaper. It was to be called the *British Gazette* and would be a Government publication.⁵

The great problem facing the *British Gazette* was the serious shortage of newsprint. Sir Malcolm Fraser learned at the start of the strike that only ten days' supply existed in the whole country for the projected newspaper – and, if this were used, national newspapers would be unable to print again for a week or a fortnight after the strike had ended. The Government angered *The Times* by commandeering supplies; but the main source came from abroad, when Davidson arranged for 450 tons of newsprint, enough for 13 million copies of a four-page *Gazette,* to be shipped in the greatest secrecy from Holland to the Pool of London and stored in a requisitioned warehouse across Waterloo Bridge. Since no paper-making factories were working, Davidson had to commandeer a mill at Northfleet, on the Thames, 'in a rather disaffected area', and recruit about two hundred volunteers 'from various sources'. The managers of several other big paper-makers acted as key men. Electrical experts were obtained from Callender's Cable Construction Company, and the whole contingent was heavily guarded by a company of Royal Engineers and a Naval detachment. Great care was taken that none of the barges lying at anchor could be sunk to block the river front, and thus access to London. Wooden huts were erected rapidly to house the men; and working in fierce heat on machines which were each 840 feet long they were soon producing 50 tons of paper a day – enough for 1½ million copies of the *Gazette.*⁶

Having secured its supplies of newsprint, the Government had to establish its publishing headquarters. The offices of both the *Daily Mail* and the *Daily Express* were considered, and then rejected, because both could be easily blocked by pickets.[7] Instead, the Government took possession of the *Morning Post* building. When this occurred, at 11 p.m. on 3 May, 'the building was, apart from the editorial staff, a mere empty shell with no means of stereo-typing and printing the paper, and no means of distributing it. . . . It was, therefore, necessary to obtain what key men were available, and fill in the vast gaps with volunteer assistance.'[8] Hundreds of cars and scores of aircraft had also to be obtained to distribute the *Gazette* throughout the country. In order to avoid being wholly dependent on the loyalty of the *Morning Post* composing staff, Davidson decided to have matter set in duplicate, and the machines of Eyre and Spottiswoode were used for this purpose.[9]

Davidson's caution proved well founded, for at 3 p.m. on 4 May the composing staff of the *Morning Post* were withdrawn by their union and threw away the five columns that had been set.[10] He had mistakenly believed that typists could operate the keyboards of linotype machines. Yet the Government was able to recruit enough key men from other newspapers, especially the *Mail* and the *Express*, as well as drafting specialised artificers from the Royal Navy, to keep the *Gazette* in business. Davidson's plans for its production and distribution were a model of efficiency. Hundreds of lorries and cars made thousands of journeys by scores of routes to distribute the newspaper across the country. Aircraft flew each night from Northolt and Biggin Hill, airfields near London, to Yorkshire, Liverpool and Plymouth, taking copies to the most distant regions. Nothing like this special air service had ever been attempted before, but its role was crucial. 'It was the regular arrival of news despatches at certain key points,' explained Baldwin's Secretary for Air, Sir Samuel Hoare, 'that convinced the public the Government was in control. The result was there was no panic.'[11] The air service defeated the strike by forestalling public disorder. Detailed plans covering patternmaking, ink supplies, oil, paper, transport and so on were drawn up to deal with a prolonged emergency. 'A careful scheme was got ready for use at a moment's notice,' the Davidson report noted. 'The country was divided into three areas – Northern, Central and Southern – and the paper would have been manufactured at Aberdeen, Grimsby and Aylesford.'[12] Arrangements were also made to commandeer convenient works which had their own power supplies. Midway through the strike the Government had commandeered six major publishing and paper-manufacturing plants. By the end of the strike, with a daily sale of $2\frac{1}{2}$ million copies, the *British Gazette* could claim the largest sale 'of any daily paper in any part of the world at the time'.[13]

The production and distribution of the *British Gazette* epitomised the painstaking nature of Government preparations for the emergency. But if the technical aspects of the *Gazette* were a triumph, editorially the newspaper was not a success. It was run by Churchill. Baldwin later described this appointment as 'the cleverest thing I ever did' because it kept Churchill busy at a time when his interference elsewhere might have caused trouble. Actually, there is little evidence that Baldwin had much say in the decision : Churchill simply assumed command. His early background in journalism as a war correspondent was a qualification no one else in the Cabinet could match. Despite this, he was a bad editor. 'It wasn't much of a paper,' one of Churchill's Cabinet colleagues admitted.[14] He approached his job like a war correspondent, observing with obvious enthusiasm that 'a great newspaper office, with its machines crashing and grinding away, reminds me of the combination of a first-class battleship and a first-class general election'.[15]

Thus in the first edition, on 5 May, the *British Gazette* tried to give the impression that the strike 'was by no means so complete as its promoters hoped', when the whole nation knew otherwise. Almost all the workers who had been called had come out; away from London, people knew the strike was working. From the very start, the *Gazette* handled the news provocatively or ineptly. Yet Government propaganda was clearly vital at this stage, and it is hard to see why Baldwin believed that putting Churchill in charge of it kept him out of harm's way. It gave him the chance to cause a great deal of damage. Moreover, his handling of talks with the miners in the summer of 1926, after the General Strike had failed, indicated that he might have been better employed as a negotiator rather than a propagandist during the strike itself.

As editor, Churchill found himself at odds with almost everyone – journalists, printers, Civil Servants, politicians, churchmen, even the King. Davidson wanted some censorship but no distortion, but Churchill refused to print 'a lot of defeatist trash' which might indicate that the strike was a success and so encourage 'the enemy'. He demanded 'unconditional surrender' and refused to publish the news that in Plymouth a team of strikers had beaten a team of policemen 2–1 in a soccer match at which the Chief Constable's wife had kicked-off to start the game.[16] Davidson was eager to publish the news, and Churchill's refusal to do so – though he included a column-and-a-half of Canadian ice-hockey, a sport which must have had only a handful of followers in Britain – caused a row in Cabinet.

Nevertheless, Churchill tried to foster the idea that all was well by

9a. Herbert Smith, without his usual cap (right), conferring with W. C. Bridgeman, a former secretary for mines, who acted as Government mediator before Red Friday in 1925.

9b. A. J. Cook, secretary of the MFGB, with a group of Nottinghamshire miners in 1926.

10a. Ernest Bevin, leader of the transport workers and dockers, who made his name at the TUC by his conduct of the 1926 strike.

10b. Walter Citrine (right) and Arthur Pugh, general secretary and president of the TUC, leave Downing Street after the surrender on 12 May 1926.

making the *Gazette* appear as much like a normal newspaper as possible. So sport figured prominently, while headlines often bore little relation to the story they advertised – all normal Fleet Street practice. The editor also included Zoo Notes and Latest Wills – but showed no discretion in the wills he chose to publish. Thus the first edition reported that Alderman William Pease, a former Darlington MP, had left £271,796 on his death.[17] Pease was one of the largest mineowners in the north-east of England, and this item was a gift to propagandists on the side of the miners and the TUC who were struggling to keep the miners' average wage at £2 10s a week.

Churchill's efforts to interfere in the production and distribution of the newspaper were equally unhappy. 'He butts in at the busiest hours,' wrote Tom Jones, 'and insists on changing commas and full stops until the staff is furious.'[18] Davidson complained that 'He thinks he is Napoleon, but curiously enough men who have been printing all their life . . . happen to know more about their job than he does'.[19] Jones added that the private secretaries at 10 Downing Street 'are all trying to get Winston put in charge of transport'.[20] His clumsy attempt to suppress an appeal by the Archbishop of Canterbury and other Church leaders for a negotiated settlement caused another storm. Finally, his announcement on 8 May that any action taken by the armed forces in aid of the Civil Power 'will receive, both now and afterwards, the full support of His Majesty's Government', was a dangerous incitement to violence which embarrassed the Government and alarmed the King.

Under Churchill's erratic editorship, the picture of the strike which appeared in the columns of the *British Gazette* was inconsistent. The line at first was that the General Strike was a threat to the Constitution which no Government could tolerate. The Prime Minister's message in the first edition of the *British Gazette* on 5 May expressed the Government's view clearly :

Constitutional Government is being attacked. Let all good citizens whose livelihood and labour have thus been put in peril bear with fortitude and patience the hardships with which they have been so suddenly confronted. Stand behind the Government, who are doing their part, confident that you will cooperate in the measures they have undertaken to preserve the liberties and privileges of the people of these islands. The laws of England are the people's birthright. The laws are in your keeping. You have made Parliament their guardian.

G

The General Strike is a challenge to Parliament and is the road to anarchy and ruin.[21]

It was a powerful message in Baldwin's best style, which showed how clearly he had seen the way to swing uncommitted opinion behind the Government.

Until the weekend, the Government newspaper tried to present the strike as a consciously revolutionary, wholly subversive, but only half-successful enterprise. Asquith, a former Liberal Prime Minister, and Balfour, a former Tory PM who was now Lord President in Baldwin's Cabinet, wrote signed articles for Churchill denouncing the strike as a revolutionary threat to Constitutional Government directed by a 'relatively small body of extremists' who wished 'to deprive the people of food'. Their tone suggested to many that Churchill himself had actually written the articles, but another Liberal, Lord Grey, wrote in similar vein. J. M. Keynes, the distinguished economist and a shrewd observer of politics (and, incidentally, another Liberal), dismissed such talk as 'foolish non-sense', criticised Baldwin's 'fatal blundering' and denounced Churchill's 'revolution stunt'. After Sunday, the line suddenly changed. There was no more talk of revolution. Lord Grey admitted he had been mistaken.[22] By midweek the Cabinet had clearly switched tactics. The *Gazette* remained vaguely alarmist and irresponsible. But *The Times* announced firmly, 'No one suggests for a moment that any considerable number of men on strike are animated by revolutionary motives.'[23]

The appearance of the *British Gazette* gave the Opposition the chance to score some political points in the House. Lloyd-George called it 'first-rate indiscretion' but 'third-rate journalism'. At question time on 5 May, a Labour MP, Lieutenant-Commander Kenworthy, asked Joynson-Hicks whether the Home Office took responsibility for statements made in the paper, and who was to pay for the costs of its production. Jix replied that the Government accepted full responsibility, and that the cost of pub-lication would be borne on the Treasury Vote.[24] The paper was sold for 1d; but since it carried no advertising this must have covered only a small fraction of the production costs, especially as the rail strike meant it had to be distributed by fleets of motor vehicles and large aircraft.[25] Ramsay MacDonald, as Leader of the Opposition, asked pointedly which Minister would be responsible for answering questions about the *Gazette* in the House, and Kenworthy, in a supplementary question, asked Jix to identify under what section of the Special Powers Act the Government was acting in producing propaganda which attacked one section of the community, but levied a charge on the whole community to pay for it.[26] Jix made no satisfactory reply, and was clearly uneasy about Churchill's part in the developing crisis. When Thomas, referring to Churchill, asked Jix privately afterwards if he could see where 'your Mussolini is driving you', the Home Secretary shook his head dolefully and agreed it was a 'a very worrying time'.[27]

One development the Government had not anticipated, which caused Joynson-Hicks further unease, was the TUC's decision to counter the Government's propaganda with a newspaper of its own. The TUC's newspaper was called the *British Worker*. It looked better, read better and was far less provocative than the Government's own propaganda journal. This was one of the pieces of union improvisation which really worked well from the first day. The *British Worker* was planned and produced in 24 hours, despite Government attempts to suppress it. Churchill was surprised to find he had competition. He had expected to have the field to himself. Instead, he was being challenged and answered by a really well produced and effective national strike newspaper. Every edition carried a message which tried to scotch the Government's Constitution issue. 'The general council does not challenge the Constitution,' it read. 'It is not seeking to substitute unconditional government. Nor is it desirous of undermining our Parliamentary institutions. The sole aim of the council is to secure the miners a decent standard of life. The council is engaged in an industrial dispute. There is no constitutional crisis.'[28]

The *British Worker* was edited by Hamilton Fyfe, editor of the Labour *Daily Herald*, and produced at the *Herald* office in Gray's Inn Road. Joynson-Hicks did everything he could to stop it. He signed a warrant holding Fyfe and the *Herald* general manager Bob Williams responsible for publication and giving the police power to search the premises.[29] A senior police officer and about 100 policemen, some of them mounted, surrounded the office on the evening of 5 May and ransacked it for evidence of subversion.

Citrine, Bevin and Ben Turner got through the crowd and the police cordon and offered themselves for arrest as directors of the *Daily Herald*.[30] A Special Branch inspector who was occupying the editor's office telephoned the Commissioner of Police with news of what he had found, or failed to find, and a summary of what the first edition contained. Six early copies of the *British Worker* were submitted to the Commissioner, who read them hurriedly. But the decision had to be taken at the highest level. Arthur Pugh had already left for the Commons to tell his leader what was happening, and later MacDonald, his deputy Arthur Henderson, and Pugh himself persuaded Baldwin to cancel Jix's order to close the paper. Baldwin believed that, as the Attorney-General had not been consulted, the closure would probably have been illegal.[31] More important, he wanted to do everything he could at this stage to keep the moderates on the union side in a mood in which they would be prepared to trust him as Prime Minister to settle the strike on fair and acceptable terms.

If Baldwin was thinking of how best to secure a peaceful end to the crisis, not everyone involved was hopeful of peace. When the Commissioner telephoned the *Herald* office to say that the newspaper could appear after all, the TUC leadership felt that they had won an important, but potentially dangerous, victory. Citrine described his mixed feelings as the low rumble of the presses re-started in the machine room in the basement, and the large crowd outside broke into tremendous cheering and choruses of the *Red Flag*. 'Men who had probably never heard [it] sung before were joining in with gusto,' Citrine recorded in his diary. 'I got to bed at 12.30 a.m., feeling very tired and not a little concerned as to where it will all end.'[32]

One common assumption about the General Strike is that it stopped all newspapers and that the *British Gazette* and the *British Worker* were the only ones to appear. This is incorrect. True, on the first day all the London nationals virtually ceased. *The Times* alone among regular London newspapers managed, despite the absence of its influential editor Geoffrey Dawson on holiday, to produce a paper from its own office on the first day of the strike – a tiny, single sheet printed on six specially installed multigraph machines which could only turn out 48,000 copies instead of the usual 150,000. Few of these could be distributed outside London because there were no trains running and the management had not been able to organise effective distribution by road. Nevertheless, the paper's appearance was apparently seen as a threat by some extremists, because there was a deliberate attempt to burn the office down on 5 May, when petrol was poured through a loading ramp and then ignited from outside.[33]

Despite this, *The Times* continued to appear daily, giving loyal, though not completely uncritical, support to the Government. Dawson, the editor, 'Secretary-General of the Establishment' in the 1920s and 1930s,[34] was one of Baldwin's closest cronies. But he was far too good a newspaperman to indulge in the kind of crude propaganda which characterised Churchill's *British Gazette*. 'The journalistic triumph of the strike,' in Julian Symons's opinion, 'was undoubtedly the production of *The Times*.'[35] It rose from 48,000 copies on the first day to 170,000 on 8 May, to 342,000 on the final day of the strike, to 400,000 on 14 May – nearly three times its usual sale. In addition, the paper managed to produce its only afternoon edition in history on 12 May, reporting the news that the strike was over.[36] This record was all the more creditable as Churchill and Davidson had commandeered supplies of the paper's newsprint to produce the *British Gazette*. Though Dawson was a close friend of the Prime Minister, he objected to this seizure, which he blamed on Churchill, and wrote an editorial criticising the policy, which others echoed in more intemperate tones.[37]

Nevertheless, as Davidson observed, 'Great care was taken that *The Times* should always have plenty of paper'. It had sufficient newsprint left at the end of the strike for more than a month. Moreover, Dawson's protests seemed to show that the Government was not being partisan by making anti-Government newspapers, like the *Daily Herald*, suffer and leaving newspapers that generally supported Baldwin alone.[38] But *The Times* was not alone. Many other newspapers, both national and provincial, managed to appear in some form or other during the emergency. The Conservative *Morning Post* was produced by blackleg labour, while other nationals, such as the *Daily Mail*, also managed to get out special strike editions.

The Communist Party transformed its usual *Workers' Weekly* into a *Workers' Daily*, and, when this was suppressed by the police, continued to bring out a clandestine *Workers' Bulletin*. Lloyd George, still hungry for power and hopeful that the strike might help ressurect him as a 'man of destiny', made an abortive attempt to bring out his own newspaper, by merging the resources of three Liberal journals at Luton. All over the country, in such centres as Birmingham, Manchester, South Wales and Sheffield, dozens of morning and evening papers appeared, most of them produced by blackleg labour and expressing extreme right-wing views. To counter these, strike committees and Councils of Action everywhere brought out their own lively, satirical strike sheets and bulletins.

For the two newspapers, produced by Government and TUC, revealed how the situation had polarised. Yet the really significant point about the rival propaganda was that the *British Worker,* for all its technical superiority, did little to help the cause of the unions and the miners. It appealed to the converted. It was distributed to strikers through their trade union branches, strike committees and so on. Few copies fell into the hands of those who were not on strike but wanted to learn what the strike was all about and how it was progressing. The *Gazette*, on the other hand, though aimed at middle-class opponents of the strike, was also read by uncommitted people who needed to be won over by the strikers or the Government. Churchill's intemperate attacks on the strikers may not have helped in converting the uncommitted; Baldwin's line that the Constitution was in danger was probably more effective. His use of radio broadcasting was both more effective and more ruthless.

Chapter Twenty-two

The Control of Radio

In 1926 radio was still in its infancy. Yet its potential power, soon to be dramatised by the strike, was already understood by a few men, including Baldwin himself and the young managing director of the British Broadcasting Company, John Reith. This thirty-six-year-old Scot, very tall and with a huge frame and craggy face, was to develop into one of the most outstanding and influential men of his time. Churchill, who often clashed with Reith, called him 'that Wuthering Height'. Trained as an engineer, he had been badly wounded in the First World War and taken his present job in charge of the newly-formed BBC in 1922. 'By sheer force of character and intellect,' as one observer put it, '[he] established himself as an autocrat in a new realm of human expression.'[1]

Yet his role in the General Strike, and that of the BBC, has frequently been misunderstood. When the miners had been locked out at the end of April, Reith was involved in long and acrimonious arguments with the Government and Whitehall. These discussions concerned recommendations made by the Crawford Committee a few months earlier on the future of broadcasting. Crawford had recommended that broadcasting be taken out of the hands of the General Post Office and placed in control of a virtually independent, Government-backed, public corporation partially financed by licence fees paid by radio users.[2] These talks about the details of the charter proposed by Crawford were suddenly interrupted by the national emergency. For three days the country was virtually without newspapers and Baldwin demanded that the BBC make an immediate announcement about the coal stoppage and General Strike.

Such was the background against which the events of the next two weeks must be judged. Reith knew that his conduct during the crisis would have an important bearing on his personal position as the most likely head of the proposed corporation and on the whole legal structure of broadcasting, with profound implications for the nation.[3] Personally, Reith had no sympathy with the mineowners and felt the Labour Party had the best chance of applying his own beliefs about practical Christianity to national and international politics. He would have supported the miners against the owners. But he was certainly not prepared to support the TUC against the Government and deplored the whole idea of a General Strike.

Still, his official policy so far had been one of strict neutrality. He had refused to allow the OMS to broadcast propaganda or recruiting messages. 'We felt it would prejudice our reputation for being non-political unless we allowed a prominent trade unionist to make his observations on the OMS,' Reith explained.[4] When Joynson-Hicks had been Baldwin's Postmaster-General in 1923, he had clashed repeatedly with Reith. As Home Secretary two years later, Jix had approved Reith's refusal to let the OMS broadcast unchallenged. Now, as chairman of the crucially important Cabinet strike committee, Jix could have an important influence on broadcasting policy during the strike. Moreover, Mitchell-Thompson, the Chief Civil Commissioner in charge of Government machinery for combating the strike, was also Postmaster-General with control of broadcasting – and he had already leaked the contents of TUC telegrams to the Cabinet. So Reith faced threats from Churchill, and more subtle pressure from Baldwin. At times during the crisis Reith felt he was destroying himself and the BBC by his refusal to let Churchill dictate to him and his determination to try to preserve his independence from Government control.

On Friday, 30 April, Jack Payne's dance band had been faded out for an announcement at 11.45 p.m. that negotiations had broken down and a coal strike would begin at midnight. As the strike started in the early hours of 4 May, Reith personally broadcast from his own home a special message written by the Prime Minister. 'Keep steady,' the message said, and was repeated over and over again. 'Remember peace on earth comes to men of good will.'[5] This was the 'pompous voice' that Beatrice Webb complained of in her diary. The message then explained that the refusal of the printers at the *Daily Mail* to set Marlowe's 'King and Country' leader involved 'the Constitutional rights and freedom of the nation'. Before continuing negotiations with the miners the Government required repudiation of the 'overt acts' which had precipitated the break and immediate and unconditional withdrawal of the General Strike notices.[6]

Davidson, who was running the Government propaganda machine, lived, most conveniently, next door to Reith.[7] He had assumed that the nation's newspapers would virtually disappear, at least during the early part of the strike, and that radio would become vitally important as the only means of disseminating news and Government propaganda. From the legal point of view there was no question that the Government had the authority not only to order the BBC to broadcast whatever it wanted, but also actually to commandeer the company's premises, as it had already commandeered the offices of the *Morning Post* and the newsprint of *The Times*. The few newspapers which managed to appear, and the TUC, all announced that the Government had actually taken over the BBC for the emergency. These reports were officially denied. For Davidson was quite clear on this point. 'I formed the opinion that if it [the BBC] were to retain public confidence and to cover the widest possible field its independence must be safeguarded.'[8]

What Baldwin was anxious to do, of course, was to exercise a more subtle influence over broadcasting, in which his own personal messages would be of paramount importance. On the first day of the strike he lunched with Reith at his club, The Travellers, and explained his policy. He was especially anxious that the BBC premises should be properly protected, and Reith assured him that police guards were adequate though unobtrusive. Baldwin and Reith then made arrangements for at least five daily news bulletins to be issued from London and Daventry at 10 a.m., 1 p.m., 4 p.m., and from all stations at the usual times of 7 p.m. and 9.30 p.m.[9] News would be supplied from the agencies and from official Government sources, especially Davidson's office, where reports were received from the ten districts into which the country had been divided.[10] The BBC also suspended copyright, so that newspapers could print BBC news bulletins and publish what was revealingly called by one local newspaper editor 'official news' during the emergency.[11] Davidson acted as go-between for Baldwin and Reith, and at a further conference on 5 May Reith tried to impress three points on the Government: that it was better to consult than to order; that the BBC should remain impartial in order to influence the peaceful settlement which would have to be made sooner or later; and that if the BBC did become partisan, as the *British Gazette* had clearly already become, strikers could easily paralyse broadcasting.[12]

The following day, Reith met the Cabinet strike committee. 'Throughout the period of the strike I vetted almost every item of every bulletin myself,' Reith explained.[13] 'It was made clear that, though the civil commissioners or departments might ask for this or that to be broadcast,

G*

the final decision rested with the BBC.' Churchill objected forcefully that this position was not at all satisfactory and that the BBC should be commandeered immediately. It was monstrous, the Chancellor argued, not to use such a potent influence on public opinion to the best possible advantage. 'Jix, to my surprise,' Reith noted, 'said mildly that if anybody felt strongly about it the whole question had better be discussed at full Cabinet.'[14] The Cabinet was supposed to discuss the problem the next day, but never got to it. Churchill was fully occupied with the *Gazette*, and with efforts to step up troop movements in London's dockland. Baldwin was as usual ready to delay dealing with problems until they were no longer relevant. Reith was left in rather precarious control.

Once the strike had started, Reith told Davidson, the BBC had to be 'for the Government in the crisis'. Explaining the position, he added, 'We were therefore careful not to broadcast anything that would seem to support the Strike, or give any suggestion that we sympathised with it, or this action would have meant in all probability the taking over of the service by the Government'.[15] But Reith believed passionately that the BBC must be allowed to remain free to define in its own way how this support was to be expressed. His backing for the Government could not be in question. All he was really saying was that broadcasting was too important to be left to the politicians, especially to Churchill. Unless the BBC retained the confidence of the general public by its responsible handling of the news, 'its pioneer work of three-and-a-half years will have been undermined [and] its influence of almost unlimited potency . . . shaken'.[16]

Davidson and Baldwin both knew that Reith was right; that if the BBC tried to give the impression, as the *British Gazette* had done, that the strike was failing and not report news of the strike fairly, it would do neither the BBC nor the Government any good. So Reith's great fear – that Churchill would take over his job – was for the moment at any rate stilled. With Davidson on Reith's side, Baldwin and Jix probably neutral, and Birkenhead and Chamberlain not strongly behind him, Churchill was alone on the issue, and the controversy lapsed until near the end of the strike, when it blew up in more virulent form.[17] 'Actually, I'm making this a question of trusting the managing director,' the Prime Minister told Reith. 'Is that all right?'[18] Reith believed his independence was now assured. In fact, it meant he would have to obey Baldwin.

Baldwin's radio message, broadcast from Reith's study, was a variation on his theme 'The Constitution is in danger. Return to work and trust me.' As Reith announced him, Baldwin struck a match to light his pipe right in front of the microphone, setting the mood of informality.[19] He expressed sympathy with the miners, but said that a General Strike was not the way to win what they wanted. 'The Government is not fighting to lower the standard of living of the miners or any other section of the workers,' he declared in an attempt to undo the damage caused by his notorious indiscretion after Red Friday. 'That suggestion is being spread abroad. It is not true.'[20] His peroration, which Reith helped him draft, has become famous, and was the subject of furious denunciation after the strike had failed. 'I am a man of peace,' he told his audience. 'I am longing and working and praying for peace. But I will not surrender the safety and security of the British Constitution. You placed me in power eighteen months ago by the largest majority accorded to any Party for many, many years. Have I done anything to forfeit that confidence? Cannot you trust me to ensure a square deal to secure even justice between man and man?'[21] These words made a profound impression. But listeners did not know that the passage about 'the safety and security of the British Constitution' was not Baldwin's but Reith's. The managing director had substituted them during the actual course of the broadcast for the phrase 'dignity of the British Constitution', which Reith felt sounded pompous and stuffy.[22]

As he left Reith's home after the broadcast, the Prime Minister remarked that he was worried about the general situation, and that his anxieties were not lessened by the action of some of his colleagues – an obvious thrust at Churchill.[23] But it was now clear that Government control of radio, and Baldwin's skill as a broadcaster, was helping them to win the propaganda war. At first, the general council of the TUC had warned its members to ignore the BBC. But as the strike progressed it became clear that strikers were listening to news bulletins as avidly as non-strikers, and relying on them just as much. 'The sensation of the General Strike,' wrote Beatrice Webb, 'centres round the headphones of the wireless set.'[24] Yet the impact of broadcasting has perhaps been exaggerated. After all, there were less than 2 million licence-holders out of a total population of about 43 million. Estimates that perhaps a quarter of the population listened this way would seem optimistic. Moreover, the BBC's news-gathering organisation was certainly not infallible, and relied greatly on what it was told. Inaccurate reports of returns to work were frequently broadcast. Thus on 7 May the BBC reported that railway footplatemen at Oxford had gone back, that the strike had collapsed at Salisbury, that six food ships had been unloaded at Immingham. None of these stories was correct. Local strike bulletins denounced them and the *British*

Worker frequently published corrections. But the BBC never broadcast them.

One of Reith's great fears during the strike was that some of the militants on the TUC side might try to jam BBC broadcasts by 'oscillation', or the use of high frequency signals. But this fear proved groundless. Indeed, engineers actually resorted to over-modulation, which led to complaints after the strike that signals were weaker and explanations from the Chief Engineer as to why stronger signals could not continue after the emergency.[25] The BBC had been declared an essential service. Special transport was organised, extra scrutiny of visitors was provided at the BBC's Savoy Hill headquarters, and the Daventry transmitter in the Midlands, which would have been the target of any sabotage, was protected by a special guard of a dozen plain-clothes policemen.[26] But if the danger of jamming never materialised, the danger of the Government interfering with the independence of the BBC proved much more real. The real test came when Ramsay MacDonald, the leader of the Opposition, and Randall Davidson, the Archbishop of Canterbury, requested permission to broadcast near the end of the strike.

The draft of MacDonald's speech reached Reith on 11 May. It was so moderate in tone that it actually said that the TUC had 'rightly or wrongly' decided to call the strike. Reith was strongly in favour of letting MacDonald broadcast, but Baldwin and Davidson over-ruled him. Davidson warned Reith that if MacDonald broadcast 'it would set Churchill off again' and give his faction in the Cabinet strike committee an excuse to commandeer the BBC, which they were perfectly entitled to do at any time. So MacDonald was not allowed to address the nation, at a time of national emergency. Today, it would be unthinkable that the leader of the Opposition would be forbidden to speak by the Government at such a time. In 1926 it showed the severe limitations of the BBC's independence.

This was made even clearer in a long, acrimonious correspondence which Reith had with MacDonald and another Labour MP, William Graham, which continued after the strike. Graham wrote to Reith on 9 May complaining about the BBC bias and Government interference and asking if the BBC was a free agent. It was 'utterly unfair and certainly undesirable,' Graham argued, 'that no opportunity is given to any representative Labour or Trade Union leader to state the case for the miners and other workers in this crisis.'[28] Reith delayed answering, and in the meantime, after an exchange of letters with Davidson, refused to let MacDonald broadcast. So Graham wrote again, pointing out that

'The Government emphatically deny that they interfered with the British Broadcasting Company in any way. On the other hand the Company states that it was not a free agent. I am sure you will agree it is impossible to make anything of these two statements.'[29] Graham then wrote again, quoting gleefully an editorial which appeared in the *Radio Times*, the BBC's official publication. This explained that although the Government could have legally taken over the BBC, it had refrained because it realised 'that the BBC could be trusted'. But the editorial admitted that 'Complete impartiality during the emergency was, in the circumstances, not to be expected', and defended the refusal to let MacDonald broadcast on the grounds that 'our liberty of action was not complete'.[30]

Reith was clearly flustered, and a stream of internal memoranda followed. Finally, he called in the Labour MP and former Cabinet minister C. P. Trevelyan to try to mediate and resolve the BBC's conflicting defences. 'I *cannot* understand the continued misinterpretation,' Reith told Trevelyan in some anguish.[31] Trevelyan succeeded, Reith admitted MacDonald and Graham had a legitimate grouse, while Graham agreed after talking to Trevelyan that 'not one trace of [ill-] feeling remains' and that 'I certainly appreciate the great difficulty in which you must have been placed'.[32] Reith's tactic of tame acquiescence in Government policy was strengthened by Mr Justice Astbury's judgement on 11 May that the strike was illegal. In Reith's own words this 'somewhat simplified' the BBC's position. If the strike were illegal, 'the BBC, an organisation within the Constitution, is unable to permit anything which is contrary to the spirit of this judgement and therefore might justify or prolong the General Strike'.[33] This might have been true of MacDonald's broadcast, although Reith made it clear that his reason for refusing this was his fear of Government take-over. 'For this reason,' he wrote, 'we refused to allow the Labour leaders to broadcast statements of their side of the case, as the Government was opposed to their being allowed to do so.'[34]

But could the censoring of the Archbishop of Canterbury be justified on the ground that his speech might 'justify or prolong the General Strike'? Hardly, since the whole point of the Archbishop's appeal was to bring the strike to a speedy end. Reith really gave the game away by simply adding his defence in this case to his decision to censor MacDonald. 'Also we refused to broadcast the Archbishop of Canterbury's announcement,' he explained baldly.[35] In fact, the censoring of the Archbishop was even more humiliating for the BBC. The Archbishop was head of the Church of England, established by law as the Church of the realm. After consulting leading figures of his own Church, as well as leading Nonconformists and Jews, Randall Davidson drafted an appeal for negotiations to be resumed. He was a conventional man, as befitted one in his position, but he felt it was his duty in this crisis to end the deadlock. So he drafted an appeal based on the following three steps being taken 'simultaneously' : that the Government resume the subsidy for 'a short but definite period'; that the mineowners withdraw their new pay scales lock-out notices and restore old wage rates; and that the TUC call off the General Strike. The Archbishop submitted a text of his sermon in advance to Reith.

Commenting on the text, Lord Gainford, a Governor of the BBC and a prominent coalowner, told the Archbishop that the point about the TUC calling off the strike should come first rather than last to prevent the TUC claiming that their action had been effective in securing amended terms. Secondly, he felt that the point about the owners withdrawing the new scales was unclear, since in some districts, such as Cannock Chase, the owners had not issued new scales.[36] Thirdly, Lord Gainford felt that the Government should encourage what he called an 'open situation' and that 'if you feel that your intervention tonight could include these points I should feel encouraged. I am leaving it entirely to [Reith] to decide what should be broadcast.'[37] In fact, as Gainford knew, Baldwin had let Reith know quite categorically that such simultaneous steps as Randall Davidson proposed ran quite counter to Government policy and that in no circumstances was the Archbishop's appeal to be broadcast. Apart from anything else, it would give Churchill a perfect chance to overcome Baldwin's resistance and take over the BBC as a Government agency.

Reith thus found himself, 'at the age of 36' to use his own words, caught between Primate and Prime Minister. But he had no hesitation. He told Davidson, 'I am very pleased you are preaching tonight and you will have an enormous audience.' But it would not be as enormous as the Archbishop had hoped. 'In view of the Prime Minister's speech, and what I believe is a position of some delicacy,' Reith concluded, 'the chance of the statement going out this evening is not likely to be realised.'[38] The Archbishop's appeal was never broadcast, though after further exchanges Reith did agree to broadcast a sermon from St Martin-in-the-Fields in which the Archbishop only referred to the Church initiative. Yet even this was not broadcast until three days later, on the eve of the collapse of the General Strike. It spoke vaguely of a 'reasonable' and 'generous' settlement; and on the same day a news bulletin made a brief reference to the Archbishop's earlier appeal. These omissions were all the more glaring because the

BBC gave the fullest publicity to a sermon by Cardinal Bourne, head of the Roman Catholic Church in Britain, in which he told his flock at High Mass in Westminster Cathedral that the General Strike was without moral justification, that it represented a direct challenge to the Government, and that it was everybody's duty to return to work and uphold lawfully constituted authority.[39] The BBC news made this the very first item in its bulletin, quoted the sermon in full and put particular emphasis on Bourne's astonishing statement that the General Strike was 'a sin against the obedience which we owe to God'.

Moreover, it was not until the strike was safely over, on 14 May, that a Labour spokesman, J. H. Thomas, was at last allowed to broadcast – and even then it was simply an appeal from a union leader who was known to be a firm opponent of the strike for his own railwaymen to return to work. When the strike ended, Reith read a special message which the Prime Minister had written at Reith's request calling on the country to forget what had happened, and to look towards the future and build. Blake's *Jerusalem* was then read immediately, followed by an orchestra and choir, and the writer Lillah McCarthy commented that it was 'the most beautiful poetry I have ever heard spoken'. In the false mood of euphoria and national unity which suffused Government supporters at the end of the strike Reith emerged as a kind of hero, a young man who had acted responsibly and yet preserved the precious independence of the BBC. But though this myth persisted it has little basis in reality. As the MacDonald and Randall Davidson episodes reveal, the price of that independence was in fact doing what the Government wanted done. True, Churchill wanted to destroy every vestige of the BBC's independence and suppress all news even remotely favourable to the strikers, just as the *British Gazette* failed to report the Archbishop's appeal. But Churchill did not speak for the Government; as time went on he increasingly spoke only for himself. Middle-of-the-road opinion did not regard Churchill's *Gazette* as wholly reliable. Baldwin and Davidson saw that if they preserved the BBC's appearance of impartiality, it would be much easier for them to get their way on important questions and use it to broadcast Government propaganda. In this they were most successful. Radio was, in Beatrice Webb's phrase, 'the sensation of the General Strike'. Baldwin was able to put his own case without opposition and give listeners the illusion that they were being told 'what was really happening'.[40] It was no wonder he sent Reith a warm tribute when it was over.

Even Churchill came to see this before the end. He and Reith had a useful argument which helped clear the air, and Reith wished they had

had a proper set-to at the start of the strike. 'He came to the car [and said]
. . . he had heard I had been badly wounded in the war. "In the head
wasn't it?" he asked. I said yes, but that my present attitude was not trace-
able thereto.'[41] An even more striking demonstration of the severe limits
of the BBC's independence was the controversy aroused by the Company's
broadcast editorials. Editorial comment had first been tried as early as
April and September 1923, but there had 'been some trouble' and the
experiment had been discontinued. Newspapers were, of course, jealous
of their monopoly of editorial comment, and the *Morning Post*, for
example, had asserted that the 'expression of anonymous and irresponsible
opinions should be prohibited'.[42] The virtual cessation of newspaper
production at the start of the strike encouraged the BBC to resume its
editorials, but they were at first strictly non-controversial. Hints on
transport arrangements, how to behave, how to get about and how to
keep calm had a 'soothing effect on the nation's nerves'.[43] But when the
coal strike dragged on after the collapse of the General Strike the
editorials 'began to deal with more serious matters and approach
dangerously near controversial ground'.[44] They were now mostly being
written by Lance Sieveking, a young man who later made a brilliant
reputation directing radio drama. Davidson and the Prime Minister
believed both miners and owners were being equally unreasonable in the
coal dispute, and that 'the BBC might do some good by preaching the
doctrine of cooperation'.[45]

But they had not been prepared for Sieveking's notorious editorial of
24 May. This was believed to betray a 'negative attitude' to the mineowners. It supported the creation of a Board to deal with miners' wages
and inland coal prices, and invited the Government to declare immediately
and enthusiastically in favour of such Samuel commission recommendation as pithead baths and family allowances. The newspapers, especially
the *Westminster Gazette*, were once more alarmed at this intrusion into
their territory, especially by such radical opinions. Lord Rothermere's
Evening News denounced 'the jaunty BBC', with its 'light-hearted
explanation of a serious development'.[46] Mitchell-Thompson angrily rang
up to protest. After that, all future editorial broadcasts were sent to him
or his deputy, J. C. C. Davidson, while the next day the Government
informed the Commons that in future the editorials 'would be suppressed
if controversial'.[47] Their title was changed to 'editorial reviews' and then
'reviews' in an effort to placate the newspapers, and their frequency
declined. 'A few were broadcast after the trouble with the Postmaster-
General,' a BBC memorandum reported ineffably, 'but as they had to

be submitted to him, they had a way of piling up in his wastepaper basket and not getting returned, and eventually they faded away altogether.' The last editorial – about fuel oil – was broadcast on 7 June. But they were important forerunners of such influential talks as J. B. Priestley's *Postscripts*, which, broadcast after the nine o'clock news during the Second World War, became a national institution.

Reith undoubtedly benefited personally from events in 1926. Later that year he reluctantly accepted a knighthood, and in 1927 the Government granted the BBC its charter and made Reith first director-general.[48] This was a position of enormous influence for a man 'at the age of 36' to occupy during the formative years of broadcasting, and Reith used it to leave a characteristic and indelible mark on British radio. But the pattern had already been set in 1926. Compared to what happened to radio broadcasting in other countries, such as Australia and the United States, where commercial interests were allowed to dominate from the start, Reith created a system of which Britain could be proud. But although the BBC was arguably the best such organisation in the world it still tended to give the illusion rather than the reality of an objective and impartial approach. Reith's paternalistic and high-minded mission to elevate the level of mass culture revealed itself in his policy towards popular programmes, music and so on. In religion the public was given a careful balance of all denominations, but nothing from the humanist or agnostic viewpoint. Similarly, current affairs and discussion took place within a carefully limited and controlled context. What those announcers in their dinner jackets, black ties and impeccable 'BBC accents' really gave the audience was 'the official news'. Nothing really controversial or abrasive was allowed to intrude, and this tradition was strengthened by the propaganda role which the BBC played during the Second World War after Reith had resigned.[49] Though this tradition was dented during the Suez Crisis of 1956, it was not until the 1960s that it was finally destroyed and replaced for a time by a more open and controversial approach. It was one of the long-term, indirect legacies of the General Strike which has received little attention.

Chapter Twenty-three

King and Country

By the weekend it was clear to the Government, the TUC and the nation as a whole that the General Strike had been far more successful than anyone had really expected. The response had been overwhelming, and the solidarity of the strikers remarkable. There had been some rioting and a few thousand arrests, but nothing approaching a serious breakdown of law and order in the country as a whole. Faced with this situation the Government were forced to consider tougher methods to end the strike. The leaders of the TUC, aware that the Government might introduce more extreme measures and fearful that the situation might then get out of hand, began to make serious preparations for ending the strike as soon as possible. For all its undoubted success, it was clear that the strike had not brought the nation to a standstill or the Government to its knees, and was not likely to do so for a long time. By then the unity of labour might have crumbled, extremists on both sides might have taken control, and lives have been lost. The real problem for the TUC was how to get the miners to agree to any settlement which might include a reduction of wages.

Throughout the strike King George V observed events closely and anxiously, while playing a moderating role. Indeed, he emerged from the crisis with great credit. An old-style conservative, with the manners of a landed aristocrat, he knew nothing of the life of ordinary people at first hand. Yet he regarded himself as an 'ordinary little man' and understood that the strikers were his subjects to whom he owed an obligation. He had earlier faced major Constitutional crises over the Parliament Act in 1910–11 and the Home Rule Crisis of 1914. He had expressed real hostility to strikes and strikers during the years of labour unrest before the war. But dealing in 1926 with a crisis as grave as any he had experienced before he revealed some sympathy and astute political judgement. Though a few left-wing critics put it about that the King was more concerned with the fate of the pit ponies than he was with the sufferings of the pitmen, the strikers in reality had much to thank him for during the emergency. As one Cabinet member put it, 'Throughout the dispute the great influence of George V was exercised on the side of peace and conciliation.'[1]

Before the strike started, the Cabinet had discussed possible ways of dealing with the situation. In a record of Cabinet discussions sent only to the King and not circulated to Cabinet members after the meeting, the minutes reveal that 'Suggestions were made that in the event of a General Strike legislation should at once be introduced either to make a secret ballot necessary and/or that in the event of a sympathetic General Strike, as now contemplated, legislation should be introduced to remove the immunity of strike funds in such cases and make picketing illegal.'[2] This gave the King an early indication of the drift of Government thinking, and he did not like what he saw. By the second week of the strike, with no return to work apparently in sight, Baldwin decided to act. He arranged for a question to be put down in the House on Tuesday 11 May, asking 'Does the Government intend to deal with the position of the trades unions?'

Baldwin's answer was that 'The Government are not now contemplating any modification in existing trades union legislation, but they are considering the desirability of making clear what they believe to be now the law, namely that a General Strike is illegal.'[3] Baldwin's answer was less than frank. The Cabinet had in fact drawn up a 'most secret' draft Illegal Strikes Bill 1926, which Baldwin had wanted to introduce while the strike was still in progress. The Bill made it an indictable offence to use trade union funds in a strike 'which is intended to intimidate or coerce the Government or the community'.[4] While the Bill was being rushed through Parliament, the Government planned to introduce an order-in-council under the Emergency Regulations forbidding banks to pay out strike pay to unions conducting the General Strike. The draft of this provocative measure was marked 'to be kept under lock and key'.[5] Despite this, it proved to be one of the most open Cabinet secrets of all time, and, after Tom Jones had done some discreet lobbying, the King's criticism that the Bill was 'a grave mistake' and obviously the work of Baldwin's 'hot-headed colleagues' which would have 'disastrous effects' on the strikers, persuaded the Government quietly to drop it.[6]

The whole question of the legality of the General Strike was one which preoccupied the Government. Though it denounced the strike as an attack on the Constitution, the Government was unable to identify precisely why the TUC's action was a breach of the law. This was left to the Liberal MP, Sir John Simon, and a High Court judge, Mr Justice Astbury. Simon, a former Liberal Attorney-General, was an austere but ambitious politician who saw the strike as an opportunity to claim the Liberal Party leadership. Asquith, who had never really recovered from the blow of 1916, was now in physical and mental decline. Though he condemned the strike, his words carried little weight. Lloyd George, though in eclipse, still had hopes of recovery. He had played the Tory card as leader of the Coalition. Now he was trying to play the Socialist card, putting out feelers to moderate Labour leaders such as Snowden and MacDonald. He offered the Labour Party both his moral support and the assistance of his own large personal political fund if they could come to agreement over policy.[7]

Against this background Lloyd George, who had taunted Baldwin for backing down on Red Friday in 1925, now expressed sympathy with the strikers. Simon, on the other hand, grasping for the Liberal leadership, delivered the most resounding condemnation of the strike. It was, Simon contended, 'an utterly illegal proceeding' directed against the State and not against any employers. The strikers were therefore not protected by the Trade Disputes Act of 1906. Every railwayman on strike was in breach of contract and every trade union leader was 'liable in damages to the uttermost farthing of his personal possessions'.[8] Simon's speech received wide publicity and was not effectively rebuffed by the Labour Party in the House. The following Tuesday it received authoritative backing from the High Court in Mr Justice Astbury's judgement in a case involving the seamen's union.

This union, led by the maverick Havelock Wilson, was one of the few which had voted against the strike at vesting day. When some branch officials had called out members in defiance of the union decision, Wilson had sought an injunction restraining them. Mr Justice Astbury could have decided the case on the narrow grounds that the branch officials were clearly acting in defiance of the union's decision. Instead, he decided to rule on the legality of the General Strike. In his judgement he supported Simon's view that the strike was illegal because no trade dispute existed anywhere except between the miners and the mineowners and that the orders of the TUC were therefore illegal.[9]

The views of Simon and Astbury were thought to have rattled moderate opinion at the TUC and in the labour movement throughout the country, although there is little evidence that they did. The effect on uncommitted public opinion, taken in conjunction with Baldwin's effective radio broadcasts, was probably more serious. Whatever their immediate impact, the opinions were shot to pieces afterwards by legal authorities, notably A. L. Goodhart, who argued that sympathetic strikes were protected by the law and that to prove that the TUC was acting against the State it must be proved that its leaders were guilty of treason, felony, seditious conspiracy or seditious libel, or criminal conspiracy, which was 'obviously idiotic'.[10]

With the legality of the General Strike thus questioned, the Government felt bound to consider new methods of handling the emergency. Churchill's announcement that any action taken by the armed forces would receive full Government backing looked likely to lead to a 'pogrom' against the strikers. The King denounced Churchill, but the announcement undoubtedly influenced public opinion. In a message to all trade unionists, apparently issued with the authority of the TUC general council on 12 May, Islington trade council announced, 'The Government has threatened the arrest of the general council of the TUC. The council desire it to be known that in any event they have made all arrangements for carrying on until a successful conclusion has been reached.'[11] Rumours to this effect were widespread, although Hamilton Fyfe, the editor of the *British Worker*, discounted them, and there is no evidence that the Government thought seriously about arrests.[12]

On the other hand, Hamilton Fyfe also discounted rumours that the Government was planning to prevent payment of strike pay, and these rumours were undoubtedly true. The Government also took action to stop the transfer of funds from trade unions abroad which were being sent to support the strike. Under the Emergency Powers the Government argued that where money was transmitted to Britain from abroad 'for any purpose prejudicial to the public safety or the life of the community' the secretary of state could 'prohibit the Bank from paying any such monies'.[13] The Government was particularly angered by the approval which the Soviet Government gave to money sent to the British miners by the Russian Council of Trades Unions. Birkenhead and Churchill wanted to break off diplomatic relations with the Russians and stop the money, but the King was much more moderate. He drew a clear distinction between money sent to aid the General Strike, 'to which we could unquestionably take exception', and that sent to the miners. 'It would be disastrous,' the King concluded, 'if the Government's action could in any way justify a cry from the Socialist Party that the former were attempting to stop financial aid from Russia or from any other country to save the miners' women and children from starvation.'[14]

In fact, the Labour Party was remarkably inactive during the strike. Indeed, Parliament as a whole played little or no part in solving the crisis. The strike sharpened existing tensions within the Liberal Party and accelerated the fall of Asquith from leadership.[15] It strengthened the hand of those in the Conservative Party who had long wished to toughen the law on trade unions and weaken the link between the unions and the Labour Party. But the strike embarrassed the leadership of the Labour Party. They deplored it and tried to dissociate themselves from it as much as possible. They did not try to blame Baldwin's Government for the part it played in precipitating the crisis, though the Government's record was very vulnerable. Instead, the party contented itself with somewhat futile attempts to assist a negotiated settlement. MacDonald, Snowden, Henderson, Thomas and Clynes were in daily contact with Conservative leaders, and though the talks were unproductive they were enough to raise suspicions on the union side. When MacDonald claimed he had been 'in hourly conference' with the Government 'regarding a settlement of the strike', and the *Manchester Guardian Bulletin* reported 'It is understood that Mr Baldwin and Mr Thomas are again in formal conversation with a view to seeing whether some understanding can be reached without delay',[16] the *British Worker* issued a categorical denial and the general council of the TUC sent MacDonald a sharp rebuke.[17]

As the strike continued, pressure mounted from uncommitted opinion for some kind of negotiated settlement. Letters and telegrams from local councils, academics like A. D. Lindsay, the Master of Balliol, and above all from Church leaders poured into the Cabinet and the TUC urging peace. The pressure from Churches was particularly marked. All denominations were represented, but the attitude of the Church of England was probably the most effective, given its established position under the law. The Archbishop of Canterbury was a conservative-minded man. But he felt the miners had been harshly treated and expressed sympathy with the strikers. A priest from a Warwickshire mining area said, 'I am all with anyone who will fight for the maintenance of the miners' wages. . . . They simply cannot live on less. They feel – and I fully agree with them – that much of the subsidy was grabbed. They see the wasteful luxury of some of the owners.'[18] Baldwin had managed to prevent the Archbishop of Canterbury from broadcasting his appeal for peace along lines similar to the Samuel memorandum. Not surprisingly, though, a Government which had suppressed Randall Davidson gave full publicity to Cardinal Bourne.

Chapter Twenty-four

Surrender

Archbishop Davidson and all those who had been pressing the case for a negotiated settlement never had any really serious chance of success. Their efforts were unlikely to succeed because the Government was not interested in a negotiated settlement. Unconditional surrender were the only terms they could accept from the TUC. Churchill was not making such belligerent points at the end of the strike as he was at the start, and the *British Gazette* was admitting that the strike was not really a revolutionary threat. But the Government had clearly exploited the Constitutional issue fully from the start while Baldwin's monopoly of the broadcasting medium seemed to have rallied an important section of public opinion behind the Government. However, Baldwin was also afraid that Davidson's campaign might lead to a shift in public attitudes, or a change in opinion among the better informed sections of the community, which could upset his policy. It was this fear which explains his determination to suppress the Archbishop's broadcast appeal for peace.

For its part, the TUC was fearful that if the strike continued much longer there might be a danger of violence and bloodshed and of the leadership of the strike at the local level falling into the hands of left-wing extremists. Many informed people and much of the general public not involved directly in the strike now believed that the General Strike represented such a challenge, and the general council of the TUC recognised this. The problem was really how to call the strike off without complete loss of face. Any terms which did not look like complete capitulation would do. The object must be to try to win concessions from the Government which the owners would accept and which the miners would not feel amounted to the betrayal they felt they had suffered in 1921.

Once again, Sir Herbert Samuel was called in to act as honest broker, as he had acted in 1925. His entry was dramatic. Like Geoffrey Dawson, the editor of *The Times*, Samuel was in Italy when the strike began. He was working on a book about philosophy which he had had to abandon when he agreed to act as chairman of the royal commission in 1925. He called Baldwin, offering his services, when the strike started. The Prime Minister rejected the offer, but Samuel came home anyway, disembarking at Dover on 6 May. A telegram to Sir William Mitchell-Thompson, the Postmaster-General and Civil Service Special Commissioner who was head of the Government machine for defeating the strike proved more fruitful than his telephone call to Baldwin, for Mitchell-Thompson arranged for a car to meet him at the quayside. The car was driven by the world champion racing driver Major Henry Segrave. Samuel reached London within the hour and started work.

His first approach was to his former colleagues on the royal commission, Sir William Beveridge, Sir Herbert Lawrence and Kenneth Lee. They were unenthusiastic about Samuel trying to bring the three sides together. Jimmy Thomas was much more agreeable, and arranged to put Samuel in touch with the TUC negotiating committee, whose members, especially Bevin, were anxious to get meaningful talks started. When word of this reached the Cabinet, Steel-Maitland wrote to emphasise that the Government 'would never try to procure the end of the strike by a process of bargaining' and that the strike notices must be unconditionally withdrawn first. 'The Government are bound most carefully and sympathetically to consider the terms of any arrangement which a public man of your responsibility and experience may propose,' Steel-Maitland continued, 'but it is imperative to make plain that any discussion which you think it proper to initiate is not clothed in even a vestige of official character.'[1] A Government committee, consisting of Baldwin, Lane-Fox and Steel-Maitland himself met Samuel and emphasised this point. It was a position which enabled them to enjoy the best of both worlds. The Government remained completely uncommitted, but could be sure of receiving a steady stream of information about the TUC's thinking through informal contacts with Samuel. Suggestions Samuel made to the TUC, on the other hand, lacked any authority.

Samuel's discussions with the TUC took place over the weekend in secrecy. Their meeting-place was a house in Bryanston Square owned by Sir Abe Bailey, a South African mining millionaire and friend of Thomas. The furnishings were ornate, with many valuable paintings. The absence of any miners' representatives made the talks insubstantial. Any agreement reached would not be worth the paper it was written on unless it was firmly endorsed by Smith and Cook. When these two leaders learned of the talks on Saturday, 8 May, they were suspicious and demanded to know what was going on at Bryanston Square. Once again, the full implications of vesting day seemed to have been lost on them. Bromley, secretary of the train driver's union and a member of the general council, tried to clarify them. 'We are all in this now, and I want to say to the miners in a brotherly, comradely way, but straight – but *straight* – that this is not a miners' fight now. I am willing to fight along with them and to suffer the consequences, but I am not going to be strangled by my friends.'[2]

Smith replied that if Bromley wanted to return to work he was free to go, but made no secret of the contempt he had for supporters who would cry off like that. What the exchange revealed was that once the miners had agreed to hand over all responsibility for conducting the strike to the TUC they would be no stronger than the weakest link in the TUC's armour. And there was no doubt that the railway unions were the weakest link. Bromley's locomen had a great deal to lose, in terms of seniority, pension rights and even reinstatement. The railway companies were already making it clear that unless the employees returned to work at once they might find themselves sacked or punished by loss of seniority and pensions.[3] The endemic divisions between the footplatemen, railway clerks and other grades meant that, faced with this kind of pressure, their unity was likely to crack at any time. This is a point which other historians seem to have missed. It was true that there was no mass return to work on the railways before the strike ended. But there was a real danger of such a return which responsible union leaders like Bromley could not afford to ignore. When the railwaymen did go back after the TUC had called off the General Strike they found they had to sign humiliating admissions of guilt and accept worse terms.[4] They were more vulnerable than the miners in many ways, and when the General Strike failed, many railwaymen lost valuable benefits, such as seniority and pension rights, and even their jobs in some cases.[5]

Now they had learned of the talks the TUC was having with Samuel, the miners' executive decided to have nothing to do with them until some more explicit proposals emerged. But Samuel's proposals were couched in terms which the miners were bound to reject. First Samuel asked the TUC negotiating committee if the miners would be prepared to accept wage cuts if talks were resumed between Government, owners and miners. The TUC assured him that they would – providing the Samuel commission's proposals for reorganising the industry were begun immediately and with the prospect that they would be effective. This had been the crucial point since the Samuel commission reported. But there was really no basis for the belief that the miners themselves would be willing to accept pay cuts in any circumstances. An even more serious objection was the question of how reorganisation was to be financed, given the attitude of the owners and the Treasury towards capital expenditure.

However, the conference felt that these problems were not insoluble and turned to a discussion of more detailed proposals, including the Mines National Wages Board, which was to be made up of miners, owners and neutral members with an independent chairman. The Wages Board would draw up new and simplified pay scales, guarantee the wages of the lower-paid men and fix 'reasonable figures, below which the wages of no class of labour should be reduced in any circumstances'.[6] There was nothing new or surprising in any of this, except possibly for the recommendation that any downward revision of pay scales would last for one year, during which time reorganisation would be made effective. As Samuel himself explained, 'All the proposals were within the framework of the Commission's recommendations.' Indeed, they were no more than a re-statement of the proposals on which the three sides had been unable to agree before 3 May.

The miners had not been consulted, but this was still not seen to be necessary. The object of the talks was to try to get the TUC off the hook, and Samuel's intervention might help them to extricate themselves from an already difficult situation which could easily become even more difficult and dangerous. By the end of the weekend both Samuel and the TUC negotiating committee felt they could see signs of a settlement. At the end of the talks Samuel wrote to the TUC general council and the Cabinet proposing that the General Strike be called off forthwith, that reorganisation should start at once, that the TUC agree to a settlement 'generally on the lines of the report as a whole', that the subsidy be continued until the end of the month while details were worked out and that during this period the mines should be reopened on the terms operating before the lock-out of 30 April.[7]

Why did the TUC negotiators not take the miners' executive more fully into their confidence during these talks? Thomas, Pugh and Citrine by then must have known that the miners would not accept any terms which meant wage reductions. Since the TUC's overriding objective by the weekend was to look for some formula which would enable them to end honourably a General Strike they had entered with the utmost reluctance, talking with the intransigent miners would only have made their problems more acute. Others outside the TUC still believed it might be possible to get the miners to agree to wage reductions if some firm assurances were given about reorganisation. Harold Laski believed Herbert Smith 'would consent to 15 per cent off the wages of hewers and 10 per cent off the rest',[8] while Horace Wilson, one of the Government negotiators, told Tom Jones that Smith's view was that 'having had his men out he would be willing to face a wage reduction but would want something firm in the way of reorganisation, as a set off'.[9]

Thomas preferred talking to Establishment figures rather than to the miners' leaders. So he went straight from the TUC's meetings with Herbert Samuel to lunch with Lord Wimborne, a former Lord-Lieutenant of Ireland. Other guests included Lord Londonderry and Lord Gainford, two important coalowners, Lord Reading, a former Liberal Attorney-General, Osbert Sitwell, a writer whose family had large interests in the mining industry, J. A. Spender, the Liberal journalist, and Ethel Snowden, wife of the former Labour Chancellor who was sick himself and unable to attend. The purpose of the lunch was to try to reach terms which all three sides might accept. Reading convinced Thomas that not all Liberals were like Simon, anxious to punish Labour leaders as rebels.[10] Thomas assured everyone that the miners were prepared to accept the Samuel Report as a whole, provided they were given some firm assurances about improvements and reorganisation, and even though this would mean pay cuts. Reading reported this to Tom Jones, who passed it on to Baldwin just before the Prime Minister met his Cabinet at 5.45 on Saturday, 8 May. Baldwin had good reason for knowing that the miners were in no mood to accept pay cuts.[11] All Thomas's assurances did was confirm his belief that the TUC was already looking for a quick way out.

In Cabinet, Birkenhead encouraged Baldwin's interpretation of Thomas's approach, while Churchill was simply scornful of the whole idea. Other sources were suggesting other terms of settlement. Sir Allan Smith, chairman of the engineering employers, wanted 10 per cent cuts pending final arbitration, while Lord Astor, the rich and influential Conservative politician, writer and diplomat, put forward more detailed suggestions, which Baldwin seemed more inclined to treat seriously than Smith's proposals. Astor, who was a close friend of Tom Jones, wanted withdrawal of the lock-out notices, acceptance of the Samuel report as a basis for discussion by all three sides, extension of the subsidy for two weeks while talks continued and acceptance of coal commission arbitration on all the points still outstanding after a fortnight's further discussion. Astor also envisaged further financial assistance from the Government to cushion the blow which would fall hardest on some mining areas when the subsidy ended. Jones argued for this proposal 'with all my might. . . . My policy was to split Ecclestone Square in two with the aid of a gesture from the PM which would help the moderates.' Steel-Maitland was favourable if nervous. 'I rather like it,' he told Jones, 'but I think it is too soon.' The Minister of Labour then left to confer with Horace Wilson, leaving Jones alone with a silent Baldwin.

Jones urged the Prime Minister to 'draw on the last ounce of his personal influence and conviction' in facing 'terrific opposition' at what might be 'the most critical Cabinet of his life'. Part of the 'terrific opposition' appeared later, when Churchill gave Jones 'one of the fiercest and hottest interviews of my life'. The Chancellor, who knew the Treasury would never agree to pay a penny more to the mining industry, erupted in 'a cataract of boiling eloquence impossible to reproduce'. He told Jones, 'We are at war. Matters have changed from Sunday morning. We are a long way from our position then. We must go through with it. You must have nerve.'[12] Jones protested that he had plenty of nerve, but that it was a terrible mistake to regard the general council of the TUC as traitors. 'Pugh and Thomas . . . are as loyal as you are to the State,' Jones pointed out, at which point Churchill retorted, 'Well, I've done my duty by you,' and strode off late to Cabinet.

Meanwhile, Samuel had been busy drafting a memorandum which he believed could be used to provide the basis for a settlement. When he presented it to the TUC on Tuesday, 11 May, the general council found that it incorporated all Samuel's original points about wage cuts, reorganisation, a pay board and a basic minimum. Although no one had yet consulted the miners properly it was clear that both sides were anticipating an early end to the General Strike. Thomas had made a significant speech at a weekend rally in Hammersmith, reiterating his well-known opposition to the idea of a General Strike and his belief that the parties had been on the brink of a settlement when the Government had broken off negotiations after the *Daily Mail* incident. Thomas added that whatever the outcome the nation was bound to suffer as a result of the strike. 'The responsibility is indeed a heavy one,' he concluded. 'But there will be a graver responsibility on whichever sides fail to recognise the moment when an honourable settlement can be arrived at. That moment must be accepted and everyone must work to that end.'

The clear implication of this speech was not lost on the Government, and Thomas's remarks were quoted in successive issues of the *British Gazette*[13] and in BBC radio news bulletins. By now it was clear too that the majority view on the general council had swung behind Thomas's desire to end the strike as soon as possible. Divisions, doubts and uncertainties among member unions were now becoming apparent. The leaders of the railwaymen's unions were worried about the danger of a mass return to work in a few days. Smaller unions had exhausted their strike-pay funds. Workers were worried (as were the Government) about what to do with volunteer workers who had replaced men who were out on strike. More important, the threat of tougher Government measures clearly worried the moderate members of the general council. The King may have repudiated Churchill's notorious 'pogrom' announcement, giving Government backing to anything the military chose to do. The opinions of Simon and Astbury that the strike was illegal may not have rattled experienced union leaders. Doubtless they were even prepared to risk arrest and possible imprisonment under the emergency regulations.

On the other hand, success seemed as dangerous as failure. For what really worried the general council as the strike entered its second week was the possibility that the situation might rapidly lurch out of control. As a show of strength the General Strike had not persuaded the Government to extend the subsidy temporarily or bring pressure on the owners to moderate their terms. Nor had it persuaded the miners that they would have to accept some pay cuts, if only temporarily. At a local level, however, the general council was clearly worried about the reports of friction between strike committees and the Co-ops over the issue of permits, the wider problem of permits and the danger of more widespread outbreaks of violence. The general council, fearful of divisions and a drift back to work, had always been hostile to the idea of a General Strike. Paradoxically, its very success by the second week only strengthened those fears that the TUC might lose control and persuaded them to call it off quickly. The TUC was being inundated with reports during the second week which indicated that support for the strike showed no signs of slacking, that morale was excellent and that strikers were confident of victory. Second-line workers in the steel trades, textile industry and shipbuilding were demanding that they be called out too, and there were few signs of weakness from any of the main regions.[14]

On Tuesday the TUC did call out the second-line unions, as it had planned to do the previous Friday. But by Tuesday it was clear that the general council was already thinking in terms of a speedy return to work. Pugh and Bevin agreed with Thomas: it was too dangerous to let the strike continue much longer. Thomas still took the view 'Never mind what the miners or anybody else says', while Bevin reflected similar views when he remarked, 'I am not concerned with what the miners may think about it. . . . My union came into this business on very definite terms. . . . The dockers will stick out for weeks, and so will the miners, but I don't think it is right to go on asking men to make sacrifices if we can get justice any other way. The other side does not want to fight the matter out to a finish.' Thomas agreed that 'Some of them do, but the businessmen do not' – an obvious reference to the more enlightened employers and coalowners.[15]

The whole problem, however, was, were the miners going to get justice? When the general council met the miners' executive at 8.30 on Tuesday evening, Pugh urged Smith to accept the Samuel memorandum as the basis for a return to work. Smith asked if it might be amended, and Pugh snapped back, 'No. You must take it or leave it.' Smith was worried about the danger of victimisation if they went back on those terms, and Cook asked what guarantee the miners had that reorganisation would begin quickly and that miners' pay would be quickly restored. Of course, there were no guarantees, and Thomas was reduced to pleading, 'You may not trust my word. But will you not take the word of a British gentleman who has been Governor of Palestine?'[16] Even this was really beside the point. The miners had been caught before. They could remember Bonar Law's promise to carry out 'the spirit and the letter' of the Sankey proposals in 1919. Neither Samuel's word nor Thomas's word was what really counted. Baldwin's word alone would be decisive. If the strike were called off, would the owners withdraw their lock-out notices and allow the colliers to resume work at the old rates and hours on the basis of the Samuel memorandum?

When the full general council of the TUC met its negotiating committee this was the decisive question. It was asked categorically three times, Bevin later testified, 'and in each instance the answer was "Yes". . . . We took their word. . . . The Prime Minister was actually waiting in Downing Street to know whether we accepted the document or not. . . . I felt, in view of the heated nature of the miners that night, that we should see them next morning and really try to get a united body. Nevertheless, I was under no qualms about calling off the strike on the assurance received on the Samuel document. . . . I voted for calling off like any other man would have done under similar circumstances.'[17] The diary of Ben Turner, another member of the general council, confirms Bevin's version,[18] while Hamilton Fyfe reported that 'The general council members who are not among the negotiating seven have been anxious to be assured that the terms provide for "simultaneous" calling-off of the strike and withdrawal of lock-out notices. Three times, I hear, this was raised; each time the required answer was forthcoming.'[19]

Once again, as with the *Daily Mail* incident which precipitated the strike, a late-night telephone call played a decisive part at a critical juncture. Sir Patrick Gower, Baldwin's private secretary, rang Citrine at TUC headquarters to say, 'The Prime Minister has been sitting up for you. Do you want to see him this evening?' Citrine explained that the general council was still considering the question and asked Gower to wait. He rang back a few minutes later and arranged for a TUC delegation to meet Baldwin the following day. Bevin was reassured. He believed Gower's phone call meant that Baldwin must know about the Samuel memorandum and was ready to use it as a basis for settlement.[20] But what he did not know was that Thomas had already passed word to Baldwin that 'though he was encountering the most formidable obstacles, he would, he thought, by 2 a.m., be in a position to call off the General Strike'.[21] Thomas and other TUC leaders later hotly denied that they had taken a decision to end the strike before meeting the miners.[22] Citrine argued in defence of the TUC's decision that 'We called the strike off, definitely and finally made up our minds at the general council, about ten minutes before we met Baldwin on Wednesday, 12 May'.[23] But his diary was more realistic. After speaking to Gower on the telephone, Citrine recorded, 'Our fate was decided in those few seconds. Our decision to see the Prime Minister meant plainly calling off the General Strike.'[24]

The only question which remained was would the TUC try to get any conditions? Next morning Bevin saw the miners' executive, who had refused to talk to Thomas again. They had left the TUC before Gower's phone call the night before, bearing 'the unmistakable symptoms of the most profound dejection'. But the strength of their position – indeed its only strength now – was its consistency. They refused to budge in the face of Bevin's appeals for unity. Smith met these appeals with the remark that 'there was more enthusiasm for the General Strike amongst the rank-and-file than there was amongst the general council', and it was the truth of this remark which explains the haste with which the TUC was now moving to end the strike. Before leaving the miners for Downing Street, Bevin reiterated the basis of the agreement he sought. First, the strike was to be called off. Secondly, they had to discuss the resumption of work in an organised manner. And thirdly, arrangements must be made for negotiations on the basis of the Samuel memorandum.[26]

But when the TUC delegation of Pugh, Turner, Swales, Citrine and Bevin met the Cabinet strike committee at 10 Downing Street a few minutes later, Bevin found he had been living in a fool's paradise. Citrine believed Baldwin must have already learned from the news agency wire services that the miners had refused to accept the Samuel terms and that the labour movement was hopelessly split once more. Sir Horace Wilson met them at the door and announced, 'The Prime Minister will not see you before the strike is called off.' Bevin muttered angrily, 'For Christ sake let's call it on again if this is the position,' but Thomas confirmed 'We have come to call the strike off' and the delegation went in and sat down. Flanked by Birkenhead, Neville Chamberlain, Steel-Maitland and Lane-Fox, Baldwin received unconditional surrender from Pugh. 'I thank God for your decision,' the Prime Minister replied with obvious relief.

But Bevin then listened with growing anger and incredulity to the rest of the discussion. Neither Thomas nor Pugh said anything about the Samuel memorandum, the withdrawal of the lock-out notices, the subsidy or miners' pay. Swales, the representative of the Left, said nothing at all, and neither did Turner. Even more serious, from the point of view of the TUC and its member unions, notably the railwaymen, nothing was said about the way in which the strikers would return to work or about protection against victimisation. Thomas deplored the possibility of 'guerilla warfare' by the employers, and assured Baldwin 'We trust your word as Prime Minister'. Baldwin replied in equally vague terms, even when pressed by an astonished Bevin, who was the one member of the delegation to try to get some of the assurances from the Government they had all earlier agreed were essential. Bevin urged the PM to use his authority to insist on general reinstatement of all the strikers and to persuade the mineowners to withdraw their lock-out notices so that 'free and unfettered negotiations' could begin 'very speedily'. Bevin wanted some firm undertaking on these two points 'before we left the building'. Instead he got Baldwin's characteristic mixture of bromide and rebuff. 'You know my record,' he said, recalling his radio statement. And when Bevin requested another meeting soon on 'these two points' Baldwin simply refused, adding, 'Whatever decision I come to, the House of Commons may be the best place in which to say it.'[27]

This was a complete *débâcle*. The delegation had received no assurances whatsoever about any of the points they had been arguing and negotiating about for weeks and months. It took some time for the full implications to sink in across the country as a whole. Indeed, the first reaction of

11a. Strikers in the East End of London stop a van and remove the driver.

11b. Troops in battle order march along the East India Dock Road, London, during the strike.

12a. Armed soldiers on their way to occupy London docks in May 1926.

12b. An army convoy transfers food from the docks to the Hyde Park depot.

Conservatives and strikers throughout the land when the end of the strike was announced was that the TUC must have won a complete victory, or at least some significant concessions. Only later, when the full nature of the TUC's capitulation became clear, could Government supporters express their joy and the strikers their sense of shame and betrayal. But there was little they could do about it.

By the end of the week the return to work was complete. The general council's message, after all, had been 'Stand Firm. Be Loyal to Instructions and Trust Your Leaders.' The same loyalty and solidarity which had brought the strikers out on 3 May sent them back nine days later. There was a good deal of victimisation, especially on the railways and in transport generally. As Bevin put it to Thomas and Pugh as they left 10 Downing Street, 'We have committed suicide. Thousands of members will be victimised as a result of this day's work.'[28]

The damage and demoralisation experienced by the trade union movement as a result of the failure of the General Strike was very serious. Membership dropped by more than 500,000 and funds by a quarter, from £12½ million to £8½ million in the year after 1926, though they later recovered. The search for scapegoats not only wasted time and energy but was a further source of disunion and weakness. But though the TUC and organised labour were severely shaken by the disaster of 1926, the miners suffered more than anyone.

H

Part Five:
Never Again—
Or Never On Our
Knees?

Chapter Twenty-five

The Miners' Defeat

With the collapse of the General Strike on 12 May it was clear that the miners' attempt to use the TUC to put pressure on the Government and force the owners to withdraw the notices had failed ignominiously. The employers and the Government were victorious; morale in the organised labour movement had slumped disastrously. Coal stocks were unprecedentedly high, and the Government had made secret arrangements with Germany, the United States and other countries to import coal. The Emergency Regulations, which Baldwin had withdrawn on 12 May, were reissued again on 29 May and remained in force for the duration of the miners' lock-out.[1] The MFGB was in such a weak position, isolated and alone, that the executive should have accepted the owners' new terms, ended the lock-out and returned to work at once. Black Friday in 1921 had been a grim warning of what could happen when a long mining campaign failed. The union itself had suffered serious dissension. Cook himself had warned then that any strike which lasted longer than three months was doomed.[2]

But now, under Cook's own leadership, the miners stayed out longer than they had in 1921. They did not return to work for nearly seven months. Their courage has often been praised. But their pride and obstinacy was equally apparent. Cook tried to get them to budge, but Smith remained intransigent and the great bulk of the membership would not give an inch. The General Strike had failed. Samuel's new formula for a settlement had been rejected. Neither Government nor owners were willing to make the smallest kind of gesture or concession which might help the MFGB to return to work and still retain some self-respect. The result was disaster. When in November the lash of hunger finally drove the miners back, they had to accept far worse terms than they might have had in May. They returned pit by pit instead of together. They had to work longer hours for less pay. Even worse, district settlements had now replaced national settlement.[3] The miners had lost everything. The MFGB was now penniless and powerless. Moreover, they had inflicted severe damage on the union itself. Unity had collapsed and the old regional rivalries had begun to assert themselves again. During the long dispute many miners, especially in Nottinghamshire, Derbyshire and the East Midlands, had begun drifting back to work and left the MFGB to form their own breakaway Spencer Union, founded by the Nottingham Labour MP George Spencer on the basis of collaboration with the owners.

Why did the miners' lock-out of 1926 last so long? The intransigence of the miners certainly did not encourage them to go back to work. But even more important was the fact that the Government, with the exception of Churchill, seemed uninterested in putting pressure on the mineowners to offer terms which would make an orderly and speedy return to work more likely. The owners were even more unreasonable. It became clear that they were determined not only to drive the miners back on the worst terms possible, but to destroy the MFGB too. In such a situation protracted negotiations led to nothing. Lord Irwin, the Viceroy in India, wrote from Simla urging that the subsidy be extended for five years until the mines were really effectively reorganised, with uneconomic pits closed and displaced men re-employed.[4] No one took this seriously, although Churchill was worried about the cost of the strike to the Exchequer. 'I believe that had we legislated on 1 June,' he wrote to Baldwin, 'to the effect that any mine that can pay the existing rate (or some lesser quite defensible rate) may work 8 hours during (say) a 3-year period of re-organisation we should now be nearer to a break among all the coalfields and to a series of district settlements.' And even if the Chancellor was wrong, how could they be worse off? 'We are relying solely upon economic pressure administered regardless of cost,' he pointed out, 'content to wait from day-to-day and week-to-week in the hopes of the miners' resistance collapsing. But I am bound to point out to you the *terrible* cost to the nation.'[5]

Baldwin remained unperturbed. During the Prime Minister's holiday in France, Churchill took charge of negotiations, and behaved with more moderation than his conduct during the General Strike might have suggested. His apparent willingness to act in a conciliatory manner encouraged the Prime Minister to explain his strategy. 'My desire . . . is to wean the coal industry from the Government,' he wrote from Aix-les-

Bains. 'Any agreement must be between owners and men.' The miners wanted the Government to be party to such an agreement so that they could blame them 'if anything goes wrong' and use Government responsibility as 'a peg for nationalisation and all that the dreams of the wild men stand for'. Any declaration of Government policy, such as help for displaced miners, 'should be a separate understanding'. Finally, and of crucial importance to the Prime Minister, 'No settlement should contain the seeds of any future trouble within measurable distance of the General Election,' which would mean an agreement for five years.[6]

Arthur Steel-Maitland and G. R. Lane-Fox, respectively Minister of Labour and Secretary of the Mines, combined to write a draft in support of Baldwin's position. They blamed the miners for the deadlock, and argued that 'The more the Government try to manufacture a settlement, the more the miners are encouraged to stand firm'. Therefore the best Government policy was inaction. However, longer hours were 'the primary object' and hours could only be increased by Act of Parliament. So the Government should use this leverage to force the owners to make some concessions. They doubted that another inquiry would fix better wage rates in the districts 'which are the crux of the problem'. The memorandum concluded with a full statement of Government wage policy. 'It is the minimum *percentage* of all workers which is the real issue,' the document emphasised, 'not the minimum *wage* of the lowest paid worker. . . . We think there are fatal objections to laying down an Act of Parliament fixing minimum wages. Protection would be given not by prescribing a particular wage but by prescribing the machinery by which the wages should be fixed.' They felt that district conciliation boards would be sufficient to do this. Mineowners would pay a special minimum percentage plus special subsistence rates, which would be determined by these boards or by some outside authority.[7]

As the strike dragged on, the more generous owners began to fall into line with the poorer colliery companies and with Government policy. In July the Yorkshire owners, for example, agreed to cut their wage offer closer to the offers being made in other less profitable districts. This was a decisive step. The Yorkshire coalfield was one of the biggest and most important in the country and the South and West Yorkshire coalowners, led by C. B. Crawshaw and W. Burton Jones, were among the more enlightened employers. By August, reports from Nottinghamshire and Derbyshire indicated a growing desire among miners there to return to work. Conciliatory miners' MPs, such as George Spencer and Frank Varley, were very unpopular with the militants and targets for bitter vituperation from the Communists and others. Despite this, there was a steady drift back to work in Mansfield and other mining areas. The 3,500 men working in the local pits spelt the end of the strike and threatened the very existence of the historic Nottinghamshire Mineworkers Union.[8]

By the end of the month the drift back to work had become steady and irreversible. More important, it was spreading to other districts. Notices posted at many Nottinghamshire collieries offering pre-stoppage rates for a 7½-hour day were quickly copied elsewhere and met an eager response. One-sixth of the 36,000 Nottinghamshire miners signed up on the first day alone, and in the Mansfield area the proportion was as high as two-thirds.[9] In Derbyshire the owners were insisting on an eight-hour day, but 10 per cent of the men were back. Elsewhere the stoppage was reported to be 'crumbling' in Scotland, while in such areas as North Staffordshire, Warwickshire, Worcestershire, Cannock Chase and the Black Country in the Midlands there was 'a steady and general return to work'.[10] Even in such rock-solid regions as South Wales the Home Office was reporting a feeling that the stoppage might collapse in a week or two. While admitting that this was probably too optimistic, the report agreed that a majority of men would return to an eight-hour day at the old rates. This particular Home Office report showed its position clearly. 'In order that the Owners may not only own but also be allowed to *manage* their mines,' it declared, 'the principal leaders of the men must be thoroughly exposed and . . . discredited, so that the men may have an opportunity of returning to work with some prospect of continuing.'[11]

Faced with this disunity, Cook tried to persuade Londonderry, Mond and Samuel to bring pressure to bear on the Government to force a settlement on the owners before the rift in the miners' ranks widened.[12] In September Churchill met Evan Williams and encouraged him and the owners to change their minds about district settlements and make a better offer. 'But two hours' talks with the Association's representatives was profoundly unsatisfactory,' Churchill told W. C. Bridgeman at the Admiralty. 'They were obviously determined to break up the Federation and their arguments against any form of national agreement were clearly disingenuous. I asked them what harm it would do them if all the district agreements when concluded had to be ratified by the Federation and the Association nationally. . . . E. Williams said, "But what good?" I said, "Peace (for 5 years)", but that did not appeal to him.'[13]

Churchill's efforts alarmed other mineowners like Lord Londonderry. 'The situation I fear is not all that encouraging,' Londonderry wrote to the Prime Minister in Aix. 'I saw Winston when I was in London and was hopeful then that a good settlement would be reached. But I feel Winston's meeting with the owners was not altogether fortunate. . . . Winston was naturally endeavouring to persuade the owners to come to a joint conference and his efforts appeared in my judgement to follow the lines of Cook and Smith. . . . Cook's capitulation on his main points was due to his fear that the Federation would break up and nothing else.' Londonderry then argued that the break-up of the MFGB would be no bad thing. 'I am really becoming convinced,' he assured Baldwin, 'that without effective district agreements the coal trade will collapse. The sole function of the Federation is to . . . press forward with nationalisation and the break-up of the system which Conservatives and Liberals believe in. . . . I know Winston has striven strenuously . . . to end the deadlock, but Winston has never been a good doctor. He has all the attributes of the Quack and his training under Lloyd George was disastrous.'[14]

Beaverbrook urged Churchill to resign and 'rally . . . moderate opinion behind him'. But he remained loyal to Baldwin, 'a man of peace,' observed Beaverbrook, 'who worked with Birkenhead over the General Strike, and with Winston over this business, and made them both accessories to a policy of moderation'.[15] Despite this, Churchill went on to meet Cook and MacDonald. As a result of these discussions the MFGB attended a meeting with the Cabinet Coal Committee in London to examine alterations in wages and hours. Birkenhead agreed to participate, despite expressing his 'great personal contempt for Cook and Smith' in a letter to the Prime Minister.[16] The conference achieved nothing. Cook and Smith were angry because the Government had brought in the Eight-Hours Act in flat contradiction to the Samuel Report and then insisted on immediate wage cuts.[17] Smith pointed out that, 'We have said all the Report has asked us to say . . . but we are not prepared to say at once we will give a reduction in wages to help the employers'. Smith concluded belligerently, 'I am going to fight a bit yet. I am nearly sixty-five and there is a bit of fight in the old dog still.'[18]

By the end of September Baldwin had returned and resumed direct conduct of Government negotiations. He told Churchill, 'I wish it had been possible to see a separate Notts Agreement', before resuming talks with the MFGB, 'but I dare say it was impossible to wait.'[19] He offered the miners some faint hope of preserving the principle of national agreements if they would accept lower wages and longer hours. But the MFGB rejected this by a substantial majority – the last point at which a negotiated settlement might have been reached. After that the Government stood aloof while the miners drifted back to work steadily and in ever-

H*

increasing numbers. With the onset of winter there was a distinct danger from the MFGB's point of view that this steady retreat might become a rout. It was already clear that although the stoppage in South Wales, for example, might last another month, the pits there could never open again on a seven-hour basis. Moreover, George Spencer's breakaway union was making serious inroads into MFGB membership in Nottinghamshire and Derbyshire, the main centres of the drift back to work.

The success of the Spencer Union encouraged the mineowners to stick out for even tougher terms in the hope that they would be able to deal the MFGB a crippling blow if the lock-out was allowed to continue. Spencer's ideas about settlement of the present dispute and joint consultation about the general problems of the mining industry were far more acceptable than the militant intransigence of Smith and Cook. Though denounced by the Left as 'class collaboration', the ideas of George Spencer anticipated the lines of the Mond-Turner talks in 1928, which had a substantial influence on long-term TUC thinking. By November the MFGB had clearly had enough and was ready to call off the stoppage. On 5 November a delegation representing the TUC general council called at 10 Downing Street to prepare the way, and later in the day Birkenhead, Churchill, Lane-Fox, Steel-Maitland and Worthington-Evans of the Cabinet coal committee received the MFGB executive's surrender.[20] The lock-out seemed to be over. But this time the owners would not accept the terms. Evan Williams explained their reluctance in a personal letter to the Prime Minister expressing his 'grave alarm' at the Government offer of a national tribunal to the MFGB to prevent minimum wages falling too low. This plan 'to review agreements entered into between free agents', Williams told Baldwin, may have looked like a harmless expedient. But in reality 'it is revolutionary in character'. Moreover, Williams felt that the miners already had 'an excessive share of the prosperity of the industry'.[21]

By the end of November the MFGB had been forced to accept the most humiliating terms, and by December the last of the miners were back at work. District settlements had replaced national ones, the eight-hour day had been imposed by Act of Parliament, and wages had been reduced below the lowest point in 1921. The new standard was to be 1914, and in Scotland the standard was taken back almost forty years to 1888. District boards were to be set up, despite owners' objections, to supervise pay, prices and hours, and in some districts a special subsistence rate was to be paid to the lowest-paid day-wage men until 31 January 1927, when their rates would be fixed by agreement or by the independent chairman of the district board. This agreement was to last four years, and so ensure against Baldwin's great fear that more trouble would break out in the coalfields before the next general election.[22] This was total defeat. The mineowners were in complete control. The numbing effects of this disaster on the miners, the loss of MFGB members to the Spencer Union and company unions elsewhere, and the fact that the large pool of unemployed miners kept wages down to a bare minimum combined to determine the future of the mining industry for nearly twenty years. Despite all the planning, talk and tribunals which had dominated discussions of the mining industry since the war, nothing was done about reorganisation, improvements or efficiency. More important in the wider view, it proved to be merely part of a general pattern of retreat which the whole labour movement was forced to follow for the next fifteen years.

Chapter Twenty-six

Survival Story

How did the miners survive? By the end of July their union strike benefit was exhausted. But in mining areas the whole community was behind the colliers. They sank or swam together, and there was no problem about keeping up appearances. Moreover, although much of the energy of the trade union movement at this time was being wasted in bitter recriminations and the search for scapegoats, the response of the labour movement to the miners' cause was still heartwarming. Trade unions continued to send donations, while local relief funds, flag days, concerts, sports, raffles and other money-raising activities by churches, clubs and firms continued to raise cash, as much as 5s per head in some cases.[1] The Co-operative Societies, which were at the centre of a long and acrimonious dispute arising out of the General Strike, were nevertheless playing an important role in many mining areas. The miners usually had big savings invested with them, and while credit, in the form of food vouchers, was not being granted to anything like the extent that was done in previous strikes, in some cases the Co-ops were distributing 1,500 loaves of bread free each day. In Somerset the Co-op loaned the MFGB £10,000, while their shops continued giving credit.[2]

Levies from trade unions abroad were also important. The miners' struggle had captured the imagination and sympathy of workers in other countries, while the British labour movement continued to lend financial support. The TUC itself had contributed £46,000 by the end of July, the General and Municipal Workers £20,000, the Weavers' Association £10,000. Russia was the largest single source of money, since the Communists were supporting the strike for political reasons, and Soviet trade unions sent £250,000 to the MFGB. Thus in June the Lancashire and

Cheshire Miners' Federation received £22,000 from Moscow, enabling the union to pay benefits of 5s per man and 6d for each child. Other federations had received nearly £30,000 from the MFGB and from local subscriptions. In South Wales, one of the most militant and hardest-hit regions, each miner was being paid 16s to 18s a week through the MFGB, of which the Government estimated that about 8s was money sent by Russian miners.[3] The Cabinet was angry at this continuing support from Russia. Birkenhead, Chamberlain, Churchill and Joynson-Hicks argued that Russian miners were paid starvation wages and lived in grinding poverty, but were forced to support this foreign strike. They believed that the Soviet Communists were simply trying to foster revolution in Britain, and that without their support the miners would have been forced to capitulate weeks before. Attempts to stop the money being transmitted proved unsuccessful, and the episode played an important part in the Government's decision to break off diplomatic relations with Russia in 1927.[4]

Soup kitchens were set up everywhere to feed the wives and children of strikers, and sometimes even the strikers themselves. In South Wales, for example, miners could get three good meals a week for nothing, and six meals if they paid 1s a week. But Poor Law relief was the main standby, the safety-net which prevented them falling into starvation. When the General Strike first started, the Government had instructed the Poor Law Guardians to relieve destitution within the limits prescribed by law irrespective of their own views on the merits of the dispute.[5] The million or more miners on strike were not eligible for Poor Law relief. But they had some three million dependents who were eligible, and the Boards of Guardians were paying £250,000 a week in relief. During the first twelve weeks of the mining strike, while children were still in school, the Guardians were paying an additional £225,000 feeding school children in mining areas. Rates were fixed at 10s to 12s a week for each wife and 2s to 4s a week for each child. The impact of the strike in the mining regions is revealed dramatically in the figures on Poor Law relief. In the Midlands, for example, the Guardians found that in one mining area they were relieving 6,028 people, where they had relieved only 441 in the same week in 1925. In another area the Guardians were paying £7,337 relief instead of £1,111 in the same week the year before, while in a third the figure of £2,148 out-relief compared with £1,401 in the same week of the 1921 mining strike.[6]

The 1926 mining lock-out strained the social security system to snapping-point. The Government estimated that from May until October

1926 there was an increase of 337 per cent in the number of people receiving out-relief. In numerical terms this meant a rise of more than 1·1 million people who lived in areas directly affected by the lock-out, which accounted for 85 per cent of the mining population. Eleven-twelfths of this increase had occurred in seventy-eight areas in which mining was the dominant industry.[7] Of course, for young, unmarried men the strike was not always such a desperate experience. In fact, in retrospect it was often remembered, like the miners' strike of 1921, as an enjoyable period. 'It was the time of my life,' one Yorkshire miner recalled. 'For one thing, I didn't have to get up at bloody 4.30 in the morning every day to go to work!'[8] Enforced leisure could be spent pleasantly in the summer sunshine, there was plenty of opportunity for sports and recreation, and even the chance of some poaching to supplement a striker's somewhat meagre diet in the evenings.[9]

But for the most part the suffering, especially for children and nursing mothers, was often desperate, and worsened as the strike progressed. Children from many mining areas, such as South Wales and the Forest of Dean, were evacuated to stay with sympathetic families in more prosperous places such as London. Poor Law relief was only given after a humiliating Means Test, and often granted as a loan, which had to be repaid. The Guardians had been instructed to relieve destitution within the limits of the law. But some of them took their responsibilities too seriously and exceeded these limits. This was especially true, of course, of those areas where Labour controlled the local politics, and through them the composition of the Boards of Guardians. Indeed, the role of the Labour Party in controlling local government in Durham, South Wales, Yorkshire and other mining regions is now recognised as having been far more important than control of national politics, especially during strikes.[10] By 28 September the Government had received fifty-seven resolutions from local Boards of Guardians asking that emergency relief be made a national, rather than a local, charge. The Guardians were having to borrow money heavily to meet their commitments, and the borrowing limit was raised from £8 million to £15 million. By November, forty-two Boards, mostly in mining areas, had been forced to reduce their scales.

But several defiant Labour councils and Boards used borrowed money to continue to pay relief at rates higher than those laid down by the Ministry of Health.[11] When the General Strike collapsed, these left-wing councils were the first target of Neville Chamberlain, the hawkish Minister of Health. In July, in an attempt to bring the miners to heel, Baldwin's

Government brought in the Boards of Guardians (Default) Act which gave Chamberlain power to dissolve them. By early 1927 the Boards at two mining areas, Chester-le-Street, in Durham, and Bedwellty, in South Wales, had been superseded, along with a third at West Ham in London, which alone owed £2 million.[12] 'No action taken by Britain's rulers in the whole inter-war period implanted more bitterness,' concludes Aneurin Bevan's biographer.[13]

In Bedwellty, for example, the new Government commissioners who replaced the Guardians compelled the poor to live on less than one-third of what it cost to feed, clothe and shelter the inmates of the local workhouses. The average cost of maintaining one pauper in the workhouse was 10s 3½d a week, whereas those on out-relief were expected to survive on a total income of 2s 9d a week. Thus an ex-serviceman who had been out of work for four years with tuberculosis with a wife and two children found that the £1 a week he had been receiving from the Guardians was stopped altogether when the commissioners took over and he had to try to support four people on 12s 6d. His wife was reduced to working as a paper-hanger when she could, though this meant leaving her husband sick in bed at home, and rummaging for coal at the local tips.[14] This story, which could be repeated countless times, was the real measure of the sacrifice the miners and their families had to make in 1926. The loss to the nation was at least £400 million in lost trade.[15] The real loss, in terms of the bitterness which the strike created, is incalculable.

Chapter Twenty-seven

The Reckoning

Chamberlain's Poor Law Act, which created so much bitterness, symbolised the miners' defeat. But the Government used its victory to strike another blow against Labour. This was the 1927 Trade Disputes Act, which made General Strikes illegal and tried to sever the financial link between the trade unions and the Labour Party created by the political levy. Pressure for such measures had been building up for years on the backbenches of the Tory party and in Baldwin's Cabinet. Baldwin had been able to resist this pressure in 1925, when he scotched Macquisten's Bill. But already in October of that year Birkenhead was writing to Lord Reading, a former Liberal Attorney-General, about rising unemployment and hints of further trouble on the railways as well as in the mines, with the comment, 'I am myself of opinion (though many competent to judge do not agree) that we shall have no peace until the matter has been fought out to victory'.[1]

That victory had now been achieved, and Birkenhead concluded, 'In my judgement we shall have to set our teeth as we should have done if six months of war had been necessary, and carry the matter once for all to a conclusion which will involve a complete reconsideration of the exceptional legal status conceded to Trade Unions, and which they seem to me, under the influence of extremist elements, to have grossly abused.'[2]

The chairman of the Conservative Party, Sir George Younger, wrote a vigorously argued and well-informed memorandum to Birkenhead saying that only by ending the political levy would the Tories be able to mobilise their latent support among the working class. 'There are tens of thousands of votes of the men who form everywhere the nucleus of our working-class organisations in the constituencies,' Younger concluded, 'who exercise a very great influence on their fellows and who will be antagonised fatally if the liberty they demand in this matter of the levy be not granted to them.'³ Steel-Maitland had earlier expressed his opposition to Mac-quisten's Bill, but added that if such a measure were passed 'it ought to be watertight'.⁴ The fate of the Draft Illegal Strikes Bill 1926, which the Government had drawn up during the emergency and then been forced to scrap because of pressure from moderates and the King, was clearly very much in the minds of Steel-Maitland, Birkenhead and other Cabinet members who wanted to strike a blow against labour.

In July 1926, for example, the Conservative Party Labour Sub-Committee drew up a report on the labour situation, which suggested the lines on which Government policy should run. 'The General Strike,' the report concluded, 'by throwing into relief the irregularities which are associated with trade union administration today, has given the Conservative Party an opportunity which may never occur again to place the trade unions of this country upon a sound foundation.'⁵ The similarity in the thinking of the Tory Party with the employers was revealed by detailed proposals made by the National Confederation of Employers' Organisations on the reform of trade union law. The employers wanted the legal immunity to action under the law of tort for breach of contract to be repealed.⁶ They also wanted a return to the 1875 definition of picketing, which would have made strikes far less effective, the introduction of compulsory secret ballots of union members before strikes, and the repeal of the 1913 regulations governing the political levy. This had put the onus on union members who did not wish to pay the levy, by making it necessary for them to contract out. The employers, like the Tory Party, wanted to reverse the position, so that union members had to contract in to pay the political levy.⁷

Sir Allan Smith, president of the Engineering and Allied Employers' National Federation, shared these views and a letter from Smith was sent with the Federation's report to the Cabinet Coal Committee.⁸ For the rest of the year the pressure mounted. By September Steel-Maitland had declared himself in favour of a Bill which would ban sympathy strikes, protect workers who refused to strike, make picketing less effective, require unions to register, and reverse the 1913 position on the political levy.⁹ He argued that the proposed secret ballot before strikes would 'not attain the objectives which are generally desired by those who make the suggestion'. Steel-Maitland obviously believed it would help solidify opinion among potential strikers. But there was no doubt in his mind about the importance of the issue – indeed, he regarded it as 'the most important matter before the country'.[10] Robert Cecil, Chancellor of the Duchy of Lancaster and an influential figure among backbenchers, wrote to Baldwin early in 1927 urging that any proposed trade union legislation should restrict itself simply to making a General Strike illegal and controlling picketing 'leading to intimidation'.[11] A letter from Lord Cave in March suggested divisions within the Government over the Bill. Neville Chamberlain wished to ban strikes in the 'public utility trades', Cave himself wished to end trade union immunity to normal legal action for tort, while the Attorney-General, Sir Douglas Hogg, wished to protect the right of a trade unionist *not* to join a strike if he did not wish to do so. The political levy was clearly a problem – 'I do not expect much from this,' Cave wrote – and the question of a secret ballot before strikes was even trickier. Davidson and Baldwin were greatly preoccupied with this question, and spent a good deal of time devising the correct strategy for presenting their policy to the Party Conference.

By March Davidson was becoming convinced of the need to appease Party pressure by bringing in a Bill which would hit at the political levy and the financial link between the unions and the Labour Party.[12] The Tory Party Labour Committee in Crewe, for example, urged that the Act should make General Strikes and all picketing illegal, separate sick and superannuation funds of trade unions from their strike funds, make it compulsory for all trade unions to register as friendly societies, make it compulsory for all trade unions to hold a secret ballot before striking, and reverse the law on the political levy. So in April 1927 the Government introduced the Trade Disputes and Trade Union Act. It banned General Strikes, imposing a maximum sentence of two years' imprisonment for those who participated in them, repealed the political levy clause of the Trade Union Amendment Act of 1913, and contained many of the other proposals which had been discussed in Tory circles in recent months. It reintroduced the common law conception of intimidation in such a way as to make picketing much more difficult, forbade Civil Service and local government workers to join unions which could affiliate with the TUC and made strikes by any local government workers illegal.[13] This was a punitive attack on the Labour Party and the labour movement which led to the angriest debates in Parliament since the Home Rule crisis in 1914.

Indeed, as the Labour leadership reminded the House, the Tories had provided ample precedent for refusing to obey the law during the Home Rule crisis. J. R. Clynes recalled that Birkenhead, who had recently denounced the General Strike as a 'criminal conspiracy against the state' and its leaders as being 'guilty of the greatest crime and treason that has ever been attempted against Parliament',[14] had himself openly encouraged Ulster Protestants to armed resistance in 1914. 'I think his Lordship must have forgotten his own high reputation as a treason-monger,' Clynes concluded.[15] Philip Snowden referred to a speech by Joynson-Hicks on 6 December 1913, when he had declared, 'The people of Ulster have behind them the Unionist Party; behind them is the Lord God of Battle; in His name and in your name I say to the Prime Minister: "Let your armies and batteries fire. Fire if you dare; fire and be damned." '[16] The rhetoric and the rudeness of Labour's opposition was to no avail, and at the end of the session the Trade Disputes Act became law.

The opposition was also in a sense misplaced. Though the Bill had aroused great bitterness in the Labour movement it was a futile measure. It had virtually no effect. The basic clause against sympathetic and political strikes was never invoked in the nineteen years of its existence on the Statute Book. No strike was ever declared illegal. The clause on intimidation was used in a few local strikes, but never with real impact. The defeat of the General Strike and the deepening of the economic depression had forced the unions onto the defensive. Despite the activities of left-wing rank-and-file vigilance movements there were no major strikes in the 1930s which might have tempted the Government to use the law. Even the attack on the political levy, which had looked like a body-blow against the Tory Party's major political opponents, had surprisingly few long-term results. Though the Labour Party's income was cut by more than a third immediately, it gradually recovered as shrewd union secretaries enrolled new members and placed the contracting-in forms among the many that had to be signed.[17] In any case, the Tory attack on the Labour Party's finances looked bad because the Conservatives themselves relied on large, secret gifts from big business, as many voters knew.

The Poor Law and Trade Disputes Act were crude expressions of the failure of the General Strike. Other consequences were more subtle and slow to reveal themselves. By 1928 it was becoming clear that the inroads which the Spencer Union had made on membership of the MFGB were deep and permanent, and that the bitterness which the strike had created among the miners was to last a generation and more. True, the activities of the Spencer Union were largely confined to Nottinghamshire and Derbyshire. But in other areas, notably South Wales, company unionism became a powerful force, hampering efforts to coordinate united action to maintain wages and improve conditions. In the 1930s the struggle against company unionism in the South Wales coalfield took a new turn with the use of the 'stay-down' strike. Miners stayed down the pit at the end of a shift, sometimes joking that the terms they wanted were 'thirty bob a week and live-in'.[18] In addition to the crushing burden of permanent mass unemployment, mining regions were further weakened by conflicts between colliers 'as bitter as anything the coalfields had known in their long ferocious history'.[19] Hopes of creating a truly united national industrial union to secure national agreements with the mineowners had to be shelved. In 1931 A. J. Cook died at the early age of forty-four and was succeeded by Ebby Edwards, a much more pliable man. The Mining Association spoke of the 'excellent relationship' they enjoyed with the MFGB. Not until April 1935, nearly ten years after the disaster of 1926, did the MFGB feel strong enough to put in a wage claim for 'the miners' two bob' – and back it with the threat of a strike. But although there was no major coal stoppage between 1926 and 1939, the story was not one of complete rout. By 1936 the strongholds of company unionism had been recaptured everywhere except in Nottinghamshire, and even here the Spencer Union had virtually ceased to exist by the end of the decade. Moreover, the average cash earnings of pitmen actually rose slightly but steadily throughout the 1930s. Apart from a dip in the depths of the depression from 43s 9d in 1930 to 42s 1d in 1932, they climbed to 44s 6d in 1934, to 50s 6d in 1936 and to 55s 11d in 1938.[20] Yet miners still remained 'the forgotten men' of industry, isolated and, since 1926, increasingly alone.

The failure of the General Strike discredited ideas about revolutionary industrial action. The Communist Party, which had doubled its membership in 1926, lost all its new recruits (many of them miners) by 1927.[21] The failure also led to a renewed interest in political activity and industrial collaboration. The political activity bore fruit with the election of MacDonald's second Labour Government in 1929, when the party actually topped the poll for the first time. The first signs of industrial collaboration had been seen the year before, when Sir Alfred Mond established a joint committee of employers and the TUC to explore means of making industry more efficient. 'We realise,' Mond wrote, 'that industrial reorganisation can only be undertaken with the cooperation of those empowered to speak for organised labour. . . . We believe that the common interests which bind us are more powerful than the apparently divergent interests that separate.'[22] At the first session of the 'Mond-Turner' talks, the industrialist indicated proposed subjects for discussion. They included rationalisation and amalgamation in industry, especially mining; housing, health and unemployment insurance; education and industry; works councils; the security, status, and financial standing of workers; the causes of disputes; and the creation of a permanent standing committee representing both sides of industry to keep an eye on problems and developments.[23]

Mondism was denounced by Cook, the Left in general and the Communists in particular as an example of class collaboration. Nothing came of the talks at the time. But they were a portent for the future. Before he died Cook switched support from James Moxton's Marxism to Sir Oswald Mosley's 1931 proposals, which anticipated many of the new ideas that transformed economic planning in the next generation. The thinking of other Labour leaders was deeply influenced by the Mond-Turner episode. Bevin in particular, who had been made to bear so much of the responsibility for the failure of 1926, took part in the discussions enthusiastically. When the Labour Government won power in 1945, and the labour movement found it position transferred from weakness to strength, Mondism was to play a more important part in TUC thinking.

Chapter Twenty-eight

Conclusion

The Mond-Turner talks raised immediate hopes after 1928 that confrontation might give way to conciliation in industrial affairs. Even Cook, who was so completely identified in the minds of the miners and the general public with the old-style conflict, seemed to be growing more moderate. But such hopes were only to be partially fulfilled in the long term. They were quickly dashed by events in the 1930s. MacDonald's second Labour Government, another minority administration kept in power by Liberal support, collapsed in the financial crisis of 1931. His Coalition with Baldwin discredited political action in the labour movement just as surely as the General Strike had discredited industrial action. Britain was forced to abandon the gold standard and the pound fell to its pre-1925 parity of $3.40 against the dollar. Unemployment, which had reached its peak of nearly 3 million – some 30 per cent of the insured population – in 1931, returned to its normal figure of around 10 per cent of the insured population. It was the end of the attempt to re-establish Britain's pre-war financial hegemony for which the mining industry had paid such a high price. But few of the pits which had been forced to close since 1925 were able to reopen.

Labour had wanted to nationalise the mining industry, but its dependence on Liberal votes between 1929 and 1931 made this impossible. Yet it was able to pass a Coal Mines Act which did something to alleviate the bad working conditions the Sankey commission had condemned twelve years earlier. The deepening depression forced many more of the marginally profitable pits to close. Striking miners were often blamed for damaging pits during disputes. But the owners were not averse to this practice if they felt it would save them money. 'Pits were . . . flooded and abandoned,' wrote the young Labour MP Hugh Dalton, who represented a mining seat, 'because the private coalowners would not cooperate in the comparatively simple job of pumping out the water. So one pit after another . . . was drowned out and the livelihood of the little mining villages was drowned out too . . . seventy million tons of the best coking coal in Britain were submerged.'[1]

The political effects of the 1931 crisis were immediately apparent. At the 1931 general election the anti-Coalition wing of the Labour Party was reduced to a rump of fifty-two MPs.[2] Trade union membership and the strike rate remained low. Militancy revealed itself in rank-and-file activities within trade unions, such as the Vigilance Movements in transport and on the railways. But such movements remained largely isolated and ineffective over the long run, and were mostly dominated by Communists. Not that this need necessarily have been a disadvantage. There was no need for the Communists to argue their case against capitalism. It was being made for them throughout the Western world, while financial and economic structures collapsed and unemployment rocketed throughout Britain and North America as the Great Depression deepened. Indeed, one feature of the 1930s was the extent to which much middle-class opinion, moderate or fearful of Labour in the 1920s, swung to the Left. The novelist, Graham Greene, who had worked on *The Times* in 1926 and enlisted as a special constable, ascribed his changing sympathies to the economic collapse.[3] The hunger-marches of the 1930s, like the Jarrow Crusade, may not have achieved much, but they educated the middle class to the realities of industrial life in a way that the conflicts of the 1920s had failed to do. The rise of Hitler, the mounting threat of war and the emergence of the Popular Front seemed to herald a new, if brittle, unity on the Left which lasted at least until the Moscow trials and purges after 1936 destroyed faith in the Communists.

Yet the dominant theme of the 1930s was not the success of the Popular Front but the overwhelmingly conservative mood of the British people, reaffirmed at the polls in 1935.[4] Despite the hunger-marches, most people in every social class felt they were better off now than they had been before – as indeed they were. The failure of united action in 1926 and the defeat of the miners had benefited the majority. Baldwin's belief about the necessity of wage cuts seemed to have been vindicated. Yet the Labour Party still retained its determination to repeal the hated Trade Disputes Act. MacDonald's attempt to restore the law which the last Liberal Government had enacted in 1913 foundered, ironically, on Liberal opposition – more evidence of that party's shift to the Right. Labour was too weak after 1931 to do anything again until 1939, when Bevin led a TUC delegation to Prime Minister Chamberlain in an attempt to bargain repeal of the Trade Disputes Act in return for trade union cooperation with the rearmament programme.[5]

In 1940 Chamberlain fell and was replaced by a wartime Coalition under Churchill. His Minister of Labour was Bevin, his antagonist in 1926, and Churchill rejected another request that the Act be repealed as a sign of national unity.[6] Nevertheless, as Nazi Germany threatened invasion and Britain mobilised to meet its supreme challenge in 1940, Bevin held a key job He tried to apply the lessons he had learned in a lifetime of industrial negotiations – not least the lesson of conciliation he had found so persuasive during the Mond-Turner discussions. His achievements were substantial. But he is often credited with having reduced, and even virtually stopped, strikes during the war. This is not true. Indeed, industrial relations grew worse during the war than they had been at any time since 1926. The strike rate had fallen sharply after the failure of the General Strike, remained low throughout the 1930s and fell again during the first year of the war. The pre-war average of 1·3 million man-days lost each year declined to just under a million in 1940. But after that the number of man-days lost in industrial disputes rose to just over one million in 1941 and actually surpassed the pre-war figure in 1942. In 1943 1·8 million working days were lost in 1,785 strikes and 1944 set a new record for the total number of stoppages, with 2,194 involving the loss of 3·7 million working days.[7]

Far from creating a sense of national unity, the return of full employment and greater job security during the war actually led to greater militancy and a determination among organised workers to get some of their own back for all the damage that they had suffered in the inter-war years. No one could be sure what sort of world they would be facing when the war ended. Everyone feared a return of the pre-war depression with mass unemployment. So both management and men tended to dig in and fight for every advantage they could get. Though bad labour relations did not help the war effort, they were perhaps an inevitable result of recent labour history. Moreover, they undoubtedly did something to help restore the self-confidence and dignity of the trade union movement, as well as improving the standard of living of the working class. The mood after 1926 may have been 'Never Again' but it always implied 'And Never On Our Knees'.

The rising number of strikes was all the more remarkable because Order 1305 of the wartime emergency powers actually strengthened the

Trade Disputes Act and made all strikes illegal. Mining was the most strike-ridden industry, accounting for two-thirds of the stoppages, and it was mining which illustrated the folly of trying to outlaw strikes. When about a thousand miners at Betteshanger Colliery in Kent struck for higher wages in 1942, three of their union leaders were imprisoned and the rest of the strikers fined up to £3. The leaders were released once the strike had been quickly won. But none of the men paid his fine. There were too many to jail them all, or even bring them to court, while victimisation of a few would simply have brought everyone out on strike again. The law had been brought into contempt, and when hundreds of thousands of miners struck in 1944 no prosecutions could be made.[8]

The notorious Order 1305, like the Trade Disputes Act, remained in force however. Indeed, in 1943 Churchill had stopped postal workers violating the Act by affiliating with the TUC when he threatened their pension rights. In 1945 he rejected another TUC request to amend the law by arguing that the great mass of the Tory Party was opposed to repeal and that the issue would have to be decided at the forthcoming general election.[9] To Churchill's surprise, and that of the nation, Labour won a sweeping landslide victory at the polls in the summer of 1945 which gave them close to a 2-to-1 majority[10] in the Commons and a chance at last to abolish the hated 1927 Act. For all its negligible effects, Labour had never faltered in their opposition. Now, despite a crowded timetable at a time of acute national crisis, the new Government gave repeal high priority. Bevin, who was now Labour's Foreign Secretary, bore the immense burden of making policy abroad in the atomic age. Yet he took time off to set the record straight at last on 1926.

'I propose this afternoon,' he told the House, 'to deal with the historical side of the General Strike. I have been waiting twenty years to do this.' He had not become an MP until 1940 and so had not had a chance to speak in the Commons Debates of 1927. 'They cast the trade unions for the role of enemies of the State,' he continued, emphasising that 'this was not a strike against the state. It was a strike in support of people whose wages were at the lowest possible level . . . and from which certain powers . . . sought, unjustly, to drive them lower . . . [by a] miserable attack on the standard of life of men in a basic industry.'[11] Though the Act had had such little practical effect it was important as a symbol of the defeat and bitterness of 1926. Moreover, it had undoubtedly created a deep sense of injustice among ordinary working men and convinced them that the courts had turned against them. As such it was a token of the humiliation of the defeat of the General Strike.

The General Strike is usually seen as a decisive turning-point in inter-war domestic affairs: as a watershed between the turbulent class-war politics of the immediate post-war period and the relative quiescent acceptance by Labour of mass unemployment in the late 1920s and the 1930s. As Duff Cooper, a young Tory backbencher at the time, put it, 'The air was cleared and from that day to this relations between capital and labour have been happier in Great Britain.'[12] Though the class war may have continued in the coal districts, it faded elsewhere. The General Strike brought into prominence a new generation of leaders, like Bevin and Citrine, who believed in conciliation and compromise rather than conflict, and who were able to follow this policy once the national stoppage and the coal dispute had been settled. On the other hand it has been argued that the General Strike was not in itself a real turning-point at all. Change was coming anyway and the crisis just happened to occur at an appropriate moment.[13]

Certainly the General Strike was an anachronism when it occurred. It was five, or even twenty-five, years too late. It was foiled by the Government's use of radio broadcasting and the motor car, technical developments that were helping to shape the new world. More important in placing it in perspective, the strike shattered the post-1921 calm with a sudden, unexpected and short-lived return to the labour unrest of the previous decade. Clearly 1919 had been the last date at which such a national industrial stoppage might have succeeded. The *Jolly George* incident was misleading. It vindicated the use of industrial action against the possibility of resuming war against Russia, not for industrial purposes. Black Friday marked the decisive turning-point rather than 1926. The collapse of the triple alliance, the defeat of the miners, the success of the employers' offensive in reducing wages, the Irish treaty and the general desire for peace and calm were the factors which shaped the history of the 1920s. Baldwin's policies after 1925 were only possible because 1921 had been a decisive defeat for Labour.

The Left has usually interpreted the events of the 1920s in terms of a class war, with a unified ruling class forcing the Government to back the mineowners against the miners in order to break the power of organised Labour, weaken its links with the Labour Party and stabilise a low-wage, high-unemployment economy. Some historians still accept this;[14] others, while rejecting this picture as too simplistic, have failed to explain the reality in sufficient detail. For the surface appearance of class-war politics is misleading. The really interesting thing about the 1920s is the extent to which so many competing factions, both within what might loosely be called the Establishment and on the side of organised labour, were fighting with each other for control. The financial world, and above all the Treasury, wanted deflation and a return to pre-war parity. Some employers, especially those who sold in the domestic market, favoured this. Those who were competing for export markets believed they were being ruined by this policy. Mining was simply the most dramatic example of this division, which can be traced to the attitudes of owners and miners' leaders too. And on the TUC side there was a struggle for control between the forces of moderation and extremism which lasted until the moderates found themselves reluctantly carrying out the policies of the extremists by leading the General Strike.

In a sense, the same process operated on the other side. Baldwin's policies began as an attempt to balance between factions. Churchill tried to resist the financial world's pressure to go back to gold at the earliest possible moment with the argument that industry would be more content if finance were less proud. His capitulation to Niemeyer, Norman and the orthodox approach was decisive. Not only did the gold standard policy mean forcing wages down. It meant that any hope of using Government money to pay for the essential reorganisation of the mining industry – which Samuel had promised in an attempt to get the miners to accept lower pay – was completely out of the question. Churchill's role is especially instructive. Once he had accepted a return to gold, he fought for it with great enthusiasm, borrowing Niemeyer's arguments against him word for word in his own arguments with Mond and other industrialists who were struggling to save Britain's most important industry from sacrifice on the high altar of orthodox finance. Moreover, though he seemed actively to seek confrontation in 1926 in order to teach Labour a lesson, he became the most conciliatory of Ministers after the General Strike at a time when Baldwin was capitulating to party pressure to pass the Trade Disputes Act.

The failure of the General Strike is primarily the story of divisions within the rising labour movement. But it also casts revealing light on the fatal divisions within the declining Liberal Party. Liberals turn up everywhere in this tale, and on almost every side. Lloyd George, making his first serious attempt to recapture power via a coalition with the right-wing of the Labour Party, backed the TUC and the strike. Asquith condemned it. Simon said it was illegal. Samuel, Beveridge and Lord Reading tried to solve it. Nothing showed more clearly the failure of Liberalism in the 1920s to add up to anything remotely coherent in philosophic or practical terms. And yet the whole episode was really the result of a misguided attempt to return the British economy to the position it had enjoyed during the Golden Age of Liberalism, when the gold standard set the pattern for a world economy in which Britain was pre-eminent.

If the 1920s had been dominated by a desire to return to the good old days before 1914, no such illusion appeared after the Second World War. The reality of Britain's loss of world power may have been masked; but the whole domestic mood of 1945 was positive and forward-looking. The Labour landslide at the polls and the maintenance of full employment in the post-war period enabled the trade union movement and the miners to sustain the gains they had fought for during the war. Though Churchill had refused to repeal the Trade Disputes Act, he conceded that the war had made the unions 'an estate of the realm'. There could be no going back to the old days now. With jobs for everyone, social security as a right, a free health service which at that time was one of the wonders of the world, wider educational opportunities and some of the old class divisions broken down by the war experience, the immediate post-war years saw a peaceful revolution in British life which, while it may have disappointed some of its more enthusiastic supporters, was nevertheless as momentous as anything in recent history.

Repeal of the Trade Disputes Act was the first order of business for the new Government. But another early measure was the nationalisation of the mining industry. These two measures seemed to close a chapter which had begun in 1926. Though a great many pits had been forced to shut, so that there were only about 800 colliery companies in existence in 1946 as opposed to some 1,500 twenty years before, nothing had been done to reorganise the industry in the way the Samuel Report had recommended. Emanuel Shinwell, Minister of Mines in 1924, who became Minister of Fuel and Power in 1945, found there were no detailed proposals for nationalisation, despite the recommendations of 1919 and 1925. Nationalisation in 1947 had great symbolic importance for the miners, who had just created their own truly *National* Union of Mineworkers. Wages were simplified. Conditions slowly improved. Reorganisation and improvements promised for thirty years were begun. But nationalisation did not solve all the miners' grievances, and the industry remained strike-prone throughout the 1950s.

The 1960s saw a dramatic change, however. As Britain finally began to wake up to the reality of its sharply diminished position in the world it also became convinced that coal, once the very symbol of British greatness, no longer counted for much. Oil and atomic energy looked like the providers of power for the future. Miners' wages, which had stood at the top of the industrial table in the 1950s, slipped steadily down as coal lost its competitive edge to cheaper fuels. Recruitment dropped, and despite protests from the NUM hundreds more pits were closed. Coal was just as critical to the economy, but the miners' leaders pursued a supine policy. Suddenly in the 1970s things changed again. Atomic energy was apparently proving a chimera. World oil prices went up by 400 per cent at the time of the 1973 Arab-Israeli October War. For a time experts tried to blame it on short-term political considerations. Then it became clear that the era of cheap oil was over. As the energy crisis began to bite in the 1970s, the nation heeded at last the warnings the NUM had delivered to deaf ears in the 1960s.

If coal was to become more important then the miners were determined to be properly paid again. The strike the NUM called in 1972 was the first national mining strike since the disaster of 1926. Within seven weeks the union had done what the MFGB had failed to do in seven months in 1926 and brought a Conservative Government to its knees, settling a big pay claim in full and promising the miners special consideration in future. This must have brought some satisfaction to older leaders. Moreover, the miners achieved all this without seeming to antagonise large or important sections of public opinion, despite the fact that it was the general public which was hardest hit by that strike. But the outstanding feature of the 1972 miners' strike, as compared with that of 1926, was not so much its success as the way that success was achieved. In the 1920s Britain had been more dependent on coal than it was in the 1970s. Coal was used for gas, electricity and power of all kinds. Every household, every train, burned coal. Yet in the 1920s the nation was twice able to withstand national coal stoppages which lasted for months. Why was this? Part of the answer lies in the timing of the strikes. The disputes of 1921 and 1926 took place in the summer, when there was much less demand for fuel, whereas the victorious strikes of 1972 and 1974 occurred in January and February, the months of heaviest use. More important, the enormous output of the industry in the 1920s certainly helped the Government to build up huge stocks of coal with which to withstand long strikes. Finally, the Government was able to import large tonnages of coal from abroad to break the strike. But what really stands out about the strike of 1972 – illustrating the social changes of nearly fifty years – was the miners' use of the so-called 'flying pickets'. These highly mobile squads of men moved round the country, picketing docks and power stations, to stop coal deliveries in a highly dramatic, controversial but effective way. In 1926 they had lacked this mobility. Instead they had remained sullenly at their pits until starved back to work. The 1972 victory seemed to show that militancy paid. To no one's surprise, the miners struck again in 1974 after a long period of negotiation and industrial action for higher pay. This time they helped precipitate a general election which led to the formation of a minority Labour Government, which immediately settled the dispute on what were substantially the miners' terms. Perhaps these two strikes reopened a story which seemed to have ended in 1926. They certainly showed that the story of the miners, with which this book opened, is still central to an understanding of modern British history.

Notes

Introduction

1. The talks took their name from the principal negotiators for management and labour, Sir Alfred Mond, creator of Imperial Chemical Industries, and Ben Turner, a leader of the wool textile workers who happened to be TUC president in 1928. Actually, Bevin did most of the talking for the TUC.

Chapter 1

1. R. Page Arnot, *A History of the Scottish Miners* (London, 1955), 1–3, and *The Miners,* Vol. 1, (London, 1949), 20–1.
2. *Calendar of Patent Rolls*, 35 Edw. 1. m. 5d, quoted in Ivor Thomas, *Coal in the New Era* (London, 1934), 31. There had been complaints about the use of coal in London and commissions of inquiry in 1285 and 1288.
3. E. J. Hobsbawm, *Industry and Empire* (London, 1968), 16, 30.
4. *Ibid.,* 94. See also A. J. Taylor, 'Labour Productivity and Technological Change in The British Coal Industry, 1850–1914', *Economic History Review*, 2nd series, 24 (1961).
5. Agriculture actually employed more, but was not an industry in quite the same sense. Coal's nearest rival as an employer was the textile industry, which employed half a million men and women.
6. *Report of the Sankey Commission on the Coal Industry* (Cmnd 359, 1919), 1–3.
7. *Minutes of Evidence Buckmaster Inquiry Concerning the Wages Position in the Coal Mining Industry* (Cmnd 2129, 1924), 22.
8. J. W. F. Rowe, *Wages in the Coal Industry* (London, 1923), 14, 17.
9. *Ibid.,* 17–18 and n.
10. *Ibid.,* 20–2.
11. *West Yorkshire Coal Owners Association Minute Book*, No. 3, 31–3, 93, 111. See also Frank Machin, *The Yorkshire Miners* (London, 1958).
12. Rowe, *op. cit.,* 24–6. See also J. E. Williams, *The Derbyshire Miners* (London, 1962), and A. R. Garside, *The Nottinghamshire Miners*, 2 vols (Nottingham, 1955 and 1962).
13. Rowe, *op. cit.,* 26–8.
14. *Ibid.,* 28–9.
15. *Ibid.,* 29–31.
16. H. S. Jevons, *The British Coal Trade* (London, 1913).
17. A. Dalziel, *The Colliers' Strike in South Wales* (1891), 23–4.
18. Rowe, *op. cit.,* 31–2. R. Page Arnot, *South Wales Miners* (London, 1967).
19. A. Cunningham, *Mining in the Kingdom of Fife* (1913).
20. Rowe, *op. cit.,* 32–4. R. Page Arnot, *A History of the Scottish Miners* (London, 1955).

Chapter 2

1. See below, Chapter 9.
2. T. S. Ashton and J. Sykes, *The Coal Industry of the 18th Century* (Manchester, 1929).
3. R. N. Boyd, *Coal Pits and Pitmen* (London, 1892), 74.
4. A. J. Taylor, 'Labour Productivity', *op. cit.,* 59.
5. Quoted in R. Page Arnot, *History of the Scottish Miners, op. cit.,* 92–3.
6. Rowe, *op. cit.,* 34–5.
7. In the Northumberland and Durham coalfields one shift of transit hands worked with two of hewers: the hewers worked seven hours, the transit hands as much as ten. The unions opposed a universal eight-hour day because they feared there would not be enough boys to make up the extra transit shifts and that rising costs could erode sales in the export market. By the same token, the north-eastern unions opposed abolishing sliding scales: export prices could *not* be controlled like prices on the home market. For a full explanation, see Rowe, *op. cit.,* 35, 37, 39, and especially Appendix v, 169.
8. Some unions actually excluded them from membership.
9 J. R. Raynes, *Coal and its Conflicts* (London, 1928), 33–4.
10. Rowe, *op. cit.,* 39–40.

Chapter 3

1. Even as penetrating a mind as Prime Minister Henry Asquith's was baffled by the complexities of wage scales in the coal industry. In 1912 he told a joint meeting of owners and miners, 'I have listened with great interest to the experts of Yorkshire and Northumberland; but the great expert at the other end of the room, Colonel Shaw, said it was all Greek to him, as it was to me.' Perhaps it should be noted that Asquith had been an outstanding classical scholar at Oxford.

2. See G. D. H. Cole, *Labour in the Coal-Mining Industry* (London, 1923), 10–15, and Rowe, *op cit.,* 39–45.
3. Cole, *op. cit.,* 11.
4. For examples of the complexity of post-war wage structure, see below, Chapter 9.
5. Cole, *op. cit.,* 12.
6. Miners tended to be concentrated into one constituency and could thus elect their own MPs without help from other unions or the Liberals. These were known as 'Lib-Labs' because they were Liberal candidates with Labour supporters.
7. Actually, another Labour MP, Richard Bell, a railwayman, was elected in identical circumstances at Derby, but Bell was virtually a Liberal and by 1903 had lapsed from the Labour group.
8. *The British Economy in Figures* (Lloyds Bank, 1969); Page Arnot, *South Wales Miners,* 18, 114.
9. Philip S. Bagwell, *The Railwaymen* (London, 1963), 305–6.
10. W. W. Craik, *Central Labour College* (London, 1967), 79–97; Henry Pelling, *America and the British Left* (London, 1956), 100–4.
11. Craig, *op. cit.,* 172–86.
12. For a revealing article on Abraham, see E. W. Evans, 'Mabon and trade unionism in the South Wales Coalfields', in *Men of No Property,* ed. G. A. Hughes (1971).
13. G. A. Philips, *Economic History Review,* 2nd series, 24 (February 1971), 55–7.
14. The Labour Party had been financed by a political levy taken from union members' subscriptions. The Osborne Judgement made this political levy illegal. The Trade Union Amendment Act restored it, but allowed union members to contract out if they wished. It took an act of will, and often courage, to do so and clearly it was easier to do nothing. The Tories made it necessary to contract in by

the 1927 Trade Disputes Act, which Labour reversed in 1946. See below, Chapter 11.

15. David Marquand, 'Heyday of the Liberals', *The Observer*, 9 January 1972.

Chapter 4

1. Britain lost more people through emigration in the years before the war than during the war itself. Yet losses were proportionately three times as high among junior officers as among soldiers. Death struck at the traditional ruling class; and the resulting loss in numbers and confidence perhaps helps to explain the faltering leadership evident in the inter-war years. A. J. P. Taylor, *English History 1914–1945* (Oxford, 1965), 120.
2. *Ibid.*, 122–3.
3. For a fuller discussion of the collapse of the post-war boom, see below, Chapter 9.
4. Robert Skidelsky, 'Gold Standard and Churchill: the Truth', *The Times*, 17 March 1969. For a fuller discussion of the return to the Gold Standard, see below, Chapter 11.
5. *The British Economy in Figures* (Lloyds Bank, 1969).
6. *Buckmaster Inquiry Minutes of Evidence*, 15. The detailed breakdown of figures for skilled workmen was as follows (1914 figures in brackets): food 49s 10d (27s): sundries 2s 6d (1s 2d): fuel and light 4s 2d (2s 4d): rent 7s 5d (7s 3d): fares 1s 2d (1s): insurance 3s 6d (no change): clothing 13s 9d (7s). Total 82s 4d (49s 3d). Increases for semi-skilled and unskilled workers were higher on the scale indicated above. The trouble, as Professor Pigou remarks, is that 'unfortunately, wage-earners do not buy exactly similar sets of goods at different times'. But Pigou (who incidentally served on the Cunliffe committee on currency and finance

in 1918) reckons the cost of living rose by 72 per cent between 1913 and 1924. A. C. Pigou, *Wage Statistics and Wage Policy* (London, 1949), 8–9.

7. *Buckmaster Inquiry Minutes of Evidence*, 18–19.
8. *Ibid.*, 81.
9. Taylor, *op. cit.*, 5n.
10. As the Conservative Party had begun to call itself after 1886, when Home Rule became the central issue in domestic politics, to emphasise its determination to preserve the traditional Union with Ireland. The party reverted to its customary name when the Union with Ireland ended in 1921.

Chapter 5

1. Harold Nicolson, *King George the Fifth* (London, 1952), 333–4; J. M. McEwan, *Journal of Modern History*, vol. 34, no. 3 (1962), 294–306.
2. Robert Blake, *The Unknown Prime Minister* (London, 1955), 412.
3. J. T. Murphy, *The Political Meaning of the Great Strike* (London, 1926), 24.
4. *The Strikes (Exceptional Measures) Bill*, Cab. paper GT 6998, summarised in Cab 23/15, 57, full text Cab 24/76.
5. *Appendix to War Cabinet 547*, 20 March 1919, Cab 23/15.
6. *War Cabinet 546A, Draft Minutes*, 19 March 1919, Cab 23/15, 53.
7. *Ibid.*, 54
8. *Ibid.*, 56.
9. Robert M. Rayner, *The Story of Trade Unionism* (London, 1929), 190.
10. A. H. Gleason, *What the Workers Want*, 69.
11. Jack Lawson, *The Man in the Cap: the Life of Herbert Smith* (London, 1941), 71.
12. *Ibid.*, 6.
13. *Ibid.*, 138–9.
14. Gleason, *op. cit.*, 69.

15. For details, see Taylor, *op. cit.*, 261n.
16. Rayner, *op. cit.*, 192; G. D. H. Cole, *Labour in the Coal-Mining Industry*, (Oxford, 1923).
17. Quoted in Rayner, *op. cit.*, 192.
18. Cole, *op. cit.*, 77.
19. Hamilton Fyfe, *Behind the Scenes of the Great Strike* (London, 1926), 8. For a full discussion of the problems of the mining industry in the 1920s, see N. K. Buxton, 'Entrepreneurial Efficiency in the British Coal Industry Between the Wars', *Economic History Review*, 2nd Series, 24, No. 3 (December 1970), 476–97. Buxton's argument that, contrary to the findings of Royal Commissions on coal mining, there was no association between the size and the total cost of mining operations is challenged by M. W. Kirby in *Economic History Review*, 2nd Series, 25, No. 4 (November 1972), who argues that Buxton has confused coal *mines* with colliery *companies*. Further articles by W. Johnson, and a rejoinder by Buxton, complete the exchange, *ibid.*, 650–69.
20. Quoted by Fyfe, *op. cit.*, 8–9. Lloyd George's Government considered such plans. See Thomas Jones, *Whitehall Diary*, vol. I (London, 1969), 91, 17 July 1919, edited by Keith Middlemas.
21. Fyfe, *op cit.*, 9.
22. *Coal Industry Commission Reports* Cmnd 359, 1919), vii–ix.
23. *Ibid.*, xxiii.
24. *Ibid.*, 40–1.
25. The owners opposed reorganisation themselves later when they regained control of the mines in 1921. See below, Chapter 7.
26. C. L. Mowat, *Britain Between the Wars 1918–40* (London, 1955), 34.
27. *Hansard*, 18 August 1919.
28. *War Cabinet 596A,* 21 July 1919, Cab 53/3, 134.
29. *Ibid.,* 136.
30. *War Cabinet 596A,* 27 July 1919, Cab 53/15, 137.
31. *Ibid.,* 138.

Chapter 6

1. David Mitchell, *1919 Red Mirage* (London, 1970), is a lively account of the revolutionary spectre haunting Europe. See also R. Page Arnot, *The Impact of the Russian Revolution in Britain* (London, 1967).
2. See Thomas Jones, *Whitehall Diary* (London, 1969), vol. I, 97–103, and *Cabinet Draft Minutes,* Cab 23/25, 4158, 69–71 and 92–3, in which military plans for dealing with a possible insurrection are discussed.
3. *War Cabinet 546A Draft Minutes,* 19 March 1919, Cab 23/15, 53.
4. *Ibid.*, 56.
5. *Ibid.*, 56–7.
6. *Ibid.*, 57.
7. *The Strikes (Exceptional Measures) Bill,* Cab. paper GT 6998, Cab 23/15, 57.
8. Cab. paper GT 6998, Cab 24/76.
9. Jones, *op. cit.*, 100. Food rationing did not end with 1921.
10. *Ibid.*, 99.
11. *Cabinet Draft Minutes,* Cab 23/25, 4158, 70–1.
12. Jones, *op. cit.*, 101.
13. *Cabinet Draft Minutes,* Cab 23/25, 4158, 101.
14. D. E. Baines and R. Bean, 'The General Strike on Merseyside, 1926', in J. R. Harris, ed., *Liverpool and Merseyside: Essays in the Economic History of the Port and its Hinterland* (London, 1969), 244–5, and Mowat, *op. cit.*, 38–9.
15. Mowat, *op. cit.*, 60.
16. Hutt, *op. cit.*, 27.
17. Gregory Blaxland, *J. H. Thomas: A Life for Unity* (London, 1964), 139.
18. Hutt, *op. cit.*, 28.
19. The Chief of the Imperial General Staff, Sir Henry Wilson.
20. General Anton Denekin, a former

Tsarist officer, was one of the anti-Bolshevik leaders in the Russian Civil War.

21. Jones, *op. cit.*, 97, 17 January 1920.

22. *Ibid.*, 98, 18 January 1920.

23. *Ibid.*

24. Mowat, *op. cit.*, 39–40; Page Arnot, *The General Strike* (London, 1926), 4–5. See also below, Chapters 7 and 13.

25. Taking 1914 as 100, their real wages in 1920 stood at 117. Taylor, *op. cit.*, 141 and n.

26. Jack Feaney from Middlesbrough in a tape recording in the possession of Clive Barker, Department of Drama and Theatre Arts, Birmingham University.

27. Thomas's partners in the triple alliance were furious with him because he had accepted the principle of the sliding scale when settling in 1919. Jones, *op. cit.*, 98.

Chapter 7

1. Skidelsky, *op. cit.*

2. *Samuel Report on the Coal Mining Industry* (Cmnd 2600, 1925), 48.

3. Arthur Horner and G. A. Hutt, *Communism and Coal* (London, 1928), 37.

4. A book by the secretary of the Mining Association, W. A. Lee, *Thirty Years in Coal* (London, 1954), is unrevealing. Some of the joint discussions between owners, miners and Government in 1926 shed a few rays of light on the owners' case. Most colliery records were apparently lost after nationalisation in 1947.

5. Baldwin Papers (hereafter BP), D.3, vol. 18, 149–54.

6. *Ibid.*, vol. 15, 137–8, and vol. 13, 466–73.

7. *Ibid.*, vol. 13, 49, vol. 15, 135, and vol. 18, 7–24, esp. 18–19 and 89–91. See also *West Yorkshire Coal Owners Association Minute Books 3–5.*

8. *B.P.*, vol. 18, 89–91.

9. *Ibid.*, vol. 13, 13. K. G. J. C. Knowles, *Strikes: A Study in Industrial Conflict* (Oxford, 1952), 185–209, compares 'strike-rates' in Durham and South Wales.

10. *Minutes of Evidence Buckmaster Inquiry* (Cmnd 2129, 1924), 19–20.

11. *Minutes of Evidence Samuel Commission* (Cmnd 2600, 1926), 61, 76.

12. *Ibid.*, 76.

13. *Ibid.*, 97.

14. Murphy, *op. cit.*, 36, prints a full table of wages on a regional basis from figures published by the MFGB. See also relevant numbers of the *Labour Gazette* and J. W. F. Rowe, *Wages in the Coal Industry* (London, 1923), esp. 98–101.

15. Lawson, *op. cit.*, 148. For the paradoxical sequel—in which Hodges and Smith seemed to have exchanged roles—see below, Chapter 8.

16. J. Parry Jones, *The Other Story of Coal* (London, 1924), 78.

Chapter 8

1. *Cabinet Conclusions 17/21*, 4 April 1921, Cab 23/25, 3.

2. *Ibid.*

3. *Ibid.*, 4.

4. This demand was not satisfied until 1967, although at the end of 1921 Bevin had created the Transport and General Workers Union.

5. Quoted in Walter Citrine, *Men and Work* (London, 1964), 130.

6. *Cabinet Conclusions 18/21*, 13 April 1921, Cab 23/25, 6.

7. *Ibid.*, 7.

8. *Appendix to Cab 19/21*, 16–17.

9. Cab. paper 4158, Cab 23/25, 69.

10. This phrase, which appears in a series of letters between the Prime Minister and the owners and miners, was the nub of an argument in Cabinet between Lloyd George and Edwin Montagu. The PM felt that without it the letters would be too permissive. Jones, *op. cit.*, 140, 142,

and Cab. paper 4158, Cab 23/25, 58–68.

11. Jones, *op. cit.*, 136.
12. *Ibid.*, 134.
13. Cab. paper 4158, Cab 23/25, 69.
14. *Ibid.*, 71.
15. Jones, *op. cit.,* 139. Cf the notorious statement by Baldwin in July 1925, quoted below, Chapter 12.
16. *Ibid.*, 133.
17. *Ibid.*, 136.
18. *Draft Conclusions and Conference of Ministers*, 13 April 1921, Cab 23/25, 118.
19. *Cabinet Conclusions 20/21*, 15 April 1921, 19. Lloyd George remarked that 'Frank Hodges presents his case like a Chancellor of the Exchequer in a most lucid, persuasive and moderate manner'. Jones, *op. cit.*, 177.
20. Frank Hodges, *My Adventures as a Labour Leader* (London, n.d.), 133 (my italics).
21. *Ibid.* (my italics).
22. *Ibid.* No shorthand writer was present, so no one can be certain what was said, an uncertainty which clearly added to the confusion of the next few hours. But there can be little doubt that this is the substance of Hodges' reply. See also his speech at the Miners' Special Conference, 22 April 1921, Cole, *op. cit.,* 211–12, and Bullock, *op cit.,* 171–2.
23. *Ibid.*, 133–4. Bullock argues that Hodges' intentions have never been satisfactorily explained, and that his own explanation to the Miners' Federation Delegate Conference on 22 April 1921 only makes his conduct inexplicable. See Bullock, *op. cit.,* 171–2 and n., and Page Arnot, *The Miners,* 315.
24. Gregory Blaxland, *op. cit.*, 154.
25. Jones, *op. cit.*, 133, 135, 138, 143.
26. Cab. paper 4158, Cab 23/25, 20.
27. *Ibid.*, 23. The reply, repudiating Hodges' proposals, was, of course, signed by Hodges himself as secretary.
28. Blaxland, *op. cit.*, 156.
29. Jones, *op. cit.*, 151.
30. Blaxland, *op. cit.*, 216.
31. Taylor, *op. cit.*, 240 n.
32. Rowe, *op. cit.*, 98–101, Murphy, *op. cit.*, 36, and *Labour Gazette*, March and December 1921.

Chapter 9

1. Mowat, *op. cit.*, 259–83.
2. Taylor, *op. cit.*, 238 and n.
3. Eric Hobsbawm, *Industry and Empire* (London, 1967), 175–6.
4. *Ibid.,* 214. Since 1945 coal exports have never reached 20 million tons a year.
5. Mowat, *op. cit.*, 266, 271.
6. Ivor Thomas, *Coal in the New Era* (London, 1934), 32–3.
7. Murphy, *op. cit.*, 36, Rowe, *op. cit.*, 98–101, and the *Labour Gazette*, March 1921 and December 1925.
8. *Labour Gazette*, March 1921 and December 1925.
9. *Buckmaster Inquiry Minutes of Evidence* (MFGB, 1924), 12–13, and *Buckmaster Inquiry Report* (Cmnd 2129, 1924), 10–16 and appendix. W. R. Garside, *The Durham Miners, 1919–1960* (London, 1971), and J. E. Williams, *The Derbyshire Miners* (London, 1962), provide much detailed evidence on wages.
10. *Buckmaster Inquiry Minutes of Evidence,* 125–6. For evidence of mining royalties and profits see 19–20, 22, 61, 76, and *Sankey Commission Evidence*, 607, 618, 625, 648, 653.
11. W. B. Reddaway, 'Was $4.86 Inevitable in 1925?', *Lloyds Bank Review* (April 1970), 19 (my italics).
12. A. C. Pigou, *Wage Statistics and Prices* (London, 1949), 9. Taking the purchasing power of the pound as 20s in 1920, it had risen to 31s 11d by 1938 – a rise of more than 50 per cent and the only rise this

century. *The British Economy in Figures* (Lloyds Bank, 1970).

13. Taylor, *op. cit.*, 176–7 and n.

14. A. L. Bowley and J. Stamp, *The National Income, 1924* (Oxford, 1927), and review in *Industrial Review* (April 1927), 6–7.

15. *Industrial Review* (April 1927), 7.

16. Ian Bradley, 'Prices and Wages Fell Together', *Observer*, 22 July 1973.

17. *Industrial Review* (November 1927), 4. The difference between these figures is within the usual margin of error.

18. *Industrial Review* (April 1931), 7.

19. *Industrial Review* (November 1927), 5.

20. Margot Heinemann, *Britain's Coal* (London, 1944), 42–3. The cost of transporting goods to isolated mining valleys tended to make things cost more. Miners' average cash earnings rose from 43s 9d in 1930 to 55s 11d in 1938.

21. *Sankey Commission Report* (Cmnd 359, 1919), vii–ix.

22. Murphy, *op. cit.*, 38.

23. *Buckmaster Inquiry Minutes of Evidence*, 10–11.

24. *Sankey Commission Evidence*, 388.

25. Margot Heinemann, *op. cit.*, 64–5.

26. Murphy, *op. cit.*, 30.

27. Roderick Martin, *Communism and British Trade Unions 1924–33* (Oxford, 1969), 79.

Chapter 10

1. Taylor, *op. cit.*, 146–9, has a full discussion of Lloyd George's welfare policy.

2. The 1922 Committee, the Tory Party's influential organisation of backbench MPs, takes its name from the date of this historic Carlton Club meeting.

3. At Bonar Law's funeral in Westminster Abbey, Asquith is said to have observed, 'It is fitting that we should have buried the Unknown Prime Minister by the side of the Unknown Soldier'.

4. Of 56 Lloyd George Coalition Liberals who were opposed by Tories (with funds provided by Bonar Law's greatest crony, the dynamic Canadian newspaper proprietor Lord Beaverbrook), 54 were defeated. Lloyd George himself did better than Asquith had done in 1918 and retained his pocket borough at Caernarvon. But just as 1918 had been a thumping endorsement of Lloyd George, so 1922 was a humiliating rejection for him. The Tories won 5·5 million votes, Labour 4·2, Asquithian Liberals 2·5 and Lloyd George Liberals 1·6. This gave the Conservatives 345 seats against 142 for Labour and 117 for the Liberals, about equally divided between Asquith and Lloyd George factions.

5. Walter Citrine, *Men and Work*, 210.

6. *Ibid.*, 211.

7. Beatrice Webb, *Diaries 1924–1932*, 116.

8. David Smith, 'The Struggle Against Company Unionism in South Wales Coalfield, 1926–39', *The Welsh History Review*, Vol. 6, No. 3 (June 1973).

9. W. A. Lee, *Thirty Years in Coal* (London, 1954), 43–4.

10. *Arthur Horner Remembers*, BBC Sound Archives, 27807.

11. Private letter from Lord Shinwell to author, 24 October 1970.

12. Of 276 million tons mined, a record 104 million tons went for export. David Lloyd George, *Coal and Power* (London, 1924), 3.

13. J. R. Campbell, editor of the Communist *Workers' Weekly*, was charged with incitement to mutiny. The Government dropped the prosecution when they remembered he was a war hero and that revolutionary phrases were the stock-in-trade of left-wing parties – which Labour still was, in theory at any

rate. But the Tories raised a hue and cry about political interference with the course of justice and put down a censure motion, which Labour lost and was therefore forced to resign.

14. Since the publication of Lewis Chester, Stephen Fay and Hugo Young, *The Zinoviev Letter* (London, 1967), there can be little doubt it *was* forged.

15. Labour ran 90 more candidates than in 1923 – a healthy sign in itself which could not cancel the loss of moderate support in crucial marginal seats.

Chapter 11

1. In Great Britain the population in 1921 was 42·7 million, in England alone, 37·8.

2. Taylor, *op. cit.*, 164–5, 301–2.

3. In 1921, 85 million working days had been lost in strikes. This figure fell to 19 million in 1922, 10 million in 1923 and fewer than 8 million in 1925 – the lowest figure since the war and less than *one tenth* the 1921 figure.

4. Keith Middlemas and John Barnes, *Baldwin: a Biography* (London, 1969), 61–2.

5. Francis Williams, *A Pattern of Rulers* (London, 1965), 13; Taylor, *op. cit.*, 125 and n.

6. His attitude towards Arthur Pugh, president of the TUC and moderate leader of the steelworkers during the General Strike, for example, was clearly that of a benevolent iron master towards a misguided union man. See below, Chapter 17.

7. The wartime boom in the steel industry had made Baldwin almost embarrassingly rich and he gave lavishly to charity. The post-war slump hit him correspondingly hard – shares worth 50s in 1920 collapsed to 3s 6d in 1927. He remained chronically in debt and really needed his £6,000 a year

salary as Prime Minister to live as he wished. Middlemas and Barnes, *op. cit.*, 53, 260.

8. *Ibid.*, 72–4; Taylor, *op. cit.*, 125 and n.

9. Interestingly, Baldwin has been compared with Henri Queille, a French country doctor and 'characteristic figure of Third Republic politics' who served three terms as Premier of the Fourth Republic between 1944 and 1958. Philip Williams, *Crisis and Compromise* (London, 1964), 36.

10. Robert Boothby, *My Yesterday, Your Tomorrow* (London, 1962), 118.

11. Though Balfour did become Lord President when Curzon died in April 1925. Curzon, despite his contemptuous dismissal of Baldwin, was eager to serve under him, as he had been with Lloyd George, another man who had humiliated him.

12. As a former Lord Chancellor, Birkenhead was entitled to a pension of £5,000 a year, which he sacrificed by taking office. To pay for his taste for high living he wrote newspaper articles which provoked strong opposition in the House. To silence him, Baldwin arranged for the Tory Party to pay Birkenhead £5,000 a year. The first payment was made just after the General Strike, in May 1926. See Confidential and secret memo and secret rate from Baldwin, 21 May 1926, in Davidson Papers.

13. Taylor, *op. cit.*, 206, 237, 255–8. 'Nearly all the domestic achievements of Conservative Governments between the wars stand to his credit, and most of the troubles also . . . there was now [in 1925] agreement . . . that poverty should be remedied by Government action. Neville Chamberlain believed this as strongly as any Labour man. . . .'

14. Chamberlain believed Lloyd George

had deliberately humiliated him by making him director of National Service in 1916–17 in impossible circumstances and then sacking him when he inevitably failed.

15. Taylor, *op. cit.*, 237.
16. *Ibid.*, 206.
17. Observing that Baldwin took no interest in foreign affairs, while Chamberlain, who did, treated Hitler like an obstreperous city councillor, Oliver Stanley said 'that to Baldwin Europe was a bore, and to Chamberlain a bigger Birmingham', Boothby, *op. cit.*, 126.
18. W. C. Bridgeman, at the Admiralty, was the only landed magnate in the Cabinet.
19. See letters to Baldwin from Chamberlain, the National Union and the Labour Committee of the Tory Party and others all strongly urging tough legislation aimed at driving a wedge between the unions and the Labour Party. BP, D.3, vol. 11, esp. 25, 73–7, 113 and 238.
20. Since 1913 trade unionists had been allowed to contract out of the political levy. Macquisten's Bill would have made it necessary to contract in.
21. 181 House of Commons Debates, *Hansard*, 7 March 1925, 839–41. Chamberlain revived the phrase to describe the Munich Agreement in 1938.
22. Taylor, *op. cit.*, 205.
23. F. Williams, *op. cit.*, 31.
24. The Cunliffe committee which met in 1918 to examine post-war financial problems had concluded that there should be a fixed fiduciary issue, with the remainder of the note issue limited to the amount of gold reserve in the Bank of England. This had been the position before 1914. So the phrase 'return to the gold standard' really meant 'Base the amount of money available mainly on the value of the gold in the vaults of the Bank of England'.
25. It is said that when Baldwin offered Churchill the post of Chancellor, Churchill (who had just returned to the Tory ranks) could not believe the prodigal was being given one of the great offices of state and thought he was being invited to become Chancellor of the Duchy of Lancaster. Sir Robert Horne had expected the Exchequer.
26. For a full discussion of this evidence, see D. E. Moggeridge, *The Return to Gold, 1925* (Cambridge, 1969); John L. Halstead, 'The Return to Gold: a Moment of Truth', *Bulletin of the Society for the Study of Labour History*, No. 21 (Autumn 1970) 35–40, and W. R. Reddaway, 'Was $4.86 inevitable in 1925?' *Lloyds Bank Review* (April 1970), both reviews of this monograph; and Skidelsky, *op. cit.*
27. Reddaway, *op. cit.*, 1, 15–16, 27.
28. *Chamberlain-Bradbury Committee Report on the Currency and Bank of England Note Issue* (1924), para. 20.
29. Reddaway, *op. cit.*, 24.
30. Churchill to Niemeyer, 22 February 1925, T172/1499B, quoted in Moggeridge, *op. cit.*, 54–5, and Skidelsky, *op. cit.*
31. *Ibid.*, and Skidelsky, *op. cit.*
32. Reddaway, *op. cit.*, 25.
33. Grigg, *op. cit.*, 185.
34. Churchill, a Free Trader, paid for these increases by restoring the celebrated McKenna duties, which Snowden had removed the year before.
35. Moggeridge, *op. cit.*, 56 n. In the Cabinet Conclusions there is only one cryptic reference to the gold standard. 'In view of the great importance of secrecy,' the memo says, 'the financial details are not recorded in the Cabinet minutes.' *Cabinet Conclusions*, Cab 23/55, 22 (25), 27 April 1925, 11.

36. *Annual Register 1925*, 40, 42–3.
37. Skidelsky, *op. cit.*
38. *Ibid*. In 1906, Niemeyer had beaten Keynes into second place in the Civil Service examination and been posted to the Treasury. Keynes had gone to the India Office. But for a last minute change-of-mind, Niemeyer would have made the India Office and Keynes would presumably have gone to the Treasury – with intriguing consequences for both men and for the nation. See obituary of Sir Otto Niemeyer, *The Times*, 8 February 1971.
39. *Ibid*., 27. See below, Chapter 12.
40. Cf. Montagu Norman's remark to Churchill justifying the return to gold. 'The merchant, manufacturer, workman etc. should be considered (but not consulted, any more than in the design of battleships).' Norman to Churchill, 2 February 1925, TI72/1499B, quoted in Moggeridge, *op. cit.*, 49, and Skidelsky, *op. cit.* As we have seen, the Cabinet was not consulted either.
41. W. A. Lee, *op. cit.*, 45–6, and Citrine, *op. cit.*, 138.
42. *Macmillan Inquiry Report* (1925), 45–6.
43. Jack Feany, a Middlesbrough railwaymen's shop steward, in a tape-recording in the possession of Clive Barker, Department of Drama and Theatre Arts, Birmingham University.

Chapter 12

1. Jones, *op. cit.*, 323.
2. Lee, *op. cit.*, 45, and Citrine, *op. cit.*, 138. See above, Chapter 11.
3. Lee, *op. cit.*, 46.
4. *The Coal Crisis*, MFGB Statement to the *Macmillan Court of Inquiry into the Coal Mining Industry Dispute, 1925* (Cmnd 2478, 1925), 9–10.

5. Bullock, *op. cit.*, 230, 273–6, 287–8, 305; Symons, *op. cit.*, 8.
6. *Report of the 56th Annual Trades Union Congress, 1924*, 68, and Bullock, *op. cit.*, 260–1. See above, Chapter 10.
7. Other members of the Macmillan court of inquiry were W. M. Sherwood of the Shipbuilders' Union, and Sir Josiah Stamp, the economist.
8. *Cabinet Conclusions,* Cab 23/50, 252.
9. *Cabinet Papers*, Cab 27/259, 6P 314 (23), 1;
10. *Ibid*., Cab 24/174, CP 356 (25).
11. Citrine, *op. cit.*, 138.
12. *Ibid*., 138–9.
13. *Ibid*., 139.
14. *Loc, cit.*
15. *Report of Macmillan Court of Inquiry* (Cmnd 2478, 1925).
16. *The Times*, 30 July 1925.
17. *Cabinet Conclusions*, Cab 23/50, 251.
18. Citrine, *op. cit.*, 139 (my italics).
19. *Daily Herald*, 31 July 1925. Baldwin afterwards denied making this statement, though it was apparently twice repeated. The discussion was confidential, but though the official minute does not record those exact words, the substance is the same. Symons, *op. cit.*, 14; Bullock, *op. cit.*, 277 and n; Page Arnot, *The Miners*, 377 and n.
20. G. M. Young, *Stanley Baldwin* (London, 1952), 99.
21. Citrine, *op cit.*, 139–40.
22. *Cabinet Conclusions*, Cab 23/50 42 (25), 30 July 1925, 291.
23. *Ibid*., 292. The need to keep troops in Ireland had hampered mobilisation in 1921.
24. *Ibid*., 293.
25. *Loc. cit.*
26. *Cabinet Conclusions*, Cab 23/50, 42 (25), 28 July 1925, 268–9.
27. *Ibid*., 30 July 1925, 291–3.
28. *Ibid*., 293.
29. Citrine, *op. cit.*, 141.
30. *Ibid*., 142. Cabinet Ministers at this

time seem to have been prone to saying some of their friends ought to be in jail. Cf. Baldwin's statement that 'a man who had made a million quick ought not to be in the Lords but in jail'.

31. Young, *op. cit.*, 99. The phrase is also attributed to the President of the Board of Trade, Sir Philip Cunliffe-Lister: Jones, *op. cit.*, 325.

32. *Cabinet Papers*, Cab 27/259, 6P 314 (23), 1–7.

33. Symons, *op. cit.*, 23–4.

34. *Cabinet Papers*, Cab 27/259 EC (24), 2–8, 15 February 1924, 3.

35. Gibson memorandum, BP, D.3, vol. 13, 3 (my italics).

36. *Loc. cit.*

37. Letter to Baldwin, 8 August 1925, BP, D.3, vol. 13, 23. It is hard to imagine which railway union leaders could be regarded as Bolshies, but this comment bears out the railwaymen's attitude quoted above, Chapter 11.

38. Chamberlain Diary, 3 August 1925, quoted in Feiling, *op. cit.*, 156.

39. Quoted in Tom Bell, *The British Communist Party: a short History* (London, 1927), 109.

Chapter 13

1. *Cabinet Papers*, vol. LIX, 4 August 1925, 515–17.

2. Baldwin appointed the commission on 25 September. Samuel's colleagues were Sir William Beveridge, another Liberal, then director of the London School of Economics, later author of the epoch-making Beveridge report which laid the foundations of the modern welfare state; General Sir Herbert Lawrence, Lord Haig's wartime chief-of-staff, now a banker; and Kenneth Lee, a Manchester cotton owner. None of them knew anything about mining, but Baldwin had gone to a good

deal of trouble to bring 'fresh minds' to bear on the problem.

3. Frank Hodges to Baldwin, 12 August 1925, BP, D.3, vol. 13, 49.

4. Churchill to Baldwin, 14 August 1926, BP, D.3, vol. 13, 33.

5. *Cabinet Conclusions*, Cab 23/50, 43 (25), 5 August 1925, 300–1.

6. *Cabinet Papers*, vol. LIX, Cab 390/25, 5 August 1925, 542–86.

7. *Ibid.*, 543–4.

8. *Ibid.*, 550. A reference to the 1919 troubles in Liverpool.

9. *The Times*, 6 August 1925.

10. Cab 390/25, 551–2.

11. *Cabinet Conclusions*, Cab 23/50, 44 (25), 7 August 1925, 316–17.

12. *Cabinet Papers*, Cab 81 (26). See also George Glasgow, *General Strike and Road Transport* (London, 1926.)

13. *Cabinet Conclusions*, 44 (25), 23/50, 316–17, 7 August 1925. Jix had already prepared a full memorandum on emergency arrangements for Cabinet use.

14. *Home Office Papers*, HO/45/ 12336/2130.

15. *Ibid.*

16. HO/45/12336/484910 and *The Times*, 1 October 1925.

17. HO/45/12336/2130, secret note of OMS conference at Home Office, 7 December 1925.

18. HO/45/12336/2130, memo from Chief Civil Service Commissioner, 5 December 1925.

19. *Ibid.*

20. HO/45/12336/2130, secret letter from C. F. Roundell to William Buckley, 30 November 1925.

21. *Ibid.*, memo from Roundell to Newsam.

22. *Ibid.*, letter from Buckley to Roundell.

23. *Daily Herald*, 13 February 1926.

24. *Hansard*, 18 February 1926.

25. HO/45/12336/484910.

26. This figure has been disputed – see Symons, *op. cit.*, 23 – but is firmly established by HO/45/

I *

12431/2130/493234, answer to circular letter dated 11 May 1926.
27. *Morning Post*, 7 October 1925.
28. HO/45/12336/2130, secret memo, 3 December 1925, and *Morning Post*, 7 October 1925.

Chapter 14

1. *MFGB Annual Delegate Conference* (1925), quoted in Bullock, *op. cit.*, 281.
2. *Report of the 57th Annual Trades Union Congress* (1925), 289–91.
3. Hamilton Fyfe, *Behind the Scenes of the Great Strike* (London, 1926), 31. Baldwin's relations with Pugh were those of an enlightened iron master towards one of his men. See below, Chapter 17.
4. Symons, *op. cit.*, 30. The whole question of the attitude of Co-op branches in various districts and the vexed question of permits had an important, and possibly decisive, bearing on the General Strike.
5. J. H. Thomas, *My Story* (London, 1937), 105–6.
6. 'The Impending Crisis'. Memorandum by W. M. Citrine. Quoted in Citrine, *op. cit.*, 146–53.
7. *Diaries*, 147–9.
8. Citrine, *op. cit.*, 143.
9. *Loc. cit.*
10. *Ibid.*, 145.
11. *Ibid.*, 143.
12. *Ibid.*, 146–7, 151–2.
13. *Ibid.*, 144.
14. *Ibid.*, 53.
15. *Ibid.*, 154.
16. *Ibid.*, 125–6.
17. See Bullock, *op. cit.*, 296.
18. Londonderry to Baldwin, 18 December 1925, BP, D.3, vol. 13, 56–8.
19. Cunliffe-Lister to Baldwin, 17 April 1926, BP, D.3, vol. 18, 89–91.
20. BP, vol. 13, 64, and *Sheffield Telegraph*, 28 July 1925.
21. See W. Mackenzie report, 30 July

1925, BP, D.3, vol. 13, 66–75. Plans to encourage emigration were popular at the time. See BP, D.3, vol. 12, Labour 6D, 10, 11, and 12.
22. BP, D.3, vol. 13, 113–32.
23. Lord Weir to Baldwin, 31 July 1925. Weir seems to have forgotten that hours were regulated by Parliament, and thus outside control of the industry.
24. Gowers to Waterhouse, 19 December 1925.
25. Witnesses included Smith and Cook, the duke of Northumberland and Evan Williams. The commission also visited twenty-five mines and received a great mass of written evidence, including reports from Mines Inspectors about more than forty pits which had been criticised by the MFGB.
26. Quoted in Michael Hughes, *Cartoons From the General Strike* (London, 1968), 21–2.
27. *Report of the Samuel Commission on the Coal Mining Industry* (Cmnd 2600, 1926), 8–9.
28. *Ibid.*, 234.
29. *Ibid.*, 235.
30. *Ibid.*, 49–62.
31. For a clear and concise summary of the report's findings, see *Ibid.*, 232–7.
32. *Ibid.*, 223.
33. Memorandum on Ending the Mining Subsidy, *Cabinet Papers*, Cab 24/179, vol. LXIII, 1926, 65–8. Since pay represented two-thirds of the cost of production, a 13 per cent pay cut made possible a price cut of two-thirds of 13 per cent, or about $8\frac{1}{2}$ per cent, which fits Keynes's view that the pound had been over-valued about 10 per cent.
34. Mond memorandum, BP, D.3, vol. 13, 181–5.
35. Report by G. R. Lane-Fox in *Cabinet Papers*, CP 62 (26), 353–5, 11 February 1926. See also CP 492 (25) and 2 (26).

Chapter 15

1. Symons, *op. cit.*, 33.
2. *The Times*, 18 March 1926; *Cabinet Papers*, Cab 23/52, 11 (26).
3. *Cabinet Conclusions*, Cab 23/50, 268. This committee met, appropriately enough, in the Moses Room of the House of Lords.
4. *Cabinet Papers,* vol. LXIII, 1926, Cab 24/179, 18 March, 281–2. See also Niemeyer's Memo to another Treasury official, Sir Warren Fisher, dated 14 March 1926, in BP, D.3, vol. 13, 153–4. Nationalisation is dismissed as a 'futile attempt to solve a miners' shibboleth', and the estimated cost of £100 million seen as 'the last straw' which might destroy the Treasury's attempts to reduce War debt.
5. *Ibid.*, annex on State Purchase, 38–9.
6. *Ibid.*, 67.
7. *Ibid.*, 39.
8. *Ibid.*, 55.
9. *Hansard*, 24 March 1926.
10. See, for example, exchanges between Lane-Fox and the Cabinet on the likelihood of the two sides accepting the report. *Cabinet Papers,* vol. LXIII, Cab 24/179, 44.
11. Feiling, *op. cit.*, 156; *Observer*, 25 April 1926.
12. Jones, *Diary*, vol. II, 12, 14 April 1926.
13. *Cabinet Papers,* vol. LXIII, Cab 24/179, 65–6.
14. *Minutes of Meeting Between the Mining Association and MFGB*, 13 April 1926 (MFGB, London, 1926), 4–5.
15. Bullock, *op. cit.*, 294; Mowat, *op. cit.*, 301.
16. *Minutes of Meeting Between the Mining Association and MFGB,* 26 March 1926, BP, D.3, vol. 13, 223–55.
17. Thomas, *op. cit.*, 111.
18. For a full discussion of the Spencer Union, see below, pp. 232, 243–4.
19. Davies to Jones, 21 January 1926, quoted in Jones, *Diary*, vol. II, 3.
20. Jones, *Diary,* vol. II, 14, 14 April 1926. Like Davies, the Llewellyn brothers were staunch Chapel men, and held moderate opinions.
21. *Minutes of a Meeting Between the Mining Association and the Executive of the MFGB* (MFGB, Co-op Printing Society, 1926), 4–8, 17–19.
22. *Ibid.*, 19.
23. The pre-war years had been unusually profitable for mining. The war drove profits still higher, from an average of £13 million in 1913 to nearly £30 million for the first three-quarters of 1918 alone. Favourable tax agreements written into the wartime act under which the Government assumed control of the industry enabled the owners to keep an exceptionally large proportion of these profits. Profits rose per ton from 1s to 4s. After the war the years 1921 and 1925 were years of loss; but the other years were years of profit, and 1923–4 was a record year when profits rose 269 per cent over the pre-war figure. Cole, *op. cit.*, 83–4.
24. *Cabinet Papers*, vol. LXIII, Cab 24/179, 23 April 1926, 811.
25. *Ibid.*, 812.
26. Notes for speech to miners, 24 March 1925, quoted in Jones, *op cit.*, 8.

Chapter 16

1. See the comment of Sir Alfred Cope, Mond's managing director, in Jones, *Diary*, vol. II, 16, 17 April 1926.
2. *Loc. cit.*
3. Mond to Baldwin, 23 April 1926, in *ibid.*, 18.
4. *Ibid.*, 19.
5. *Ibid.*, 16.
6. *Daily Herald*, 27 April 1926.
7. *Minutes of Meeting between MA and MFGB*, 32.

8. Jones, *Diary,* vol. II, 18.
9. *Ibid.,* 18–19.
10. *Ibid.,* 19. Nimmo was supported by many, including Sir Robert Horne, who had served in Lloyd George's post-war Coalition. 'What an old humbug he is,' Baldwin remarked. 'It was Horne who told Sankey that unless the Seven Hours Act was passed there would be revolution.'
11. Jones, *Diary,* vol. II, 20, 24 April 1926.
12. *Ibid.,* 14.
13. *Cabinet Conclusions,* Cab 23/52, 15/26, 14 April 1926, 244.
14. Citrine, *op. cit.,* 157.
15. Blaxland, *op. cit.,* 186–7.
16. *Ibid.,* 188.
17. *Ibid.,* 189.
18. *The Mining Situation, TUC Report of Special Conference* 29 April–1 May 1926 (London, 1926).

Chapter 17

1. Jones, *Diary,* vol. II, 24, 27 April 1926.
2. *Loc. cit.*
3. Middlemas and Barnes, *op. cit.,* 402–3.
4. BP, D.3, vol. 15, 14.
5. Letter from Sir Herbert Lawrence to the Attorney-General, Douglas Hogg, 3 May 1926, BP, D.3, vol. 15, 217–18.
6. Transcript of meeting between Mining Association and Cabinet coal committee, House of Commons, 11.30 a.m., 30 April 1926, BP, D.3, vol. 14, 466–73.
7. BP, D.3, vol. 15, 14.
8. Note of meeting held at 10 Downing Street, 11 p.m., 1 May 1926. Jones, *Diary,* vol. II, 25.
9. *Ibid.,* 17, 21 April 1926.
10. *Ibid.,* 12, 14 April 1926.
11. Citrine, *op. cit.,* 162.
12. *Cabinet Conclusions,* Cab 23/52, 21 (26), 2 May 1926, 314.
13. Jones, *Diary,* vol. II, 28–9.
14. Citrine, *op. cit.,* 166.
15. *Ibid.,* 167.
16. *Cabinet Conclusions,* Cab 23/52, 23(26), 2 May 1926, 317.
17. Jones, *Diary,* vol. II, 29, 2 May 1926.
18. *Ibid.,* 28.
19. *Cabinet Conclusions,* Cab 23/52, 23(26), 2 May 1926, 326.
20. Birkenhead memorandum on the coal negotiations, quoted in Jones, *Diary,* 36.
21. Chester, Fay and Young, *op cit.,* 94, 124–26.
22. Paul Ferris, 'The Alarming Adventures of Lord Northcliffe', *Observer Review,* 16 May 1971.
23. Taylor, *op. cit.,* 244 n.
24. *Cabinet Conclusions,* Cab 23/50, 22 (25), 27 April 1925, 10.
25. Citrine, *op. cit.,* 172. Churchill had urged his friend Lord Beaverbrook to take a tough line when the printers of his *Sunday Express* had refused to set the advertisement on Saturday, 1 May. 'Close down,' he told Beaverbrook. 'You can afford it.' Birkenhead offered contrary advice; Beaverbrook altered the advertisement and the paper appeared with a stiff leader saying the General Strike would fail. A. J. P. Taylor, *Beaverbrook* (London, 1972), 231.
26. Jones, *Diary,* 33, 3 May 1926.
27. Citrine, *op. cit.,* 171.
28. *Ibid.,* 172.
29. *Cabinet Conclusions,* Cab 23/52, 23 (26), 3 May 1926, 328.
30. *Ibid.,* appendix, 329.
31. Young, *op. cit.,* 116.
32. Citrine to Baldwin, 3 May 1926, BP, D.3, vol. II, 24.
33. A reference to a melodramatic incident when Churchill was Home Secretary in 1911 and launched a massive police operation to winkle out three suspected anarchists who had barricaded themselves into a house in Sidney Street in London's East End. The operation had been a much-publicised failure.
34. Thomas, *op. cit.,* 104.

35. A. Mason, 'The Government and the General Strike, 1926', *International Review of Social History* (Summer, 1969), 1–21.

Chapter 18

1. Bullock, *op. cit.*, 316. Support was not entirely unselfish. Baldwin had spoken of the need to cut *all* wages.
2. Beatrice Webb, *op. cit.*, 92.
3. C. L. Mowat, *op. cit.*, 313.
4. Eric Jacobs, 'It Didn't Work in 1912 or '26: Can a Political Strike Succeed Now?', *Sunday Times,* 6 December 1970.
5. These opinions were shot to pieces by other legal authorities at the time. See, for example, A. L. Goodhart, *The Legality of the General Strike in England* (Cambridge, 1927). If the General Strike was illegal in 1926, why was it necessary to pass a law making it illegal in 1927?

Chapter 19

1. Hamilton Fyfe, *Behind the Scenes of the Great Strike* (London, 1926), 7.
2. *British Gazette*, 6 May 1926.
3. Fyfe, *op. cit.*, 9–10.
4. *Labour Year Book 1927,* 113; *The Economic Journal* (September 1926), 126.
5. *British Worker*, 5 May 1926.
6. A specimen permit issued by the Ogmore Valley Council of Action in South Wales reads:
Permit No. 1:
Central Strike Committee
Permission is hereby given to J. Davies of . . . to transport groceries from the P.W.S., Cardiff to. . . .
This form is issued for a particular consignment and must be handed back to a permit committee on the conveyance of the consignment.
May 5 3.30 p.m.
Given under the authority of the Permit Committee.
Allan Potsen. Secretary.

Cabinet Information Bulletin, Cab 27/331 ST/24.
7. *Cabinet Information Bulletin,* Cab 27/33 ST (24), 3 May 1926. Cf. Taylor, *op. cit.,* 246–7.
8. Letter from Burnley and District Central Strike Committee, 10 May 1926, in *TUC Papers*, Labour GS 192 HD 5366 NW, Intelligence Committee Report. See also reports from Lancaster branch NUR Joint Strike Committee and from Kent area (South West) same date.
9. J. H. Thomas, *My Story* (London, 1937), 104.
10. Citrine, *op. cit.*, 178.
11. *TUC Papers,* HD 5366, Intelligence Committee Report.
12. Mowat, *op. cit.*, 313.
13. Citrine, *op. cit.*, 177–8, 4 May 1926.
14. Strike Organisation Committee, *TUC Papers,* HD 5366.
15. *Hansard,* 13 May 1926.
16. Symons, *op. cit.*, 64.
17. *Report of Special TUC Conference General Strike* (London, 127), 35.
18. *Ibid.*, 45.
19. Lane-Fox Report CP 62 (26). See also CP 492 (25) and 2 (26), 353–5.
20. *Cabinet Conclusions*, CP 42(25) 23/50, 291–3.
21. *Cabinet Information Bulletin*, Cab 27/331/5422, 3 May 1926.
22. See *TUC Papers*, HD 5366, and report by TGWU in *TUC Intelligence Committee Reports*, 11 May 1926.
23. *TUC Papers*, HD 5366, Reports from the Districts.
24. Michael Foot, *Aneurin Bevan* (London, 1962), 68–73.
25. *Cabinet Information Bulletin,* Cab 27/331/5422/C.16, 2 May 1926.
26. *Ibid.*
27. *Cabinet Conclusions*, Appendix II, Cab 23/25/4158, 93 and above.
28. Foot, *op. cit.*, 70.
29. *Cabinet Information Bulletin*, Cab 27/331/5422, Mines Department, No. 1, 3 May 1926.

30. *Ibid.,* Ministry of Transport, No. 1a, ST (24), 4 May 1926. The train got no further than Reading.
31. *Cabinet Information Bulletin,* Cab 27/331 ST (24), Ministry of Transport, No. 1, Railways.
32. Symons, *op. cit.,* 94–5.
33. *Ibid.,* 96–7, 100–1.
34. *Westminster Worker,* 12 May 1926.
35. *St Pancras Bulletin,* 8 May 1926.
36. Symons, *op. cit.,* 76.
37. Quoted in Lord Moran, *Winston Churchill: the Struggle for Survival, 1940–1965* (London, 1965), 247.
38. *Cabinet Information Bulletin,* Cab 27/331 ST (24), Ministry of Transport, No. 1, Railways, 4 May 1926.
39. *Ibid.,* Cab 27/331 ST (24), Ministry of Labour, No. 1a, 4 May 1926.
40. *Ibid.,* Cab 27/331 ST (24), Ministry of Transport, Nos 1a and 3, 5 May 1926.
41. Robert Rhodes James (ed.), *Memoirs of a Conservative: J. C. C. Davidson's Memoirs and Papers, 1910–37* (London, 1971).

Chapter 20

1. *Hansard,* 3 May 1926.
2. For extensive coverage in European Press see *TUC Papers,* HD 5366/ Press.
3. Quoted in Hamilton Fyfe, *op. cit.,* 71.
4. *Cabinet Papers,* vol. XXI, 326.
5. Home Office papers, HO 45 12366/ 2130, has detailed information about this.
6. G. M. Young, *Stanley Baldwin* (London, 1952), 119 n, has a useful summary of the emergency plans. Detailed information is in Home Office papers, HO 45 12366/2130.
7. *Industrial Review,* vol. 1, No. 1 (January 1927), 8, anonymous review of George Glasgow, *General Strike and Road Transport* (London, 1927), the first contemporary analysis of Government plans.
8. *British Worker,* 5 May 1926.

9. Road Transport cost the Government only £20,000 over nine days.
10. Anderson memo, 17 May 1926, HO 45 12336/2130.
11. See above, Chapter 13.
12. A. Mason, 'The Government and the General Strike', *International Review of Social History* (Summer 1969), 19.
13. Regional answers to Home Office letter, 11 May 1926, HO 45 12336/ 2130.
14. Lord Hardinge to Joynson-Hicks, 21 May 1926, HO 45 12336/2130.
15. Joynson-Hicks to Hardinge, 30 June 1926, HO 45 12336/2130.
16. Answers to Home Office Circular, 11 May, HO 45 12336/2130.
17. Taylor, *op. cit.,* 245.
18. About 4,000 arrests were made as a result of picketing incidents. This was a tiny fraction of the strikers.
19. Young, *op. cit.,* 119.
20. *Cabinet Papers,* vol. XXI, *passim.*
21. *Cabinet Conclusions,* Cab 23/52 25 (26), Cab 27/260 ST (24), 15.
22. See record in *Cabinet Papers,* vol. XXI, *passim.*

Chapter 21

1. See above, p. 162, 268n.
2. Davidson's wife, Mimi, was an equally close friend of Baldwin, his constant companion on his long summer holidays at Aix-en-Provence. 'To Mimi Davidson he was able to talk in a way which he found difficult even to other friends.' Middlemas and Barnes, *op. cit.,* 497–8.
3. Davidson strike report, 1, HO 45 12431/2130/493234, 24 June 1926.
4. *Ibid.,* 4.
5. *Ibid.,* 5–6.
6. *Ibid.,* Appendix I, 3–5.
7. *Ibid.,* 3, and Fyfe, *op. cit.,* 25–6.
8. Davidson, *op. cit.,* Appendix I, 1.
9. *Ibid.,* and *TUC Papers,* HD 5366/ GS1926/Press.
10. Davidson, *op. cit.,* Appendix I, 2.

11. Lord Templewood, BBC Sound Archives, 26024.
12. Davidson report, HO 45 12431/2130, 7, and Appendix II, *passim.*
13. *Ibid.*, 8.
14. Lord Templewood, BBC Sound Archives, 26024.
15. Philip Guedalla, *Mr Churchill* (London, 1941), 85.
16. Hearing of this, a French socialist remarked in despair: 'The British are not a nation—they are a circus.'
17. *British Gazette*, 5 May 1926.
18. Jones, *Diary*, 9 May 1926.
19. Davidson memo to Baldwin.
20. Jones, *Diary*, 9 May 1926.
21. *British Gazette*, 5 May 1926.
22. Hamilton Fyfe, *Behind the Scenes of the Great Strike* (London, 1926), 51, 58–9, 62, 69–70.
23. *The Times*, 11 May 1926.
24. *Hansard*, 5 May 1926.
25. Report of Deputy Chief Civil Commissioner, Appendix I, 7 and Appendix II, 3, 6 May 1926, HO 45 12431/2130.
26. *Hansard*, 5 May 1926.
27. Citrine, *op. cit.*, 183.
28. *British Worker*, 7 May 1926.
29. Joynson-Hicks memo, 5 May 1926, HO 45 12385/2127; Citrine, *op. cit.*, 179–82; and Fyfe, *op. cit.*, 33–5.
30. Citrine, *op. cit.*, 181, 5 May 1926.
31. Middlemas and Barnes, *op. cit.,* 412; Fyfe, *op. cit.*, 31–5.
32. Citrine, *op. cit.*, 182.
33. John Evelyn Wrench, *Geoffrey Dawson and our Times* (London, 1955), 248; Geoffrey Dawson, *Strike Nights at Printing House Square* (London) 1926; Graham Greene, *A Kind of Life* (London, 1971).
34. Lord Boothby, *op. cit.*, 131.
35. Symons, *op. cit.*, 162.
36. Geoffrey Dawson, *Diary*, 8, 12 and 14 May 1926.
37. *Ibid.*, 11 May 1926.
38. Davidson report, HO 45 12431/2130, 5.

Chapter 22
1. Obituary of Lord Reith, *The Times*, 17 June 1971.
2. J. C. W. Reith, *Into the Wind* (London, 1949), 107–9; Asa Briggs, *History of Broadcasting in the United Kingdom*, vol. I (Oxford, 1965), 248–9, 360.
3. Reith, *op. cit.*, 108. See also transcript of Reith's televised interview with Malcolm Muggeridge, *The Listener*, 7 December 1967.
4. Reith to Postmaster-General, 20 October 1925, quoted by Briggs, *op. cit.*, 367.
5. BBC Written Archives, 811.
6. Reith, *op. cit.*, 107.
7. Managing Director's Report to BBC Board of Directors, 18 May 1926, BBC Written Archives, 811.
8. Davidson report, HO 45 12431/2130/493234, 1.
9. BBC Written Archives, 811 and memo 811/1.
10. Reith, *op. cit.*, 106.
11. See telegrams from editors all over the country in BBC Archives, 811/1. Copyright was re-imposed on 18 May.
12. Reith, *op. cit.,* 107.
13. *Ibid.*, 108.
14. *Ibid.*, 108–9.
15. Report of Managing Director on General Strike, 4–12 May 1926, BBC Archives, 811, 2–3.
16. Reith to Davidson, 6 May 1926, quoted in Briggs, *op. cit.*, 363.
17. *Cabinet Papers*, vol. XXI, *passim*, esp. 360–4.
18. Middlemas and Barnes, *op. cit.*
19. Reith, *op. cit.*, 109–10.
20. Davidson report, HO 45 12431/2130, Appendix III.
21. *Ibid.*
22. Briggs, *op. cit.*, 362. Reith's pencilled correction is in BBC Written Archives, 811/3.
23. Reith, *op. cit.*, 11.
24. Beatrice Webb, *Diaries*, 11 May 1926.
25. BBC Written Archives, 811.

26. Briggs, *op. cit.*, 367–70.
27. Text of MacDonald's speech in BBC Written Archives, 811/3.
28. Graham to Reith, 9 May 1926, BBC Written Archives, 811/2.
29. *Ibid.*, 19 May 1926.
30. *Ibid.*, 31 May 1926, and *Radio Times*, 21 May 1926.
31. Reith to Trevelyan, 2 June 1926, BBC Written Archives, 811/2.
32. Graham to Reith, 11 November 1926.
33. Report of Managing Director, 3.
34. *Ibid.*, 2.
35. *Loc. cit.*
36. Lord Gainford to Archbishop, 7 May 1926, BBC Written Archives, 811/3. See also letter written by Philip Gee, PRO for the Mining Association, 21 May 1926, BBC Written Archives, 811.
37. Lord Gainford to Archbishop, 7 May 1926.
38. Reith to Archbishop, 9 May 1926.
39. News bulletin, BBC Sound Archives, 27982, and BP, D.3., vol. 18, 75.
40. Anonymous listener, quoted in Symons, *op. cit.*, 181.
41. Reith, *op. cit.*, 111–12.
42. *Morning Post*, 26 May 1926.
43. BBC Written Archives, 811.
44. *Ibid.*
45. *Ibid.*
46. *Evening News*, 25 May 1926.
47. *Hansard*, 25 May 1926.
48. Obituary of Lord Reith, *The Times*, 17 June 1971.
49. Reith left the BBC in 1938 to become head of Imperial Airways, believing with justice that he had left his stamp on British broadcasting. But he never felt, in his own words, that he had been 'fully stretched' and when Churchill, as Prime Minister during the Second Word War, failed to give him a really big job, Reith blamed their bad relations in 1926.

Chapter 23

1. Lord Templewood, BBC Sound Archives, 26024.

2. *Cabinet Papers*, vol. XXI, 316.
3. *Ibid.*, 318–20, and *Hansard*, 11 May 1926.
4. Draft Illegal Strikes Bill 1926, *Cabinet Papers*, Cab 23/52 27 (26), 360.
5. *Ibid.*
6. Harold Nicolson, *King George the Fifth: His Life and Reign* (London, 1952), 419.
7. See correspondence in Davidson Papers. Both Churchill and Commander Kenworthy, Labour MP for Central Hull, believed Lloyd George was going Left in 1926. In fact, his rebuff by Labour convinced him that he still had a role to play as leader of the Liberals. For a full discussion see M. J. Bentley, 'The Liberal Response to Socialism, 1918–1929', in K. D. Brown (ed.), *Essays in Anti-Labour History* (London, 1974).
8. *Hansard,* Commons Debates, 6th May 1926.
9. Symons, *op. cit.*, 120–1.
10. A. L. Goodhart, 'The Legality of the General Strike in England', *Yale Law Journal,* 1927.
11. *TUC Papers,* HD 5366.
12. Fyfe, *op. cit.*, 69.
13. Emergency Power Regulation 13 (a).
14. Nicholson, *op. cit.*, 420–21.
15. Roy Jenkins, *Asquith* (London, 1964), 514–17.
16. *Manchester Guardian Bulletin,* 6 May 1926.
17. *British Worker*, 7 May 1926, and *TUC Papers*, HD, 5366.
18. Rev. H. Marshall to E. F. Wise, 4 May 1926, quoted in Jones, *op. cit.*, 37.

Chapter 24

1. *Cabinet Conclusions*, Cab 23/52 (27) 26, 361.
2. Citrine, *op. cit.*, 186.
3. Home Office Situation Report, 10 May 1926, Cab 27/333/5422, and Felix J. C. Pole, *Pole's Book* (n.p., n.d.), 124–7, 127–9.

4. Both Julian Symons and Christopher Farman stress the solidarity of the railwaymen without reference to the underlying divisions or the fate many railwaymen suffered when they went back. See Symons, *op. cit.*, 208, 210, and Farman, *op. cit.*, 222. Philip S. Bagwell, *The Railwaymen* (London, 1963), 479–97, repairs these omissions.
5. Citrine, *op. cit.*, 205–6.
6. Symons, *op. cit.*, 189.
7. Quoted in Jones, *op. cit.*, 43.
8. *Ibid.*
9. *Ibid.*, 42.
10. Symons, *op. cit.*, 189–90.
11. Jones, *op. cit.*, 40.
12. *Ibid.*, 40–1.
13. *British Gazette*, 10 and 11 May 1926.
14. *TUC Papers*, HD 5366.
15. Citrine, *op. cit.*, 197.
16. *Ibid.*, 201.
17. Bevin's statement to officers of the TGWU, *TUC Papers*, HD 5366.
18. Ben Turner, *About Myself* (London, 1930), 311–12.
19. Hamilton Fyfe, *Diary*, 71, 11 May 1926.
20. Citrine, *op. cit.*, 200.
21. Osbert Sitwell, *Laughter in the Next Room* (London, 1949), 232.
22. *Special Strike Conference of the TUC,* January 1927, 389.
23. *Ibid.*, 392.
24. *Diary*, 200–1, 11 May 1926.
25. *Report of the 58th Annual TUC Conference*, September 1926, 21.
26. *TGWU Biennial Delegate Conference Report*, July 1927, 93.
27. Transcript of Meeting, BP, D.3, vol. 14, 500–6.
28. Quoted in Bullock, *op. cit.*, 337.

Chapter 25

1. Emergency Regulations, BP, D.3, vol. 15, 221–5 and 251.
2. *Miners Federation Delegate Conference*, 22 April 1921. Cook had broken with the Communist Party over this dispute. See below, Chapter 8.
3. Terms of Settlement, BP, D.3, vol. 15, 346–8.
4. BP, D.3, vol. 18, 207–10. Lord Irwin later became Lord Halifax.
5. Churchill to Baldwin, 9 June 1926, BP, D.3, vol. 18, 45–7 (italics in original).
6. Baldwin to Churchill, 5 September 1926, BP, D.3, vol. 18, 51–2.
7. Draft memorandum, BP, D.3, vol. 15, 243–9. Cf. Asquith's statement on minimum wages, *Hansard*, 1912, vols 2242–3.
8. Reports from Mansfield, BP, D.3, vol. 15, 309. J. E. Williams, *The Derbyshire Miners*, and A. R. Griffin, *The Nottinghamshire Miners*, vol. 2, and *The Mining Industry in the East Midlands* (London, 1972), all illuminate the miners' return to work in the East Midlands and the problem of non-political unionism, especially the Spencer Union.
9. Home Office Situation Report No. 110, Cab 27/333/5422.
10. Secret Mines Department Bulletin, 25 August 1926, Cab 27/333/5422.
11. *Ibid.*, 2.
12. BP, D.3, vol. 15, 309.
13. Churchill to Bridgeman, 7 September 1926, BP, D.3, vol. 18, 25–7.
14. Londonderry to Baldwin, 12 September 1926, BP, D.3, vol. 18, 149–54.
15. Beaverbrook to Lord Derby, quoted in Taylor, *op. cit.*, 233.
16. Birkenhead to Baldwin, 23 September 1926, BP, D.3, vol. 18, 5.
17. Transcript of conference, BP, D.3, vol. 14, 526–7.
18. *Ibid.*, 544.
19. Baldwin to Churchill, 5 September 1926, BP, D.3, vol. 18, 51.
20. BP, D.3, vol. 15, 169.
21. Williams to Baldwin, *ibid.*, 137–8.
22. Terms of Settlement, BP, D.3, vol. 15, 364–8.

Chapter 26

1. Ministry of Labour Report, BP, D.3, vol. 15, 266.
2. *Loc. cit.*
3. *Ibid.*, 265.
4. *Cabinet Papers*, vol. xxi, 424–7.
5. Ministry of Health Circular No. 703, 5 May 1926.
6. Ministry of Health Report, November 1926.
7. *Ibid.*
8. Conversation with Jim Bullock, a Yorkshire miner, 6 February 1974.
9. Conversation with South Wales miners. In fact, many single men worried that they were taking food from the mouths of mothers and children, and much trouble with the Guardians centred on this issue.
10. See, for example, Peter Stead, 'Working Class Leadership in South Wales', *Welsh History Review*, vol. 6, No. 3 (June 1973), 347–8.
11. The practice was known as 'Poplarism', after the London borough where it had first started.
12. Taylor, *op. cit.*, 256 and n; Foot, *op. cit.*, 80–1, 107–9, 200–1.
13. Foot, *op. cit.*, 80.
14. *Ibid.*, 81–2.
15. *The Economist*, 21 November 1926.

Chapter 27

1. Birkenhead to Reading, 8 October 1925, quoted in Lord Birkenhead, *F. E. – The Life of F. E. Smith, First Earl of Birkenhead* (London, 1960), 527.
2. *Loc. cit.*
3. Younger to Birkenhead, BP, D.3, vol. 11, 113.
4. Steel-Maitland to Baldwin, 24 December 1924, BP, D.3, vol. 11, 80.
5. BP, D.3, vol. 11, 352–7.
6. *Ibid.*, 354.
7. *Ibid.*, 355–7.
8. *Ibid.*, 358.
9. Steel-Maitland to Baldwin, 29 September 1926, BP, D.3., vol. 11, 44–5, 48–9.

10. *Ibid.*, 49.
11. Cecil to Baldwin, 9 January 1926, BP, D.3, vol. 11, 66.
12. BP, D.3, vol. 11, 73–7, 80, 245–50.
13. Melvin C. Shefftz, 'The Trade Disputes and Trade Unions Act of 1927: The Aftermath of the General Strike', *The Review of Politics*, vol. 29, No. 3 (July 1967), 397–8.
14. Birkenhead, *op. cit.*, 534–5, and *Hansard*, 2 May 1927. Birkenhead, like Churchill, had long warned against the Communist menace, and as Secretary for India feared a Russian invasion through Afghanistan. The year 1927, which saw Chamberlain's Poor Law Bill and the Trade Disputes Act, also saw Britain break off diplomatic relations with the Soviet Union. And when, in more liberal mood, the Government decided to enfranchise women, Birkenhead commented, 'The Cabinet went mad yesterday'. Letter to Lord Irwin, 13 April 1927.
15. *Hansard*, 2 May 1927.
16. *Ibid.*, 23 June 1927.
17. G. D. H. Cole, *A History of the Labour Party from 1914* (London, 1948), 195, 480–1, and Taylor, *op. cit.*, 250–1 and n.
18. David Smith, 'The Struggle Against Company Unionism in the South Wales Coalfield, 1926–1939', *Welsh History Review*, vol. 6, No. 3 (June 1973), 375.
19. Foot, *op. cit.*, 203.
20. See figures quoted in Heinemann, *op. cit.*, 43.
21. Henry Pelling, *The British Communist Party* (London, 1958), 36.
22. Quoted in Lionel Birch (ed.), *The History of the TUC 1868–1968* (London, 1968), 91.
23. G. W. McDonald and Howard F. Gospel, *Historical Journal*, xvi, No. 4 (1973), discusses the Mond-Turner talks fully.

Chapter 28

1. Hugh Dalton, *Call Back Yesterday: Memoirs 1887–1931* (London, 1953), 297.
2. The Conservatives and their supporters in both Labour and Liberal parties received more than 60 per cent of the popular vote (the highest share in history). This gave MacDonald's National Government 521 seats and the independent Liberals (who frequently backed the Government) 33.
3. Green, *op. cit.*, 174–5. A whole generation of writers – Auden, Isherwood, Day-Lewis – articulated this mood.
4. Baldwin's National Government won 432 seats, Labour 154, the Liberals 20.
5. Bullock, *op. cit.*, 636.
6. Shefftz, *op. cit.*, 404.
7. Angus Calder, *The People's War 1939–45* (London, 1969), 259, 395.
8. *Ibid.*, 396.
9. Shefftz, *op. cit.*, 403–4.
10. Labour's 11·9 million votes won 396 seats, the Tories 9·9 million 213 seats and the Liberals 2·2 million 12 seats.
11. *Hansard*, 12 February 1946.
12. Duff Cooper, *Old Men Forget* (London, 1953), 147.
13. H. A. Clegg, 'Some Consequences of the General Strike', *Manchester Statistical Society Papers* (1954). See also McDonald and Gospel, *op. cit.*
14. See, for example, Ralph Desmarais, *The Supply and Transport Committee* (Ph.D thesis, University of Wisconsin, 1970); and 'The Strikebreaking Organisation of the British Government and Black Friday', *Journal of Contemporary History* (April 1971); James Klugmann, *History of the Communist Party of Great Britain*, vol. 11, *The General Strike 1925–1926* (London, 1969).

Appendices
Select Bibliography
Index

APPENDIX I
Chronology of Main Events

1888   Miners' Federation of Great Britain founded.

1889–90 Dockers and gas workers strike. 'New unionism' among semi-skilled and unskilled workers.

1901   Labour representative Committee formed.
Taff Vale Case. Trade union funds liable for damages during strikes.

1906   Twenty-nine Labour MPs elected in Liberal landslide.
Trade Disputes Act protects union funds in strikes.

1908   Osborne Judgement outlaws union political levy for Labour Party.
Miners win eight-hour day.

1911–14 Years of 'labour unrest'.

1911   Mines Act.

1912   Miners' strikes and Minimum Wage Act.

1913   Trade Union Act legalises political levy and 'contracting out'.
Miners' Next Step published.

1914   Triple industrial alliance of dockers, transport workers, railwayworkers, railwaymen and miners formed.

1916   Lloyd George becomes PM of wartime Coalition.
Government takes control of mines as war measure.

1918   Lloyd George's Coalition wins crushing victory in General Election.

1919   Government promises to return mines to mineowners, but threat of united action by triple alliance persuades them to set up the Sankey Commission on the mining industry.
Sankey majority for nationalisation. Report shelved except for seven-hour day.

1920   *Jolly George* incident.
'Datum line' coal strike.

1921   Serious trade depression and slump in coal exports. Mineowners regain control and impose sweeping pay cuts. Smith replaces Smillie as MFGB president.

15 April – Black Friday and collapse of triple alliance. Miners fight on alone until July when they return defeated.

1921–3   'Employers' offensive' brings down all industrial wages steeply.

1922   Lloyd George falls and is replaced by Bonar Law, who wins Election for Tories.

1923   Bonar Law dies and is replaced as PM by Baldwin, who loses surprise 'Protection' election.

1924   First MacDonald minority Labour Government.
Cook replaces Hodges as MFGB secretary.
Move to Left on TUC general council.
Buckmaster Inquiry into mining supports miners' claims.
Labour Government persuades mineowners to give 13 per cent pay rise.
Tories win huge victory under Baldwin in 'Zinoviev Letter' election.

1925   Baldwin stops Macquisten's Bill on political levy. Return to Gold Standard undercuts coal exports. Heavy losses in mining as owners propose 13 per cent pay cuts. Macmillan Inquiry into mining favours miners.
Threat of coal embargo by TUC.
30 July – Red Friday. Baldwin agrees to nine-month mining subsidy while Samuel Commission investigates industry, but adds 'All the workers have got to take reductions in wages to help put industry on its feet'.
OMS is launched.
Right-wing regains control of TUC general council.
Bevin elected to TUC general council and Citrine becomes general-secretary.

1926   *6 March* – Samuel Report recommends reorganisation and pay cuts.
Mineowners propose 13 per cent pay cuts and eight-hour day from *1 May*.
Miners seek TUC support.
Government talks with owners, miners and TUC through April.
29 April – Miners give TUC full power to conduct dispute.
30 April – Owners post final terms. One million miners locked-out.
TUC holds final talks with Government.
2 May – *Daily Mail* incident. Government breaks off talks.
3 May – General Strike begins at midnight.

4 May – United response from 'first-line' workers brings $3\frac{1}{2}$ million out.

OMS merges with Government organisation.

Use of ships and volunteer road transport helps Government maintain supplies.

5 May – Churchill edits *British Gazette*. TUC brings out *British Worker*.

6 May – Reith agrees to carry out Government radio policy. Sir Herbert Samuel returns to Britain.

Sir John Simon declares strike illegal.

7 May – Samuel opens secret talks with TUC.

TUC rejects financial help from Soviet Union.

8 May – Churchill's 'pogrom' announcement alarms King.

9 May – TUC continues talks with Samuel.

10 May – Cabinet discusses plans to prevent banks paying strike benefits.

11 May – Mr Justice Astbury declares strike illegal. King persuades Cabinet to drop plan to prevent banks paying strike benefits. Miners reject Samuel memorandum as basis for settlement. Rumours that Government plans to arrest TUC general council and other strike leaders. TUC asks to see PM.

12 May – TUC calls off strike unconditionally at 12.20 p.m. Miners fight on alone. Steady drift back to work and defection to Spencer Union.

Miners return in November to lower pay and longer hours. Total defeat.

1927	Chamberlain supersedes Poor Law Guardians at Bedwellty and Chester-le-Street.
	Trades Disputes Act makes General Strikes illegal and establishes Macquisten's principle of 'contracting in' for political levy.
	Labour Party receipts fall by one-third, but recover later.
1928	Mond-Turner talks on labour-management cooperation.
1929	MacDonald's second minority Labour Government.
1929–31	Great Depression sees unemployment rise to nearly 3 million.
1931	Cook dies.
1931	Labour Government falls after financial crisis.
	MacDonald-Baldwin Coalition wins crushing victory at General Election. Labour reduced to rump of fifty-nine MPs.
1936	Spencer Union and Company unionism defeated in coalfields.

1940   Wartime Coalition. Bevin Minister of Labour.
         Strike-rate rises steadily during war.
1945   Labour wins landslide victory at general election.
1946   Trade Disputes Act repealed. 'Contracting out' re-established.
1947   Mines nationalised.
1950s   Unrest in coalfields.
1960s   Mining industry declines. Hundreds of pits close and labour force reduced to 260,000.
1972   Miners win first national strike since 1926.
1973   International oil and energy crisis.
1974   Miners win second national strike and help bring down a Tory Government.

APPENDIX II
Cast of Characters

Stanley Baldwin (1867–1947) b. son of Warwickshire ironmaster; educated Harrow and Cambridge; MP 1908; Financial Secretary to Treasury 1917; President Board of Trade 1921; Chancellor of Exchequer 1922; PM 1923, 1924–9; Lord President of Council 1931–5 and strong man in MacDonald's National Government Coalition; PM 1935–7; Earl 1937. Consummate-politician, PM during General Strike, key figure in inter-war politics.

Ernest Bevin (1881–1951) b. illegitimate, Somerset; soon orphaned; educated elementary school; leader dockers union 1910–21; 'dockers' KC' and creator of TGWU 1921, general secretary 1921–40; MP 1940; Minister of Labour 1940–5; Foreign Secretary 1945–51; member TUC general council during strike and one of the greatest figures produced by British Labour Movement.

Lord Birkenhead (1874–1930) b. F. E. Smith; educated Birkenhead and Oxford; MP 1906; brilliant barrister and advocate of Ulster's defiance in Home Rule Crisis of 1914; Solicitor-General 1915; Attorney-General 1915–19; Lord Chancellor 1919–22; Secretary for India 1924–8; Earl 1922. One of Baldwin's strong men and the cleverest member of his Cabinet.

Andrew Bonar Law (1858–1923) b. Canada; educated Canada and Glasgow; iron merchant; tough Tory leader 1911–21, 1922–3; Colonial Secretary 1915–16; Chancellor of Exchequer 1916–18; Lord President and power behind Lloyd George's Coalition 1919–21; Tory PM 1922–3.

John Bromley (1876–1944) b. Shropshire, educated elementary school; railway cleaner, fireman and engine driver GWR; general secretary ASLEF 1914; TUC general council. Most anxious to get his men back during strike.

Neville Chamberlain (1869–1940) b. Birmingham, younger half-brother of Austen, son of Joseph; educated Rugby; Lord Mayor Birmingham 1915–16; Director-General National Service 1916–17 in War Cabinet; Tory MP 1918–40; PMG 1922–3; Paymaster-General 1923; Minister of Health 1923, 1924–9, 1931; Chancellor of Exchequer 1923–4, 1931–7; PM 1937–40; Lord President of Council 1940. Notable reformer, one of Baldwin's hawks in 1926; author of Appeasement policy to Hitler at Munich in 1938.

Winston Churchill (1874–1965) b. son of Randolph Churchill and American beauty Jenny Jerome; grandson of Duke of Marlborough; educated Harrow and Sandhurst; controversial career as soldier and war correspondent; MP 1900 switched from Tories to Liberals on Free Trade 1906; Liberal Minister 1908–22. Reverted to Tories 1924; Chancellor of Exchequer 1924–9; First Lord of Admiralty 1939–40; PM 1940–5, 1951–5. Great Parliamentarian and war leader. One of Baldwin's hawks in 1926.

Walter Citrine (1887–) b. Liverpool; educated elementary school; Mersey district secretary ETU 1914–20, assistant general secretary 1920–3; general secretary TUC 1926–46; chairman British Electricity Authority 1946; Knighted 1935; Baron 1946. Best administrator produced by Labour Movement. Wrote excellent shorthand.

A. J. Cook (1884–1931) b. Somerset, son of soldier; educated Army and elementary schools and CLC; Baptist preacher at seventeen; ILP 1905; South Wales miner and miners' agent Rhondda 1919; Communist party 1921 but left over Black Friday; executive MFGB 1921–31, secretary 1924–31, Minority Movement. Spellbinding orator and demagogue, wrote *Miners' Next Step* in 1913 and was long associated with extreme Left. Reverted to ILP with Cook-Maxton Manifesto 1928 and became more right-wing before death.

J. C. C. Davidson (1889–) Tory MP 1920–3, 1924–37; private secretary and PPS to Bonar Law and Baldwin, who was a close friend; chairman Conservative Party 1929–32; Viscount 1937. Deputy Civil Service Commissioner and key figure during strike, in charge of Press and radio. Influential figure in corridors of power between the wars.

Frank Hodges (1887–1947) b. South Wales; educated elementary schools and CLC; miner, miners' agent; secretary MFGB 1918–24; served on Sankey Commission 1919; central figure in 'Black Friday' 1921; MP 1923–4 and Civil Lord of Admiralty 1924; spoke fluent French and secretary of miners' international organisation in Paris 1921–9; later head of CEGB and director of coal and steel companies; one of the most talented leaders miners ever produced, though they lost him.

Thomas Jones (1870–1955) b. Rhymney, son of storekeeper; educated Rhymney grammar school; left school at thirteen, but later put himself through Aberystwyth University and Glasgow, where he taught; deputy secretary War Cabinet 1916 and later to Lloyd George, Bonar Law, Baldwin and MacDonald. Friend and speechwriter of Baldwin's; inveterate gossip and go-between; influential figure in inter-war Establishment.

Sir William Joynson-Hicks (1865–1932) educated Merchant Taylor's; Tory MP 1908–29; Postmaster-General, Financial Secretary to Treasury 1923; Minister of Health 1923–4; Home Secretary 1924–9; Viscount Brentford 1929. Fervent evangelical and 'Reds under beds' alarmist. Known as 'Jix'.

David Lloyd George (1863–1945) b. Manchester; educated Church school; solicitor; Liberal MP 1890–1945; Chancellor of Exchequer 1908–15; Minister of Munitions 1915–16; Secretary for War 1916; PM 1916–32. With Churchill one of the greatest Parliamentarians of his day and 'the man who won the war' in 1918.

John Maynard Keynes (1883–1946) educated Eton and Cambridge; brilliant economist, member of Bloomsbury group and later father of modern managed capitalism after publication of *General Theory* in 1936 and of post-1945 world financial structure after Bretton Woods Conference. Had been Treasury official and adviser at Paris Peace Conference in 1919; in 1920s polemical journalist who opposed return to Gold Standard.

Sir Alfred Mond (1868–1930) educated Cheltenham, Cambridge and Edinburgh; Liberal MP 1906–26, Tory MP 1926–8; Minister of Works 1916–21; Minister of Health 1921–2; chairman of many industrial companies, including coal companies, and creator of the giant ICI. One of the most influential industrialists of his time; he launched the Mond-Turner talks on labour-management collaboration in 1928. Created Lord Melchett in 1928.

Sir Otto Niemeyer (1883–1971) b. Streatham of a German father; educated St Paul's and Oxford; Treasury Official and finally Controller at thirty-nine in 1922; man of outstanding intellect who played a crucial part in the decision to return to the Gold Standard in 1925.

Arthur Pugh (1870–1955) steel miller and general secretary Iron and Steel Trades Confederation 1917–36; chairman of TUC general council during strike; mild-mannered, conservative and friendly with Baldwin, who came from an iron master's family.

John Reith (1889–1971) b. Scotland; educated Glasgow Academy, Gresham's School, Holt, and Glasgow; engineer; wounded First World War; first general manager, later director-general, BBC 1922–38. Used 'the brute force of monopoly' to turn broadcasting into a mission.

Sir Herbert Samuel (1870–1963) educated University College School and Oxford; Liberal MP 1902–18, 1929–35; Cabinet Minister 1909–16; High Commissioner Palestine 1920–5; chairman of Royal Commission on Coal Industry 1925–6. Leader of Liberal Party 1931–5; created Viscount 1937.

Sir John Sankey (1866–1948) Judge of the King's Bench Division of the High Court 1914–28; Lord Justice of Appeal 1928–9; Lord Chancellor 1929–35; life member Governing Body Church of Wales; created Viscount 1932. Chairman of Royal Commission on Coal Industry 1919.

Robert Smillie (1859–1924) b. Belfast; Clyde shipyard worker at fifteen, miner at seventeen; President National Union of Scottish Mineworkers; Labour MP and president MFGB until 1921, when resigned in disagreement over union's hard line. Humorous but immensely determined and much-loved socialist, member of Sankey Commission 1919.

Herbert Smith (1862–1938) b. in a workhouse and soon an orphan; miner at ten; fighter in public houses; member of local school board 1892; president Yorkshire miners 1905–21; president MFGB 1921–38; Mayor of Barnsley; tough, kindly, laconic, intransigent, his favourite phrase was 'Nowt doin' '.

Sir Arthur Steel-Maitland (1876–1935) educated Rugby and Oxford; president Oxford Union and Fellow of All Souls; special commissioner to Royal Commission on Poor Law 1906–7; Tory MP 1910–35; created baronet 1917; Minister of Labour 1924–9.

J. H. Thomas (1874–1949) b. Newport; educated elementary school; engine driver GWR; general secretary NUR 1917–31; Labour MP 1910–31; Colonial Secretary 1924, 1935–6; Lord Privy Seal 1929–30; Dominions Secretary 1930–5; one of Labour's ablest and shrewdest negotiators, he was forced out of public life after revealing Budget secrets.

SELECT BIBLIOGRAPHY

This book is based principally on primary sources, which are listed here in full. No attempt has been made, however, to cover all the secondary work on the subject, and the books included are simply a selection of those most frequently referred to during the writing.

PRIMARY SOURCES

Government papers and documents first made available under the revised thirty-year rule provided the major source for this study. The other important source was the Baldwin Papers.

Government documents consisted of the following :

Cabinet Minutes
Cabinet Conclusions
Cabinet Papers
Cabinet Information Bulletins
Home Office Papers
Treasury Papers
Departmental Bulletins from
The Ministry of Labour
The Ministry of Health
The Ministry of Transport
The Mines Department

The second main manuscript source was the *Political Papers of Stanley Baldwin*, especially D.3, Labour, Trade and Coal etc. volumes 11–23. Other manuscript sources consulted were

BBC Correspondence and Papers
The Bonar Law Papers
The Davidson Papers
The Vernon Wentworth Papers
West Yorkshire Coal Owners Association Minutes

The major manuscript source on the union side was the *TUC Papers*, consisting of reports, correspondence and other material between various TUC committees and branches all over the country, especially

TUC Intelligence Committee
TUC Press and Publicity Committee
TUC Transport Committee
TUC Propaganda and Political Committee

Reports of Local Strike Committee
Strike Bulletins
Printed sources included
   *Report and Minutes of Evidence of the Sankey Commission on the
   Coal Industry* (Cmnd 359, 1919)
   Report and Minutes of Evidence Buckmaster Inquiry (Cmnd 2129,
   1924)
   Report and Minutes of Evidence of Macmillan Court of Inquiry (Cmnd
   2478, 1925)
   *Report and Minutes of Evidence of Samuel Commission on the Coal
   Mining Industry* (Cmnd 2600, 1926)
   Hansard, House of Commons Debates
   Proceedings of the Annual Trades Union Congress
   Proceedings of the Annual Delegate Conference of the MFGB
   Proceedings of the Annual Co-operative Congress
   Proceedings of Yorkshire Federation of Miners
   Minutes of Meetings Between Mining Association and MFGB
   The Mining Situation: TUC Report of Special Conference 1926
   Special Strike Conference of the TUC, 1927
   TGWU Biennial Delegate Conference Report, 1927
Newspapers and periodicals consulted included
   British Gazette
   British Worker
   The Times
   The Daily Herald
   The Morning Post
   The Economist
   The New Statesman
   The New York Times
   The New York World
   Labour Yearbook
   Labour Gazette
   Industrial Review
   Economic Journal
   The Sheffield Telegraph
   The Oxford Times

SECONDARY SOURCES
This list is by no means exhaustive but simply mentions those books which
have been most useful. Unless otherwise indicated, all the books are pub-

lished in London. R. K. Middlemas, ed., Thomas Jones, *Whitehall Diary*, two volumes (1969), is invaluable, as is Robert Rhodes James, *Memoirs of a Conservative: J. C. C. Davidson's Memoirs and Papers, 1910–37.* Margaret Cole, ed., *Beatrice Webb's Diaries, 1924–32* (1956), is full of mordant comments on people and events, while Arnold Bennett, *Journals 1921–1928* (1933), presents the more urbane views of a leading literary figure and London clubman. Hamilton Fyfe, *Behind the Scenes of the Great Strike* (1926), is a detailed diary kept by the editor of the *British Worker*.

Of the autobiographies, Lord Citrine, *Men and Work* (1964), is the most revealing autobiography on the union side, and includes a careful diary of the Nine Days based on Citrine's shorthand notes. A. J. Cook, *The Nine Days* (1926), is a short and emotional account. J. H. Thomas, *My Story* (1937), is disappointing, as is Frank Hodges, *My Adventures as a Labour Leader* (no date), although it does contain a long defence of his conduct on Black Friday. Ben Turner, *About Myself* (1930), adds a little on the TUC side. The left-wing miners' leaders, Arthur Horner, *Incorrigible Rebel* (1960), Abe Moffat, *My Life With The Miners* (1965), and Will Paynter, *My Generation* (1972), have written memoirs which reveal how much the events of 1925 influenced them as young men, while Lord Taylor, *Uphill All The Way*, says a little about the impact of the Spencer Union in Nottinghamshire and elsewhere.

Much more interesting, however, is J. C. W. Reith, *Into The Wind* (1949), which has an account of the BBC's policy by the man who made it under severe pressure. Viscount Samuel, *Memoirs* (1945), discusses his work on the Royal Commission of 1925 and in drafting the memorandum during the strike, while Osbert Sitwell, *Laughter in the Next Room* (1949), has details of the talks Samuel had with the TUC during the emergency. L. S. Amery, *My Political Life* (1953), throws some light on Cabinet divisions in 1926. Graham Greene, *A Sort of Life* (1971), describes his job on *The Times* during the strike, which can be supplemented by reading Geoffrey Dawson, *Strike Nights in Printing House Square* (1932). Leslie Paul, *Angry Young Man* (1951), has some vivid eye-witness accounts of scenes from the strike. Hugh Dalton, *Call Back Yesterday* (1953), describes his experiences as a young Labour MP in the mining region of Durham.

Biography is a source which has substantial gaps. On the Government side there is no good life of Lloyd George, Ramsay MacDonald or Winston Churchill during the General Strike, though Martin Gilbert's monumental study of Churchill should soon produce a further volume

K

covering this period, while John Grigg, *The Young Lloyd George* (1973), is soon to be continued with a second volume taking the story from 1902 to 1914. David Marquand's long-awaited life of MacDonald should fill an important gap when it finally appears.

For Bonar Law, Robert Blake, *The Unknown Prime Minister* (1955), is admirable, while R. K. Middlemas and John Barnes, *Baldwin: A Biography* (1969), employ a life-and-times approach which leaves little out and runs to excessive length. H. Montgomery Hyde, *Baldwin: the Unexpected Prime Minister* (1973), is probably better and certainly shorter. Lord Birkenhead, *F. E. – the Life of F. E. Smith* (1960), is a filial but useful account. Keith Feiling, *Life of Neville Chamberlain* (1946), uses his diary, while John Evelyn Wrench, *Geoffrey Dawson and Our Times* (1955), is a revealing biography of the editor of *The Times*. For the Liberals Roy Jenkins, *Asquith* (1964), is a beautifully written study which has a brief account of the impact of the strike on the man and the party. G. K. A. Bell, *Randall Davidson* (Oxford, 1935), is a life of the Archbishop of Canterbury, while Francis Williams, *A Pattern of Rulers* (1965), has biographical sketches of Baldwin, MacDonald, Chamberlain, Montagu Norman and Lord Halifax. Lord Boothby, *My Yesterday, Your Tomorrow* (1962), reprints some perceptive essays on inter-war politics, while Harold Nicolson, *King George the Fifth* (1952), tells the King's story.

There are gaps, too, among the biographies of union leaders. There is nothing on A. J. Cook, but Jack Lawson, *The Man in the Cap* (1941), provides a sympathetic picture of Herbert Smith, and Gregory Blaxland, *A Life for Unity* (1964), is perhaps too kind to Jimmy Thomas. Alan Bullock, *The Life and Times of Ernest Bevin*, vol. I (1960), is an indispensable source. Michael Foot, *Aneurin Bevan*, vol. I (1962), has a section on the strike in Ebbw Vale.

The literature on the coal mining industry is voluminous, but G. D. H. Cole, *Labour in the Coal-Mining Industry* (Oxford, 1923), and J. W. F. Rowe, *Wages in the Coal Trade* (1923), provide a good introduction. R. S. A. Redmayne, *The British Coal-Mining Industry During the War* (Oxford, 1923), is a study by the Chief Inspector of Mines, while H. S. Jevons, *The British Coal Trade* (1915), was for years the classic study. Frank Hodges, *Nationalisation of the Mines* (1920), presents the MFGB case for public ownership, while David Lloyd George, *Coal and Power* (1924), is based on a private inquiry he presided over after leaving office. Ivor Thomas, *Coal in the New Era* (1934), argues the need for reorganisation, while Arthur Horner and G. A. Hutt, *Communism and Coal* (1928), and Margot Heinemann, *Britain's Coal* (1944), are even more critical of private ownership. A defence of the owners can be found in J. R. Raynes, *Coal and its Conflicts* (1928), and W. A. Lee, *Thirty Years in Coal* (1954), the view of the secretary of the Mining Association.

R. Page Arnot's lifetime of study on the mineworkers can be read in *The Miners* three volumes (1949, 1953, 1961), *A History of the Scottish Miners* (1955) and *South Wales Miners* (1967). Other regional studies of miners include Frank Machin, *The Yorkshire Miners* (Barnsley, 1958), J. E. Williams, *The Derbyshire Miners* (1962), a monumental study, W. R. Garside, *The Durham Miners, 1919–1960* (1971), A. R. Griffin, *The Mining Industry in the East Midlands* (1971), and *The Nottinghamshire Miners*, 2 vols (Nottingham, 1955 and 1962), and Raymond Challinor *The Lancashire and Cheshire Miners* (Newcastle, 1972).

For other industries, Felix J. R. Pole *Pole's Book* (1954), is a defence of the railway companies' policy by the head of the Great Western Railway. Philip S. Bagwell, *The Railwaymen* (1963), is a comprehensive study of the growth of unions on the railways. K. G. J. C. Knowles, *Strikes – A Study in Conflict* (Oxford, 1952), is a classic study of the subject with special reference to the period 1911–47.

Of books on the General Strike itself, W. H. Crook, *The General Strike* (Chapel Hill, North Carolina, 1931), was one of the first and is still in many ways the best. Two later books for the general reader are Julian Symons, *The General Strike* (1957), and Christopher Farman, *The General Strike, May 1926* (1972). All three contain useful bibliographies. Emile Burns, *The General Strike, May 1926 : Trades Councils in Action* (1926), is based on reports sent in by trades councils and strike committees. R. Page Arnot, *The General Strike, May 1926: Its Origin and History* (1926), is a companion volume. Regional studies now in progress should deepen our knowledge of the strike at the grass roots, but meanwhile A. Mason, *The General Strike in the North-East* (Hull, 1970), D. E. Baines and R. Bean, 'The General Strike on Merseyside', in J. R. Harris, ed., *Liverpool and Merseyside* (London, 1969), and P. Wyncall, 'The General Strike in Nottingham', *Marxism Today*, 16 (1972), 172–80, are monographs and essays which help to fill in some gaps.

The role of the Communist Party can be studied in L. J. Macfarlane, *The British Communist Party: Its Origin and Development until 1929* (1966), and Henry Pelling, *The British Communist Party* (1956). James Klugmann, *History of the Communist Party*, vol. II (1969), is an official account which covers the General Strike, while Tom Bell, *The British Communist Party* (1927), is an earlier official history. Roderick Martin,

Communism and British Trade Unions 1924–1933 (Oxford, 1969), is a study of the National Minority Movement.

For the economics of the period, Donald Winch, *Economics and Policy* (1969), and B. W. E. Alford, *Depression and Recovery?* (1972), are excellent guides through some difficult historiography. A. L. Bowley and J. Stamp, *The National Income* (Oxford, 1927), is a useful contemporary source, while A. C. Pigou, *Wage Statistics and Prices* (1949), is a study by an economist who was very influential in the 1920s. D. E. Moggeridge, *The Return to Gold, 1925* (Cambridge, 1969), is a penetrating criticism of a crucial decision, which is also attacked in J. M. Keynes, *The Economic Consequences of Mr Churchill* (1925), a classic of polemical journalism.

Finally, general histories of the period must include A. J. P. Taylor, *English History 1914–1945* (Oxford, 1965), where the author's many gifts are displayed, and C. L. Mowat, *Britain Between the Wars 1918–1940* (1955), which has an admirable account of the strike. G. A. Hutt, *A Post-War History of the British Working Class* (1937), is a useful short book, which can be supplemented by G. D. H. Cole, *A History of the Labour Party from 1914* (1948). Asa Briggs, *History of Broadcasting in the United Kingdom*, vol. I (Oxford, 1965), is informative on the role of radio, while George Glasgow, *The General Strike and Road Transport* (1926), and A. L. Goodhart, *The Legality of the General Strike in England* (Cambridge, 1927), cover two particular aspects of the story.

INDEX